THE ADDAMS FAMILY THEME

Theme from the TV Show and Movie

Music and Lyrics by
VIC MIZZY

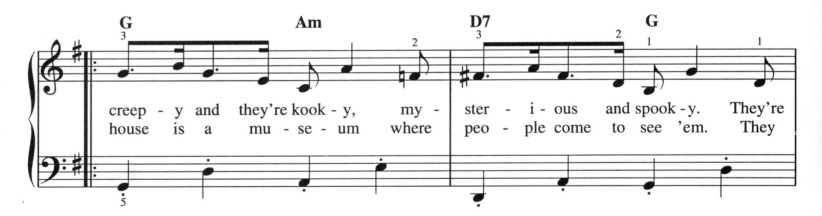

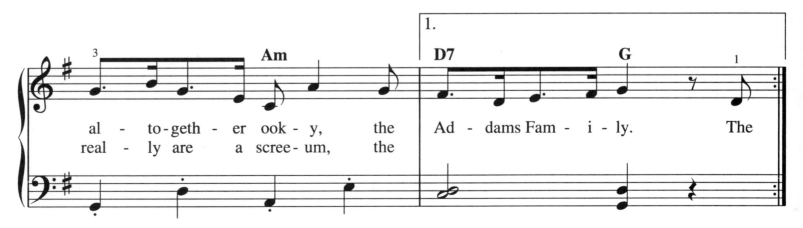

5

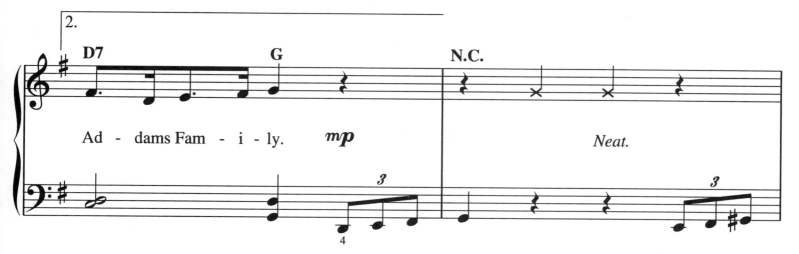

Ad - dams Fam - i - ly. *mp*

Neat.

Sweet.

Pe - tite! So *mf*

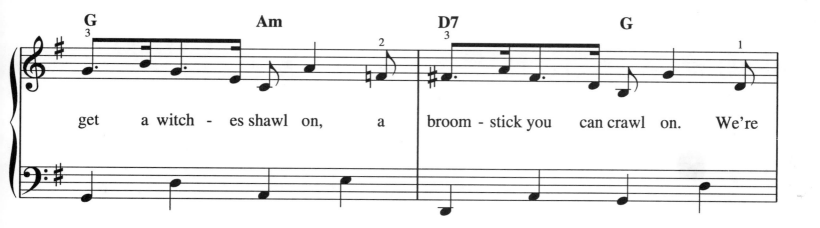

get a witch - es shawl on, a broom - stick you can crawl on. We're

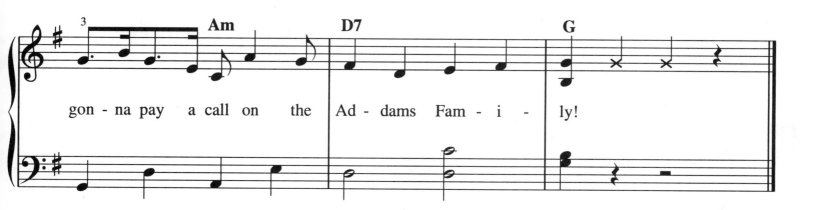

gon - na pay a call on the Ad - dams Fam - i - ly!

ALLEY CAT SONG

Words by JACK HARLEN
Music by FRANK BJORN

7

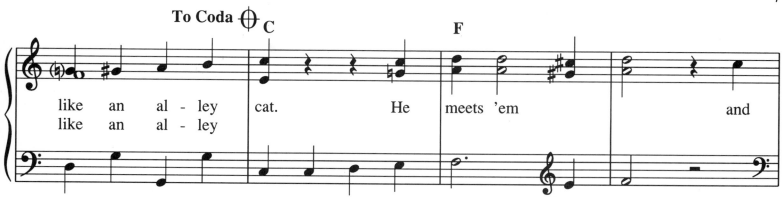

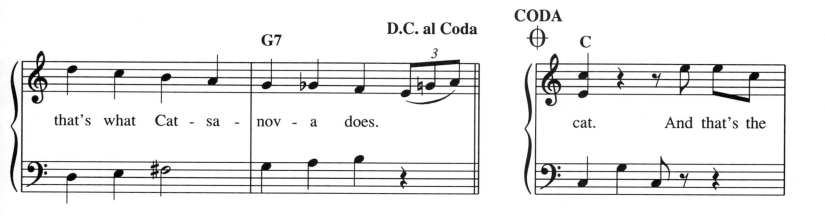

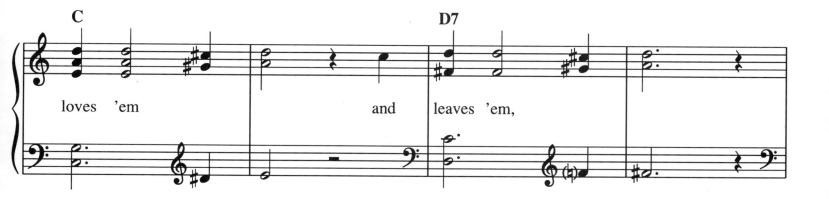

ALLEY-OOP

By DALLAS FRAZIER

Oop Oop Oop Oop Oop. Al-ley Oop Oop Oop

Oop Oop. There's a man in the fun-ny pa-pers we all know, Al-ley

Oop Oop Oop Oop Oop. He lived way back a

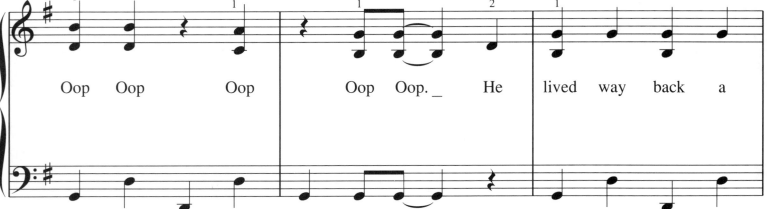

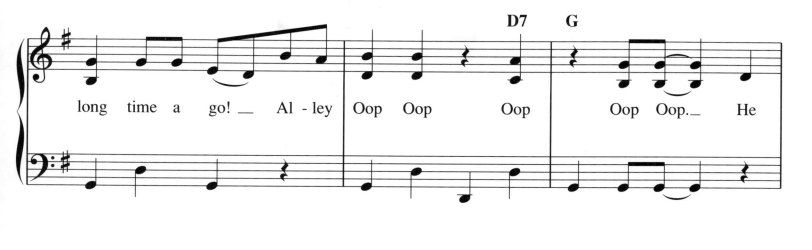

long time a go! ___ Al - ley Oop Oop Oop Oop Oop. ___ He

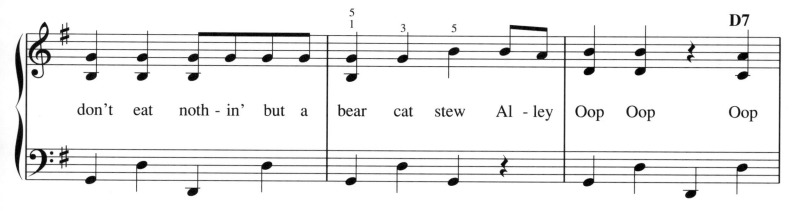

don't eat noth - in' but a bear cat stew Al - ley Oop Oop Oop

Oop Oop. ___ Well this cat's name is Al - ley Oop. ___ Al - ley

Oop Oop Oop Oop Oop. ___ He's got a Chauf - er that's a gen - u - ine
rides ___ through the jun - gle tearin'

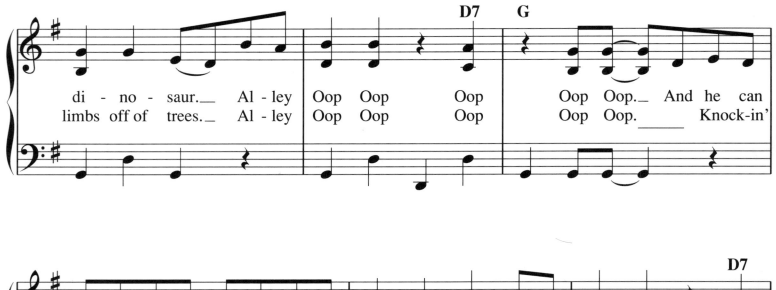

di - no - saur.__ Al - ley | Oop Oop Oop | Oop Oop.__ And he can
limbs off of trees.__ Al - ley | Oop Oop Oop | Oop Oop.____ Knock-in'

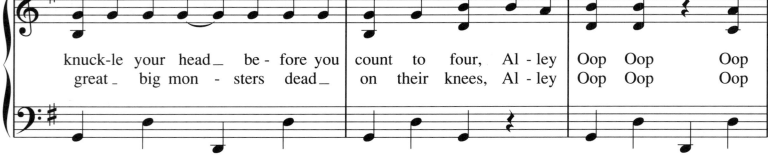

knuck-le your head_ be - fore you | count to four, Al - ley | Oop Oop Oop
great_ big mon - sters dead_ | on their knees, Al - ley | Oop Oop Oop

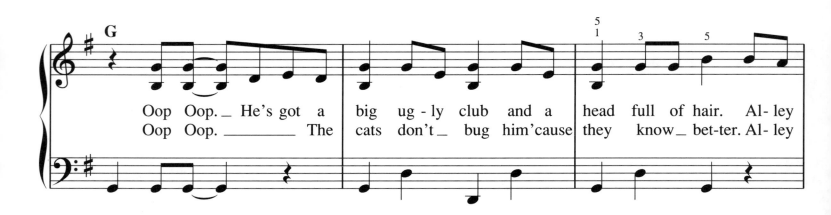

Oop Oop.__ He's got a | big ug - ly club and a | head full of hair. Al- ley
Oop Oop. _____ The | cats don't _ bug him 'cause | they know_ bet-ter. Al- ley

Oop Oop Oop | Oop Oop. __ Likes | great big li - ons and
Oop Oop Oop | Oop Oop. __ 'Cause he's a | mean mo-tor scoot-er and a

11

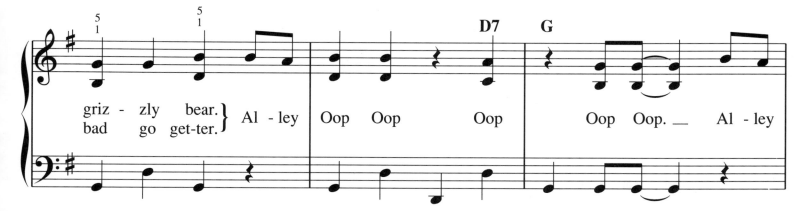

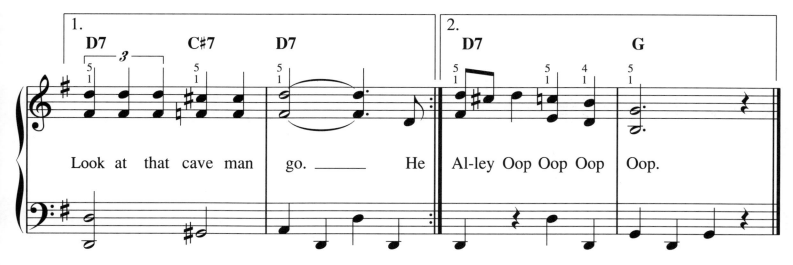

ANIMAL FAIR

American Folksong

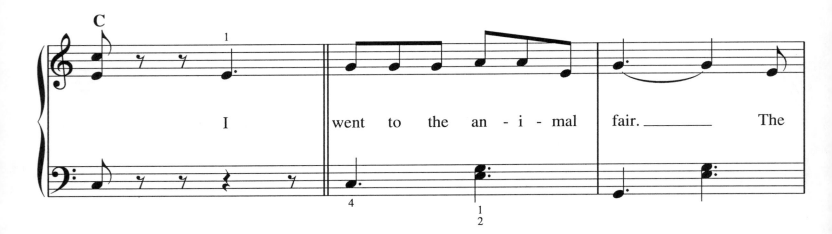

I went to the an - i - mal fair._____ The

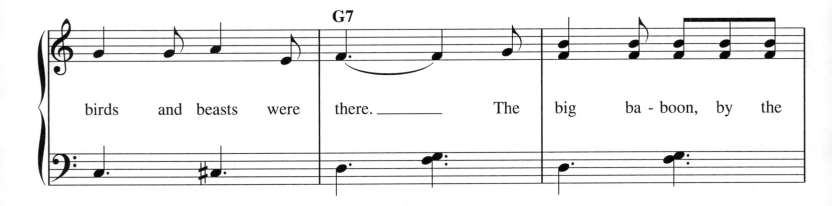

birds and beasts were there._____ The big ba - boon, by the

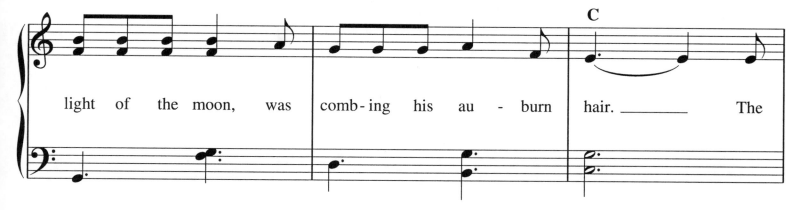

light of the moon, was comb-ing his au - burn hair. _____ The

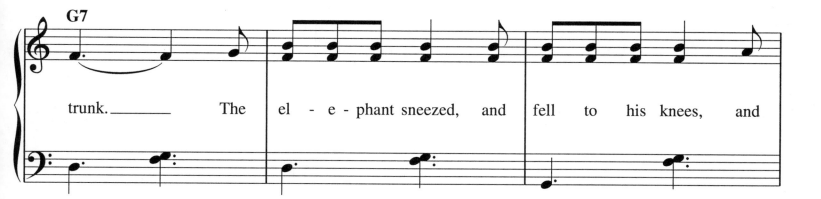

mon - key, he got drunk, _____ and sat on the el - e - phant's

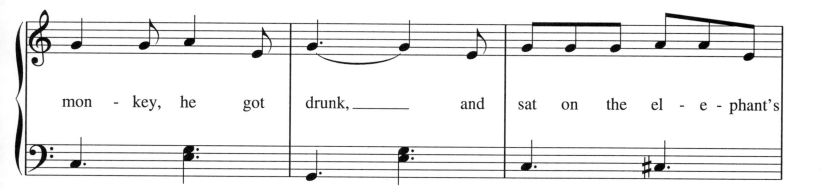

trunk. _____ The el - e - phant sneezed, and fell to his knees, and

what be - came of the monk, the monk, the monk, the monk?

ANY DREAM WILL DO
from JOSEPH AND THE AMAZING TECHNICOLOR DREAMCOAT

Music by ANDREW LLOYD WEBBER
Lyrics by TIM RICE

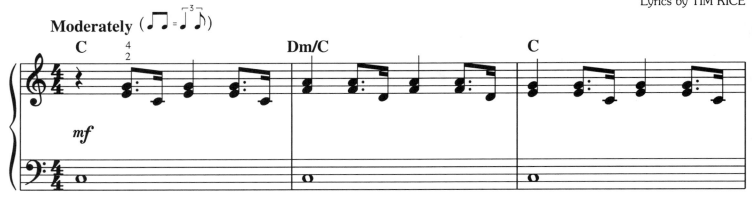

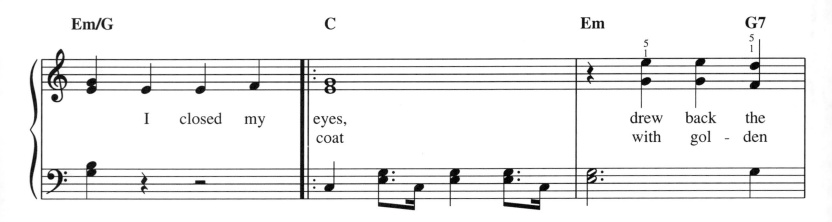

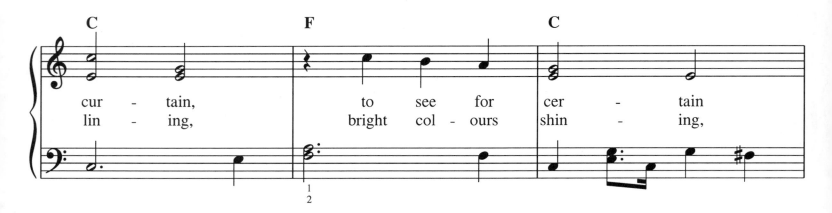

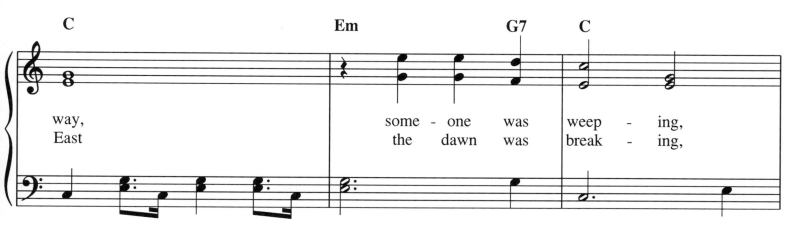

way,
East

some - one was weep - ing,
the dawn was break - ing,

but the world was sleep - ing.
the __ world was wak - ing.

An - y dream will
An - y dream will

do.
I wore my do.
A

crash of drums, __ a flash of light, __ my gol - den coat flew

16

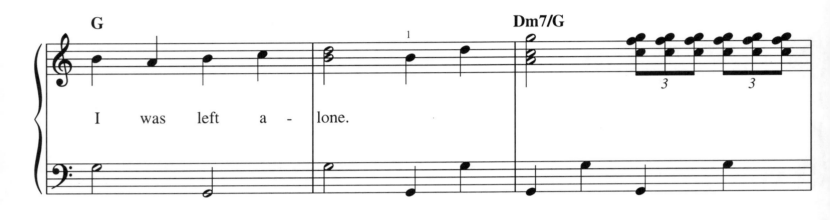

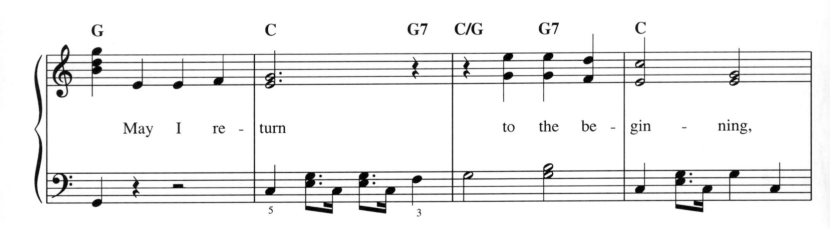

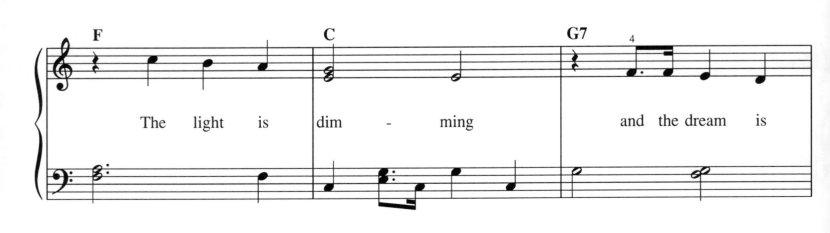

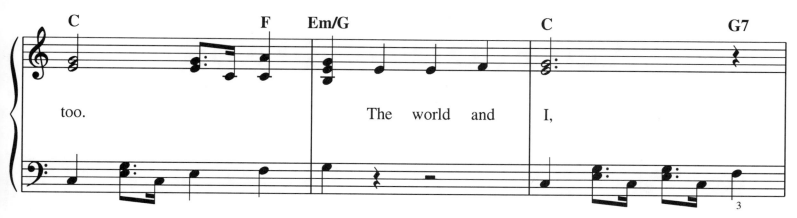

too.

The world and I,

we are still wait - ing,

still hes - i -

ta - ting,

an - y dream will do,

an - y dream will do.

BE KIND TO YOUR WEB-FOOTED FRIENDS

Traditional

Bright March Tempo

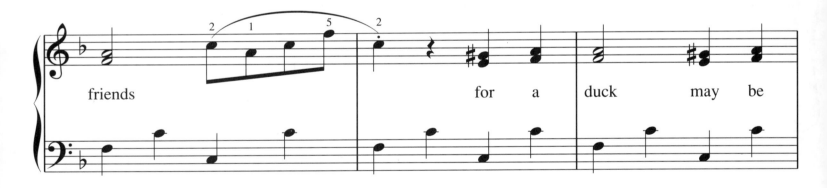

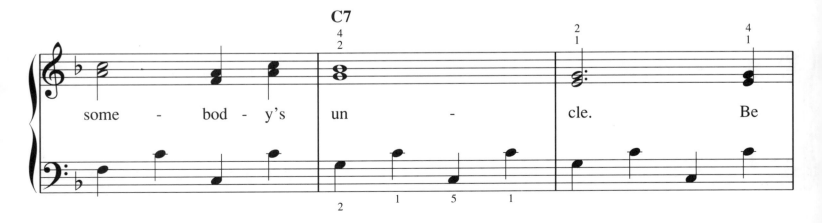

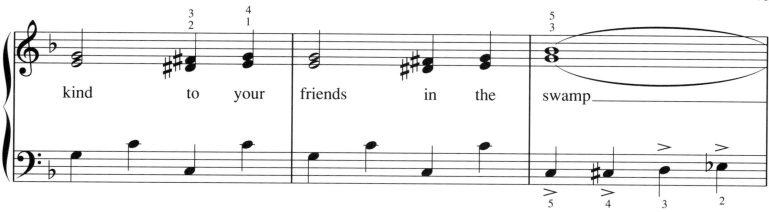

kind to your friends in the swamp

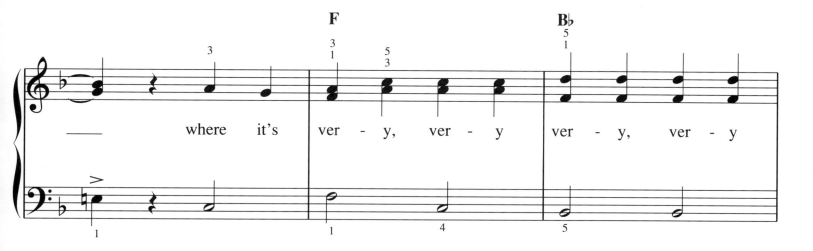

F **B♭**

where it's ver - y, ver - y ver - y, ver - y

C **F**

damp. *(Spoken:)* Two *Three* (Sung:) Now you may think that

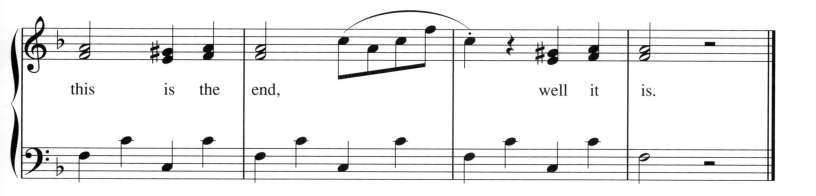

this is the end, well it is.

19

THE BEAR WENT OVER THE MOUNTAIN

Traditional

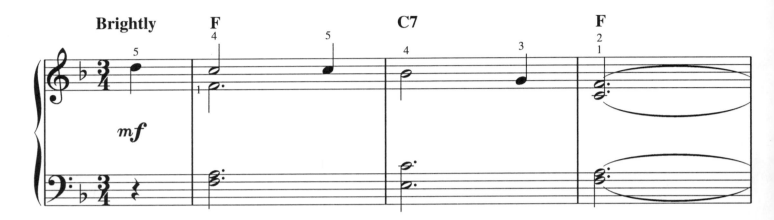

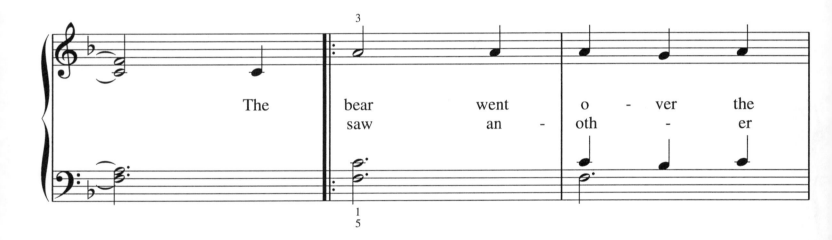

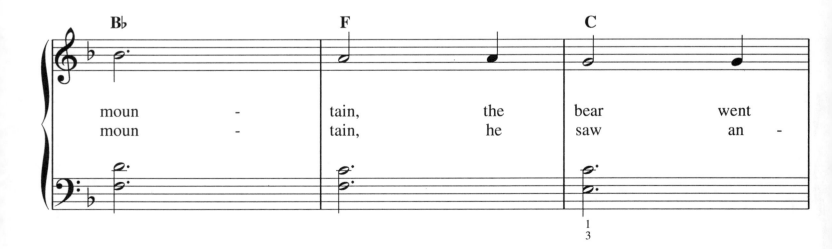

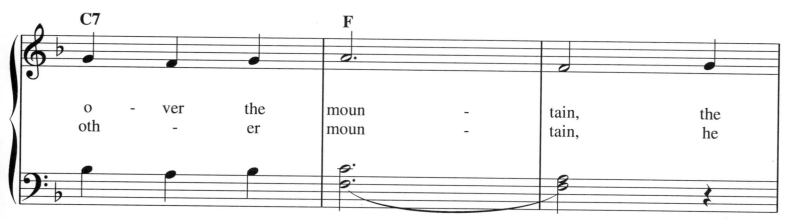

o - ver the moun - tain, the
oth - er moun - tain, the he

bear went o - ver the moun -
saw an - oth - er moun -

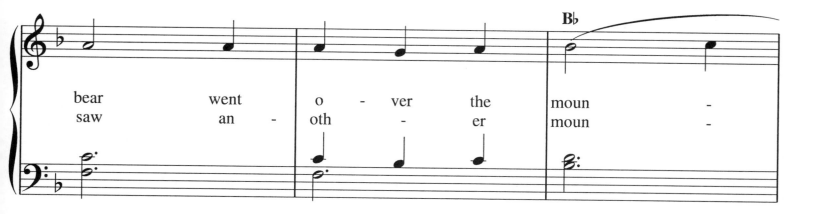

tain to see what he could
tain and that's what he could

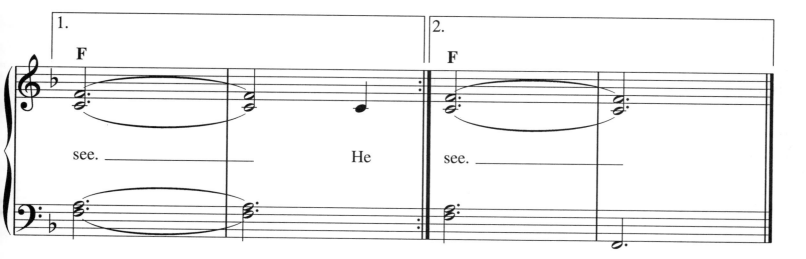

1.
see. _____ He

2.
see. _____

CAN YOU FEEL THE LOVE TONIGHT

from Walt Disney Pictures' THE LION KING

Music by ELTON JOHN
Lyrics by TIM RICE

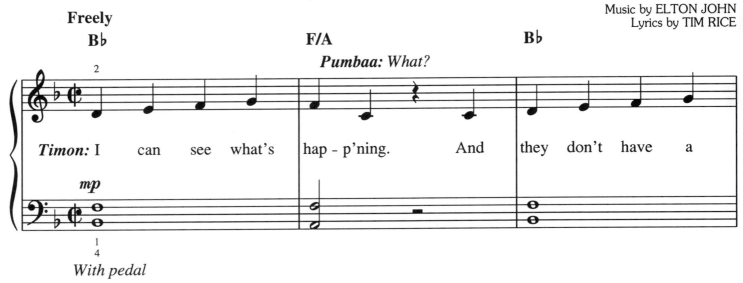

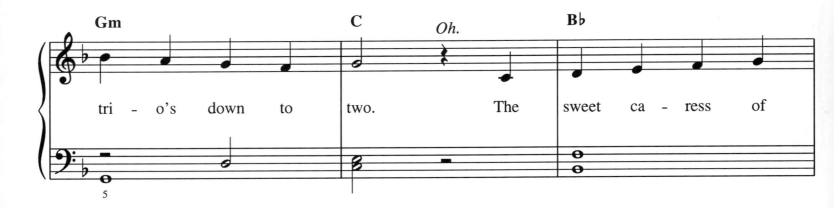

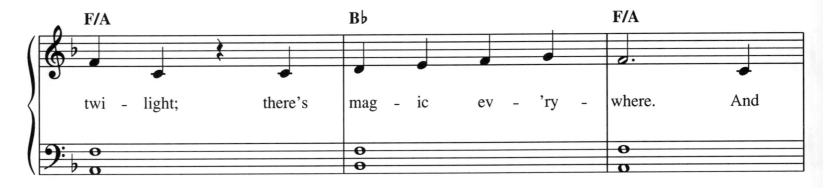

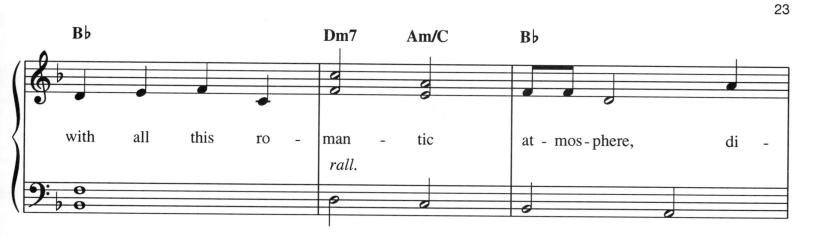

with all this ro - man - tic at - mos - phere, di -

rall.

Moderately (in two)

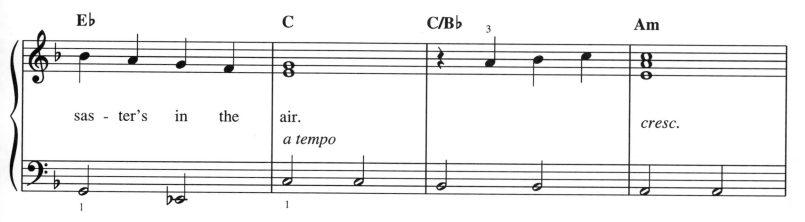

sas - ter's in the air.

a tempo   *cresc.*

Chorus: Can you feel the love

mf

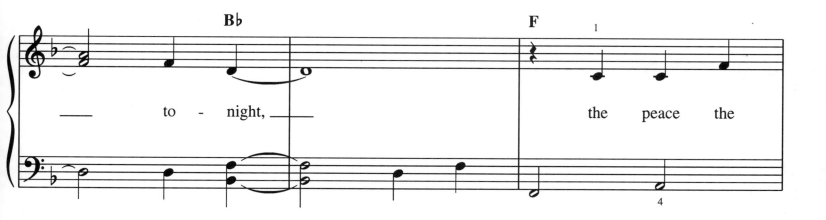

to - night, the peace the

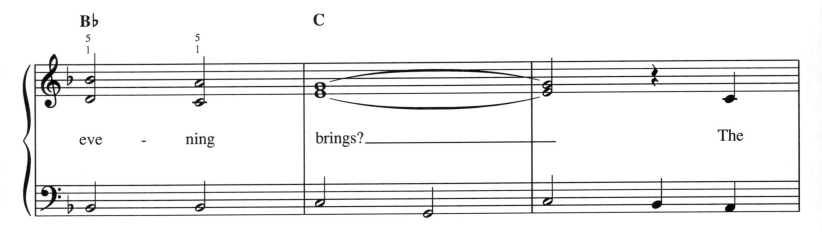

eve - ning brings?_____ The

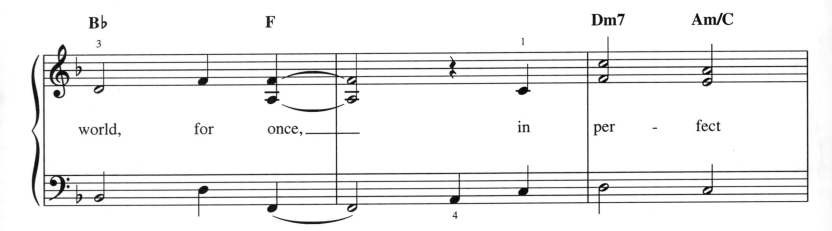

world, for once,_____ in per - fect

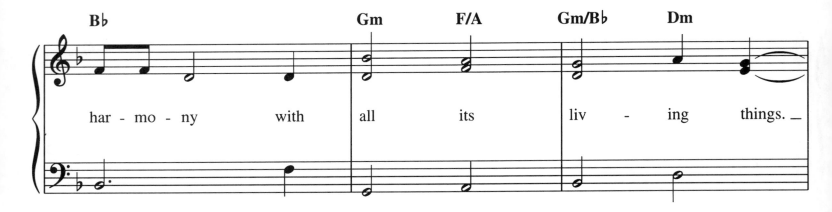

har - mo - ny with all its liv - ing things._

dim.

Simba: So man - y things to
mp

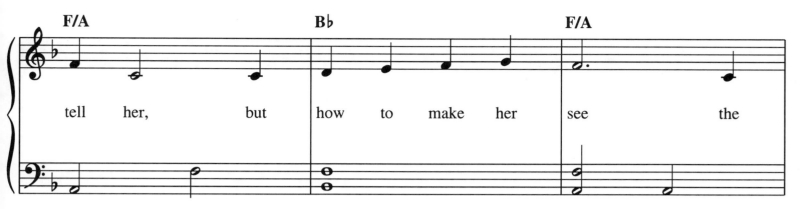

tell her, but how to make her see the

truth a - bout my past? Im - pos - si - ble. She'd turn a - way from

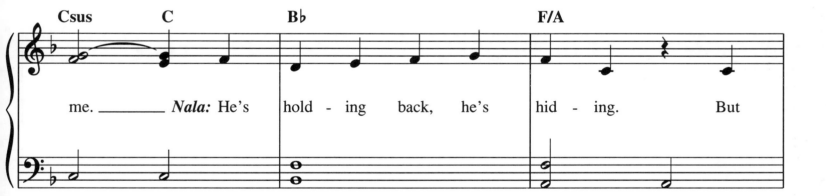

me. _____ *Nala:* He's hold - ing back, he's hid - ing. But

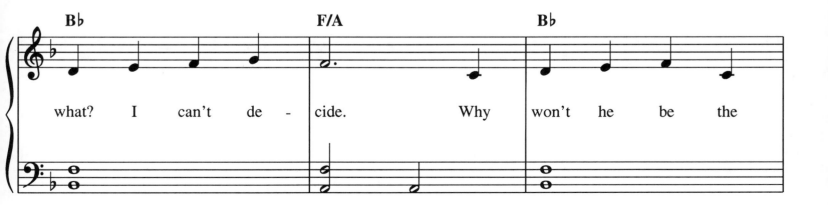

what? I can't de - cide. Why won't he be the

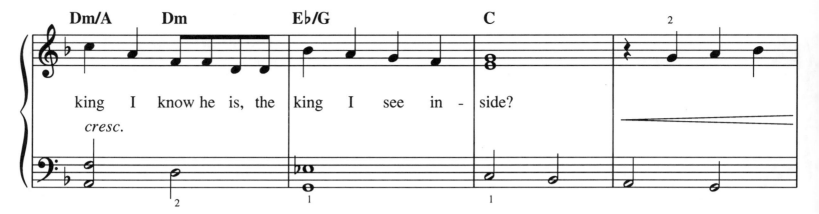

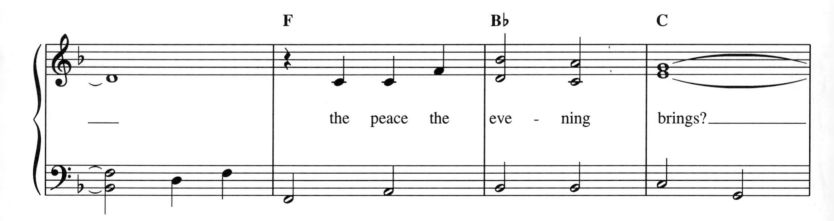

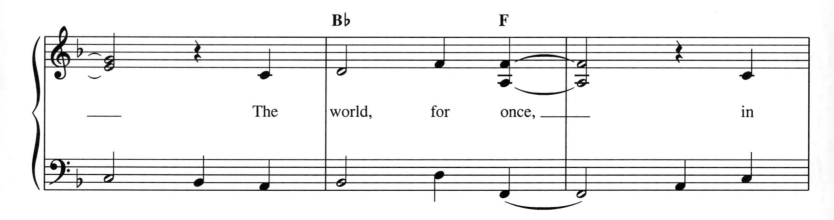

per - fect har - mo - ny with all its

liv - ing things. _____ *cresc.* Can you feel _____ *f*

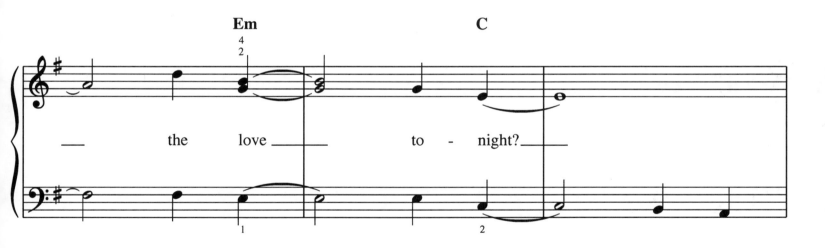

_____ the love _____ to - night? _____

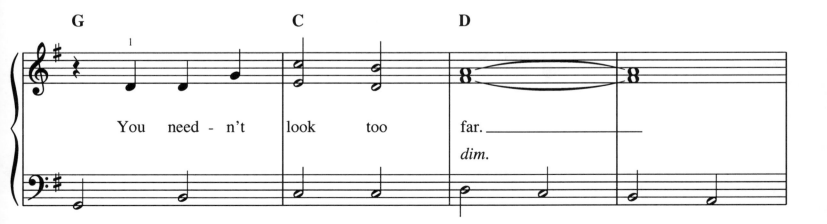

You need - n't look too far. _____ *dim.*

28

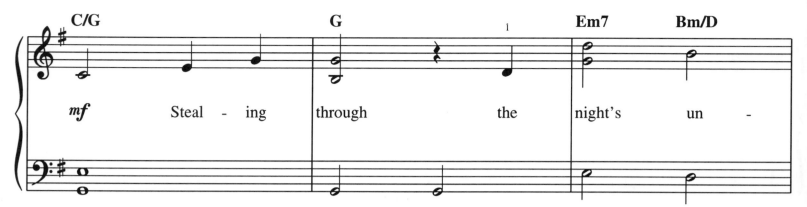

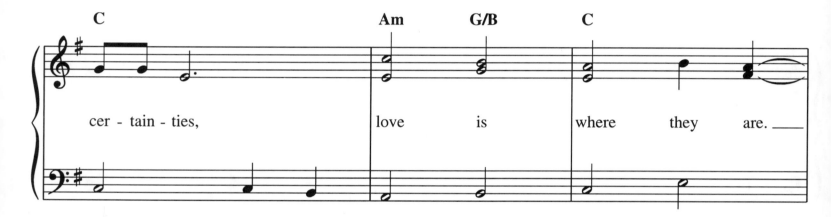

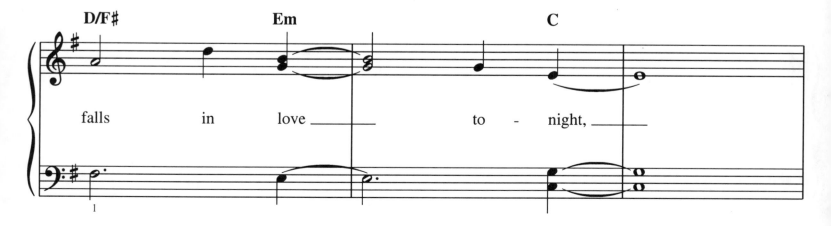

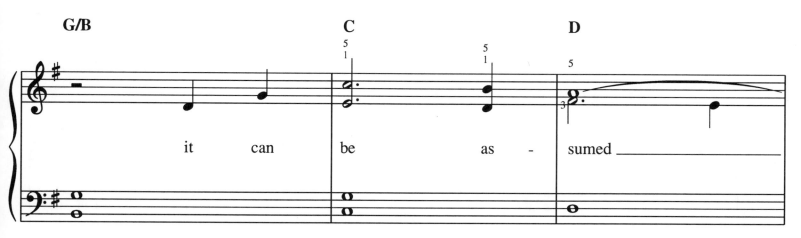

it can be as - sumed _____

_____ *Pumbaa:* his care - free days with

us are his - tory, in short, our

Timon And Pumbaa:

rall.

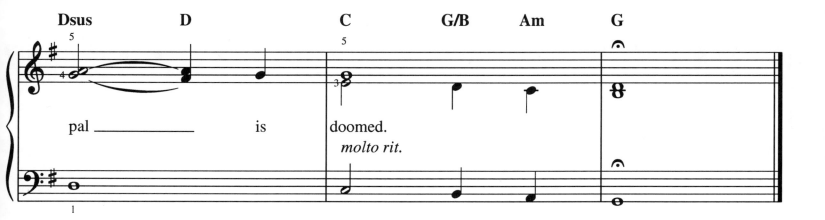

pal _____ is doomed.

molto rit.

CANDLE ON THE WATER

from Walt Disney's PETE'S DRAGON

Words and Music by AL KASHA
and JOEL HIRSCHHORN

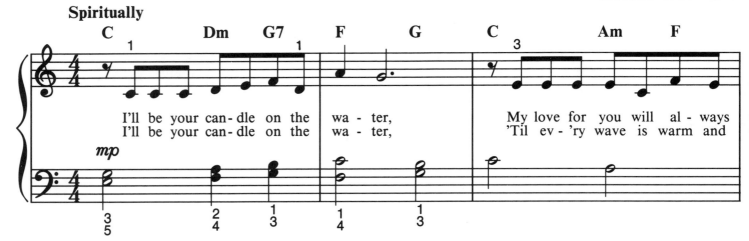

I'll be your can-dle on the wa-ter,
My love for you will al-ways
I'll be your can-dle on the wa-ter,
'Til ev-'ry wave is warm and

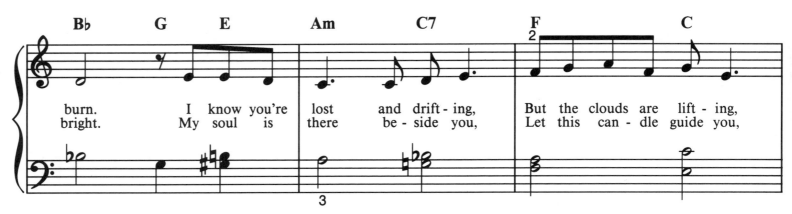

burn. I know you're lost and drift-ing, But the clouds are lift-ing,
bright. My soul is there be-side you, Let this can-dle guide you,

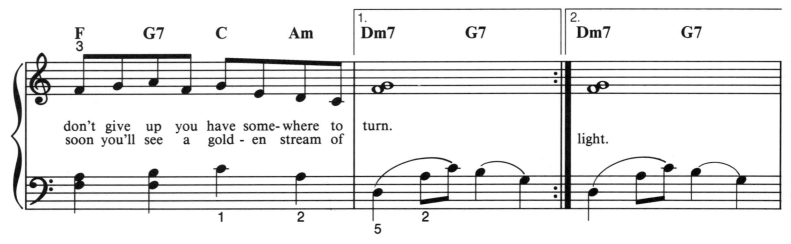

don't give up you have some-where to turn.
soon you'll see a gold-en stream of light.

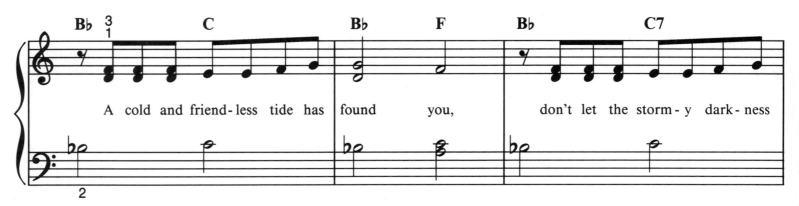

A cold and friend-less tide has found you, don't let the storm-y dark-ness

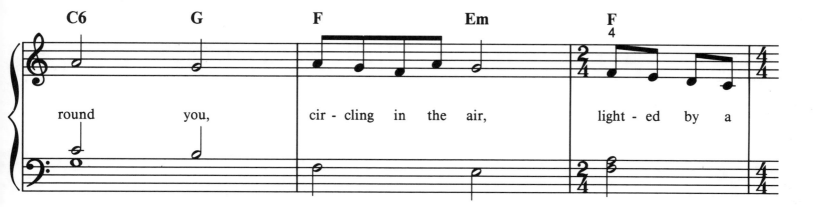

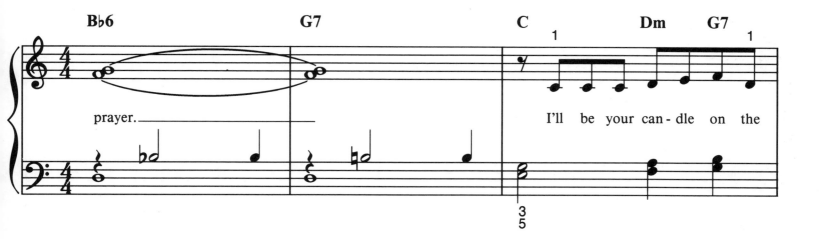

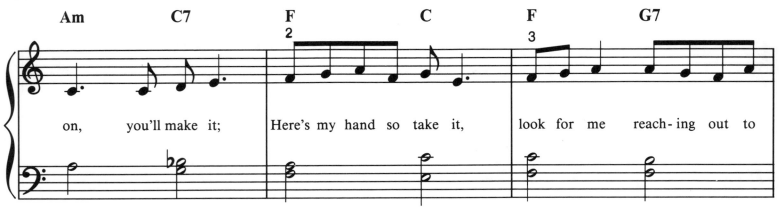

on,   you'll make it;   Here's my hand so take it,   look for me   reach-ing out to

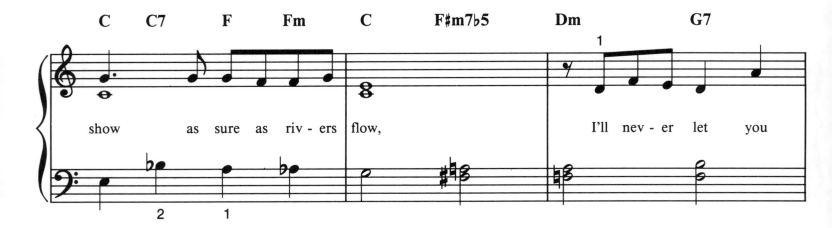

show   as sure as riv - ers flow,   I'll nev - er let   you

go,   I'll nev- er let   you go,   I'll nev- er let   you

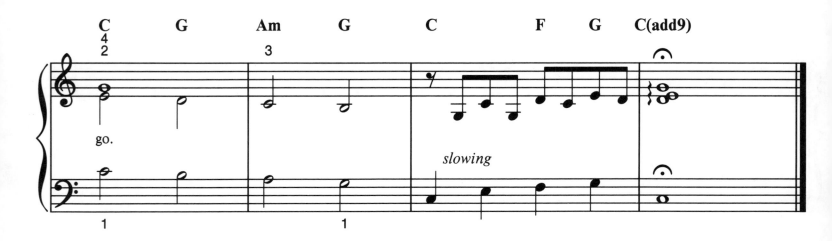

go.   *slowing*

DANCE LITTLE BIRD
(The Chicken Dance)

By TERRY RENDALL
and WERNER THOMAS

Rhythmically

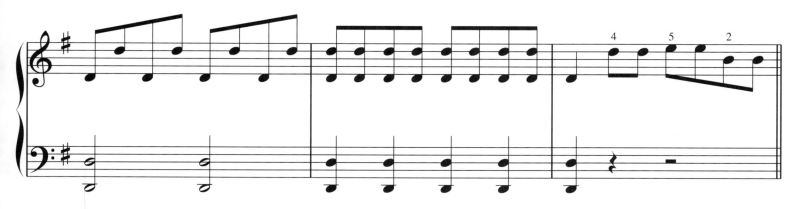

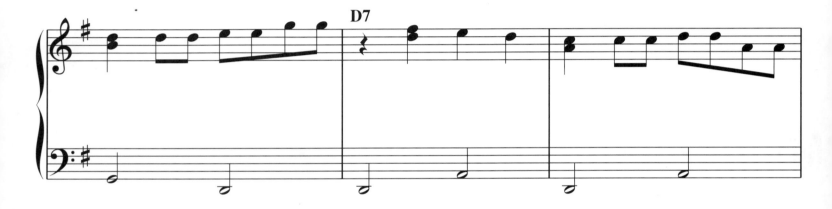

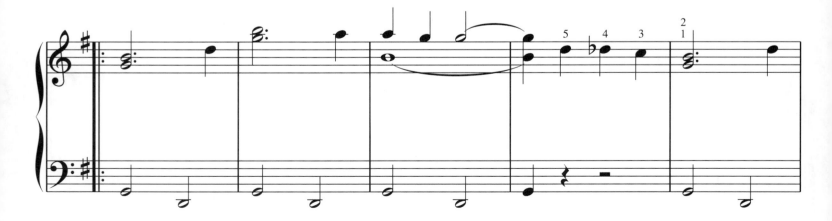

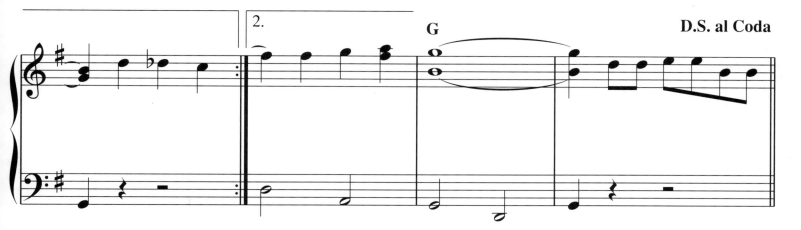

CIRCLE OF LIFE
from Walt Disney Pictures' THE LION KING

Music by ELTON JOHN
Lyrics by TIM RICE

Moderately

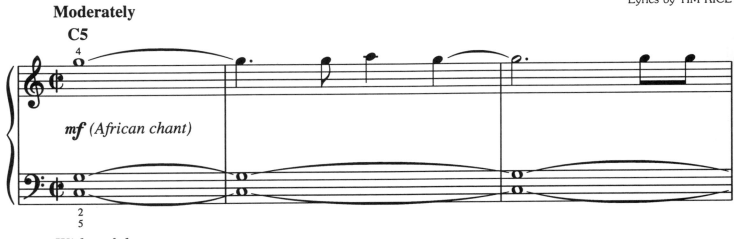

mf (African chant)

With pedal

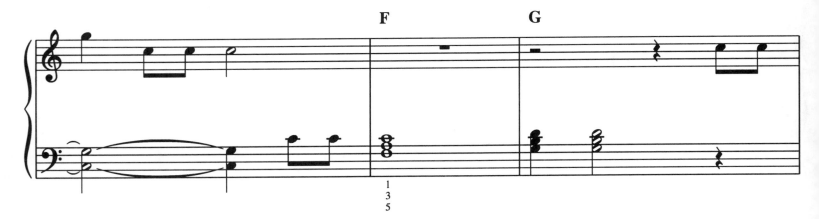

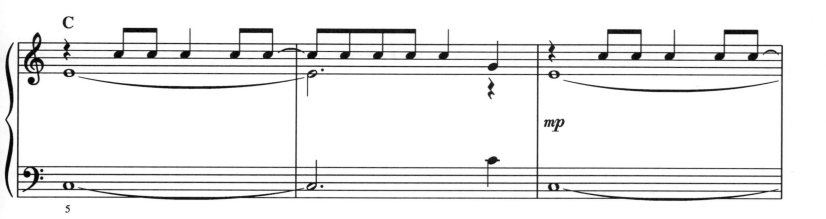

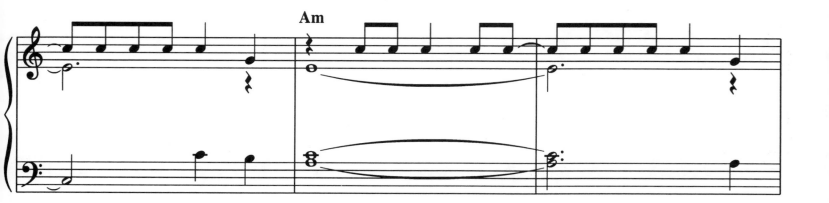

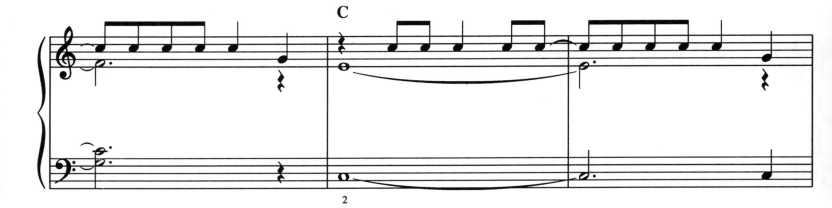

From the

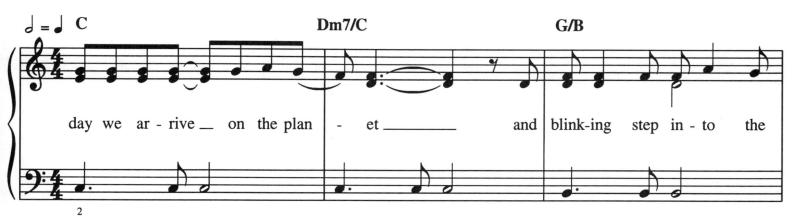

day we ar - rive __ on the plan - et _____ and blink-ing step in - to the

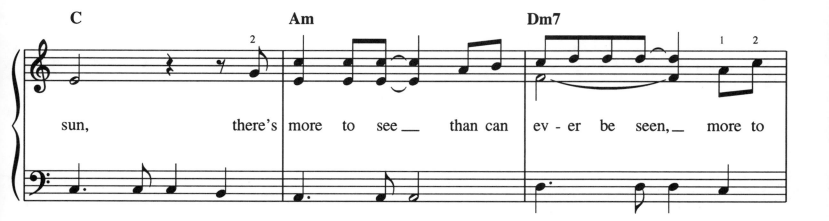

sun, there's more to see __ than can ev - er be seen, __ more to

do than can ev - er be done. _____ There's far too much __ to take

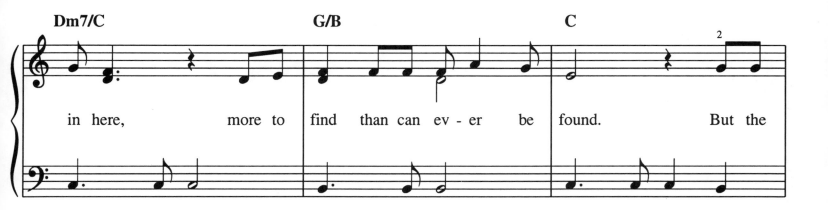

in here, more to find than can ev - er be found. But the

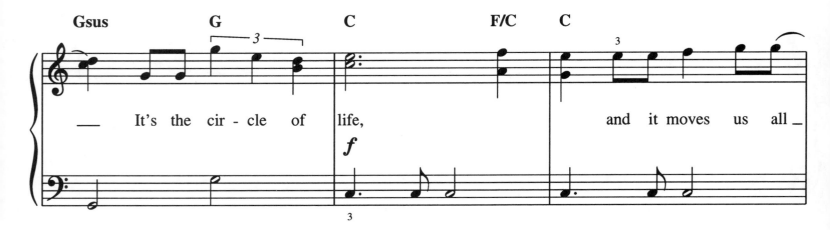

sun roll-ing high_ through the sap-phi-re sky_ keeps great and small on the end-less round._

_ It's the cir-cle of life, and it moves us all_

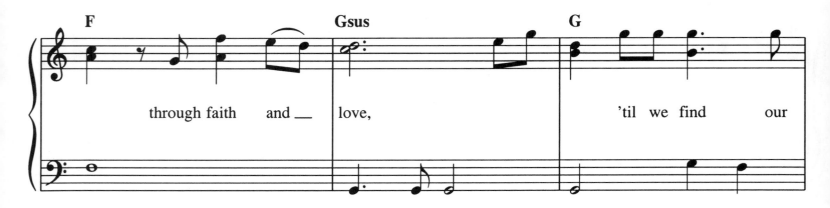

_ through de-spair and hope,_____ through faith and _ love, 'til we find our

place _____ on the path un - wind - ing

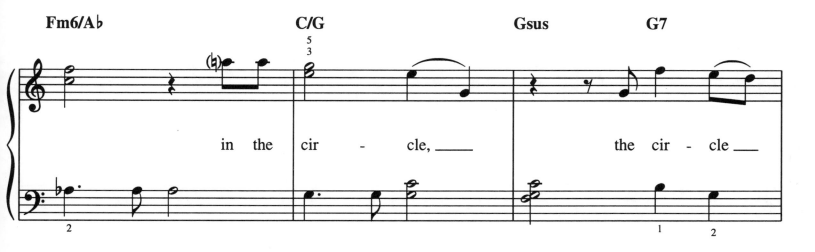

in the cir - cle, _____ the cir - cle _____

of life.

dim.

p

42

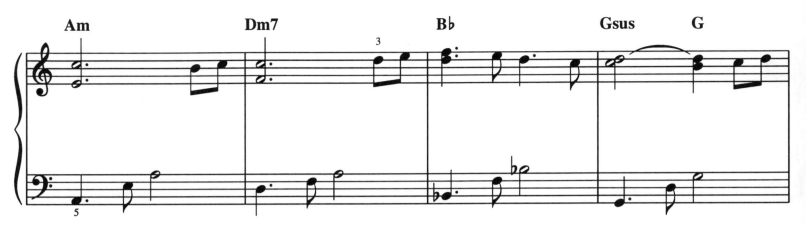

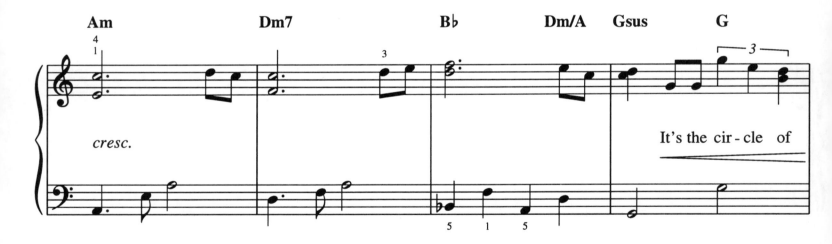

It's the cir-cle of

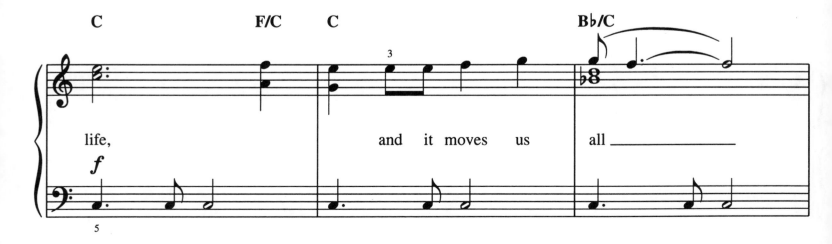

life, and it moves us all

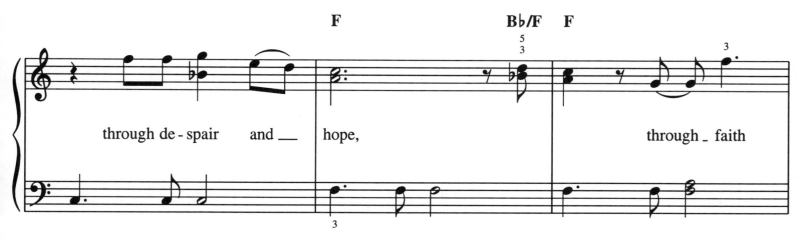

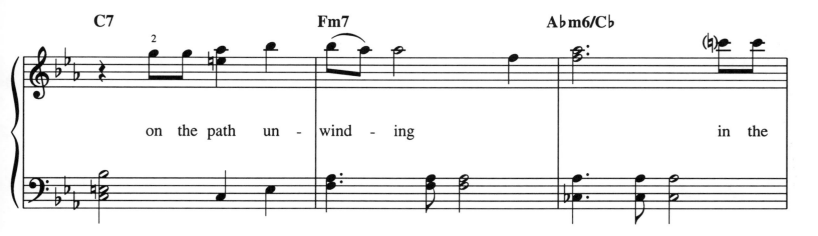
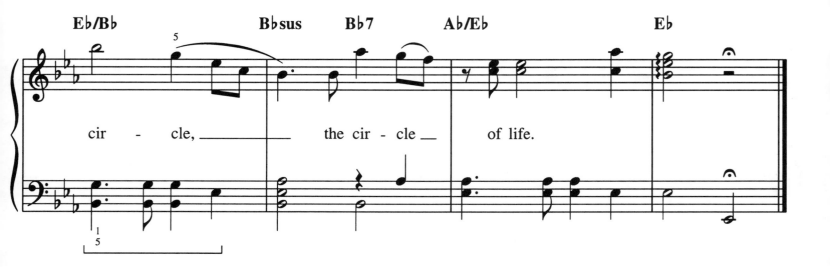

COLORS OF THE WIND
from Walt Disney's POCAHONTAS

Music by ALAN MENKEN
Lyrics by STEPHEN SCHWARTZ

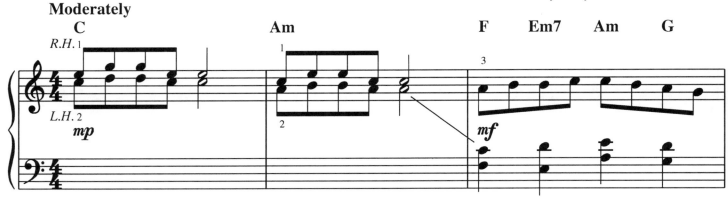

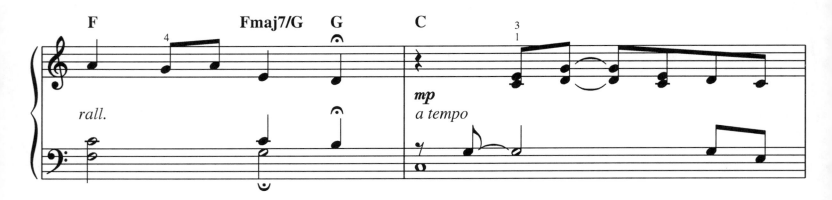

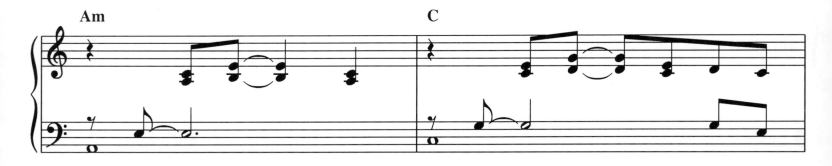

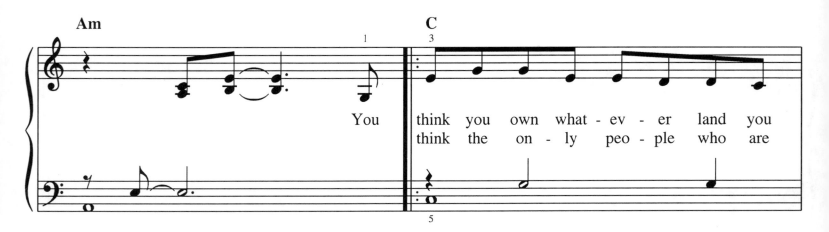

You think you own what-ev-er land you
think the on-ly peo-ple who are

45

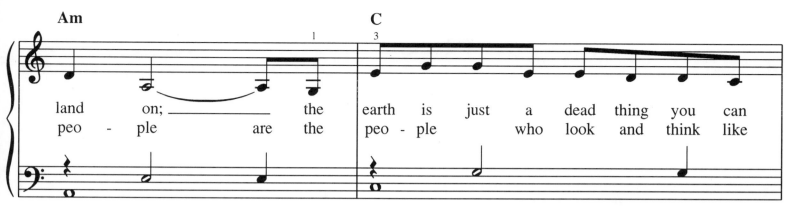

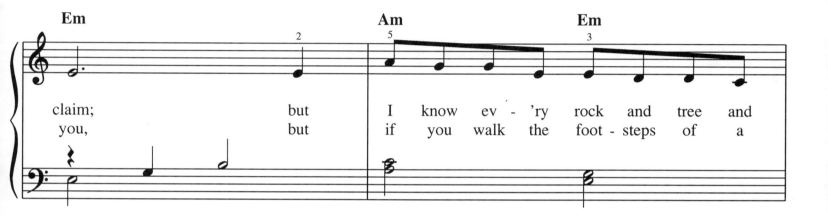

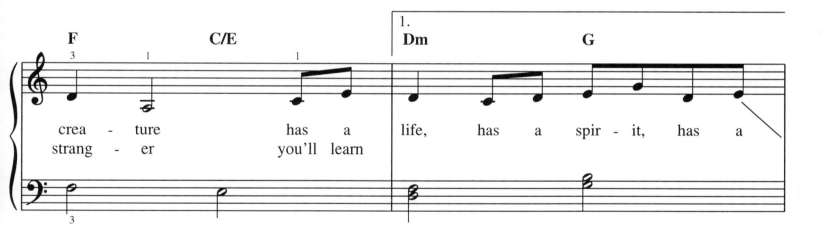

46

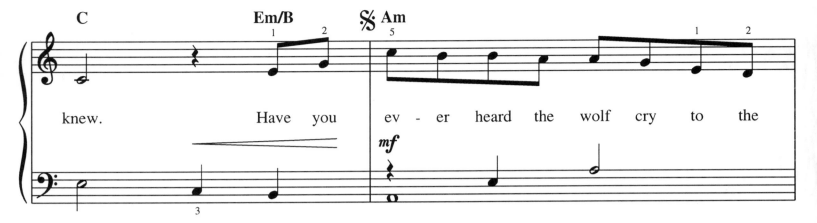

knew. Have you ev - er heard the wolf cry to the

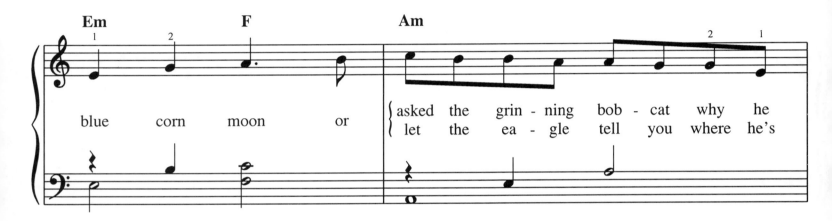

blue corn moon or asked the grin - ning bob - cat why he
let the ea - gle tell you where he's

grinned?
been? Can you sing with all the voic - es of the

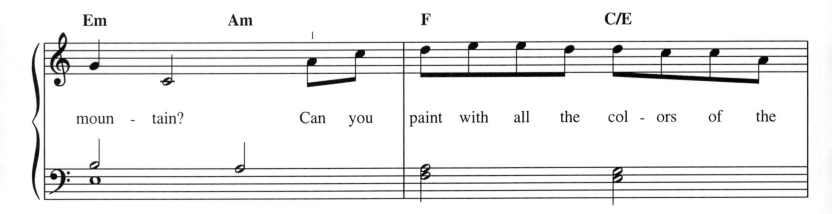

moun - tain? Can you paint with all the col - ors of the

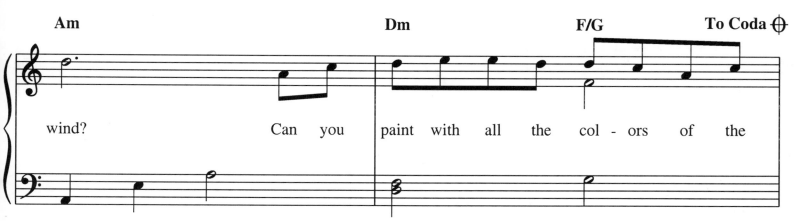

Am — wind? Can you — Dm — paint with all the col - ors of the — F/G — To Coda

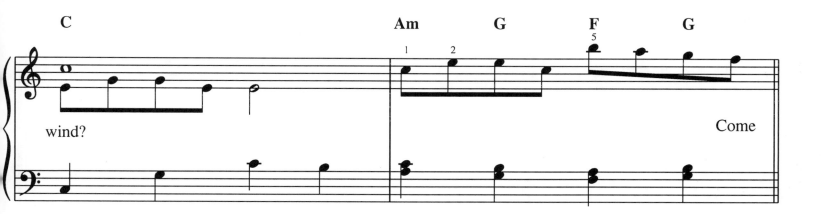

C — wind? — Am — G — F — G — Come

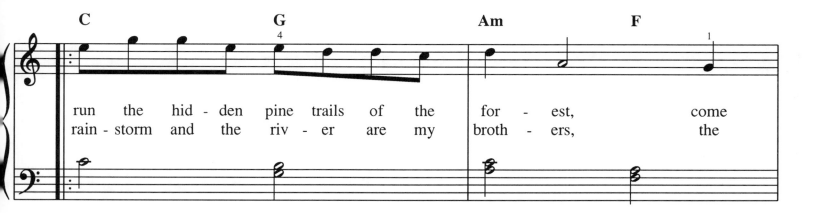

C — run the hid - den pine trails of the — G — for - est, — Am — come — F

rain - storm and the riv - er are my broth - ers, the

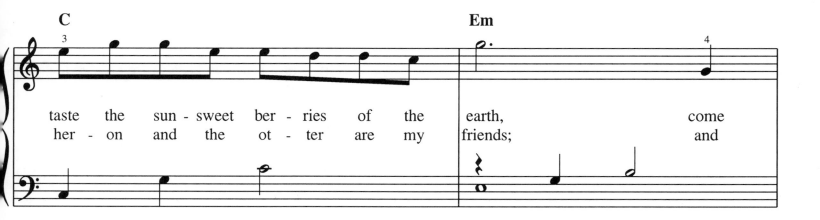

C — taste the sun - sweet ber - ries of the — Em — earth, — come

her - on and the ot - ter are my friends; and

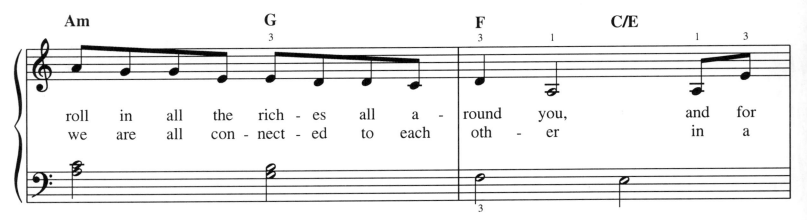

Am **G** **F** **C/E**

roll in all the rich - es all a - round you, and for
we are all con - nect - ed to each oth - er in a

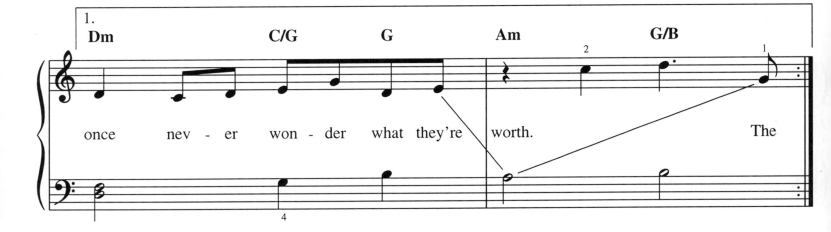

1.
Dm **C/G** **G** **Am** **G/B**

once nev - er won - der what they're worth. The

2. **D.S. al Coda**
Dm **F/G** **C** **Em/B**

cir - cle, in a hoop that nev - er ___ ends. ___ Have you

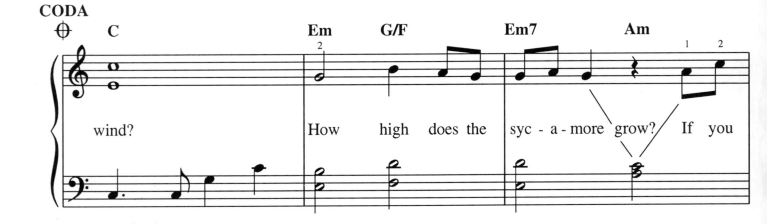

CODA
C **Em** **G/F** **Em7** **Am**

wind? How high does the syc - a - more grow? If you

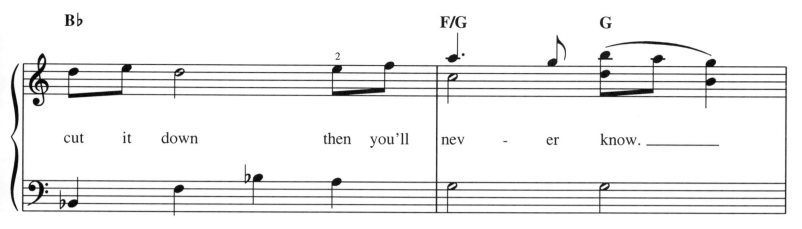

cut it down   then you'll   nev - er know. _____

And you'll nev - er hear the wolf cry to the   blue corn moon,   for

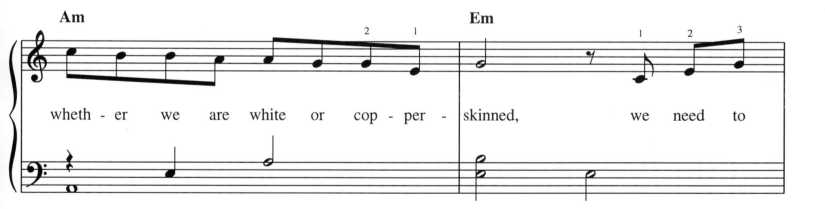

wheth - er we are white or cop - per - skinned,   we need to

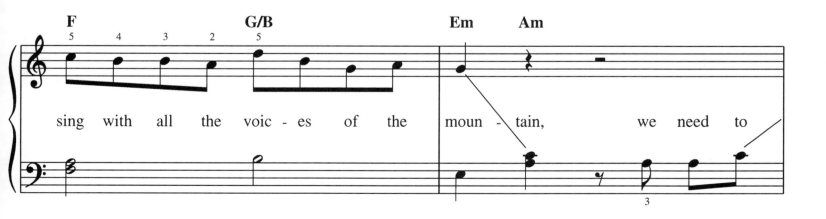

sing with all the voic - es of the   moun - tain,   we need to

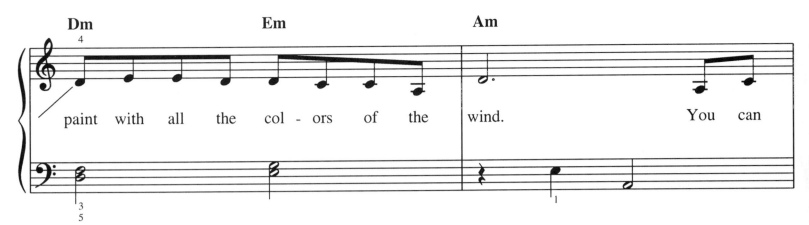

paint with all the col - ors of the wind. You can

own the earth and still all you'll own is earth un - til you can *rall.*

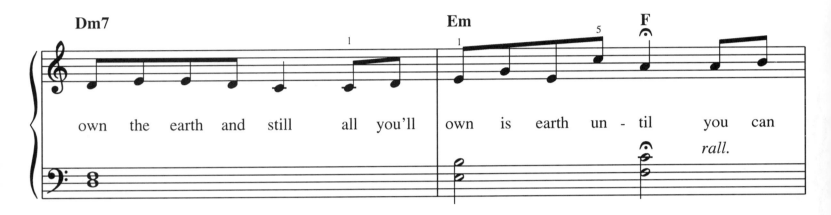

paint with all the col - ors of the wind.
a tempo

rit.

THE GROUCH SONG

from the Television Series SESAME STREET

Words and Music by
JEFF MOSS

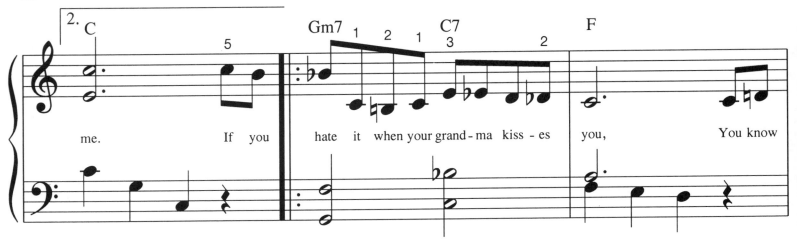

me. If you hate it when your grand-ma kiss-es you, You know

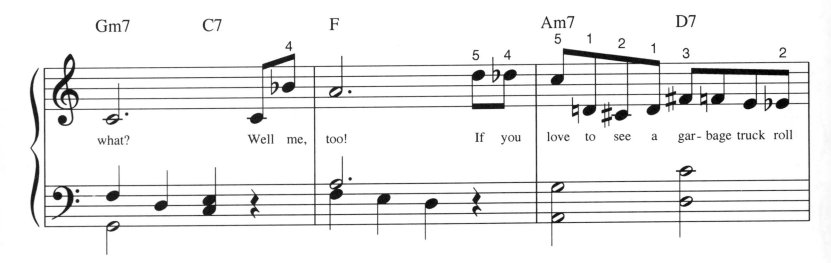

what? Well me, too! If you love to see a gar-bage truck roll

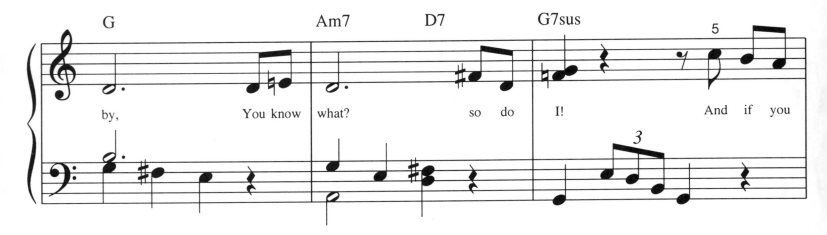

by, You know what? so do I! And if you

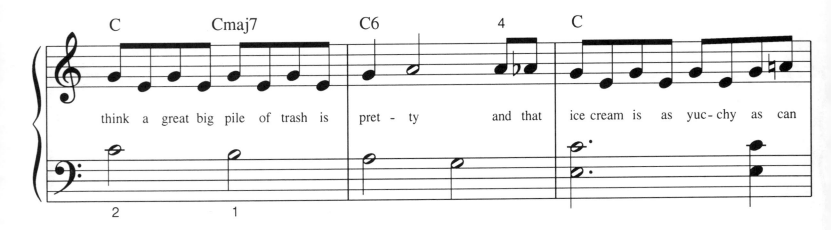

think a great big pile of trash is pret-ty and that ice cream is as yuc-chy as can

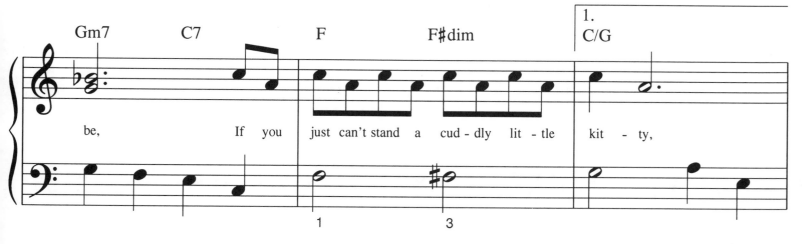

Gm7   C7   F   F♯dim   **1.** C/G

be,   If you   just can't stand a cud - dly lit - tle   kit - ty,

D7   G7   C   **2.** C   A

then you're a grouch _ like   me.   If you   kit - ty   And you'd

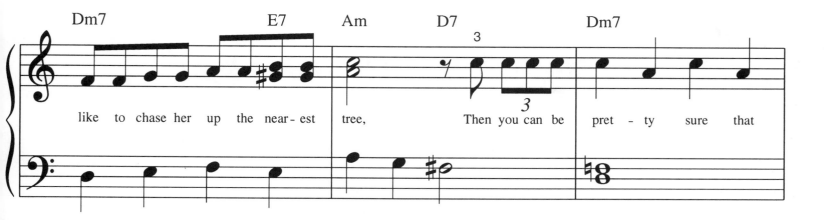

Dm7   E7   Am   D7   Dm7

like to chase her up the near - est   tree,   Then you can be   pret - ty sure that

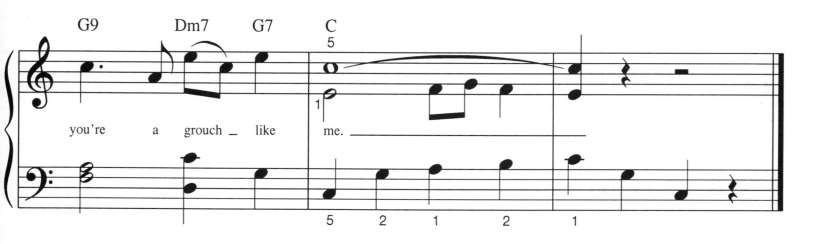

G9   Dm7   G7   C

you're a grouch _ like   me. _____

DO YOUR EARS HANG LOW?

Traditional

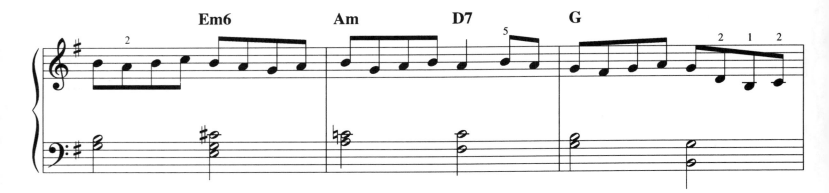

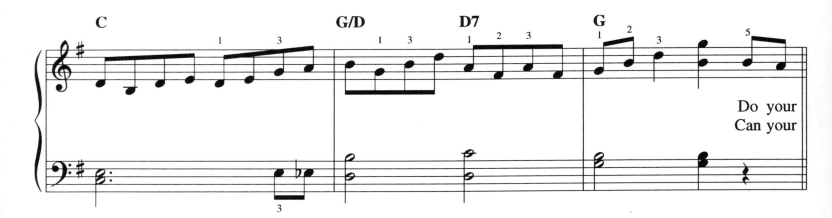

Do your
Can your

(D.S.) ears hang low? Do they wob - ble to and fro? Can you
ears stand high? Can they stand up in the sky? Can they

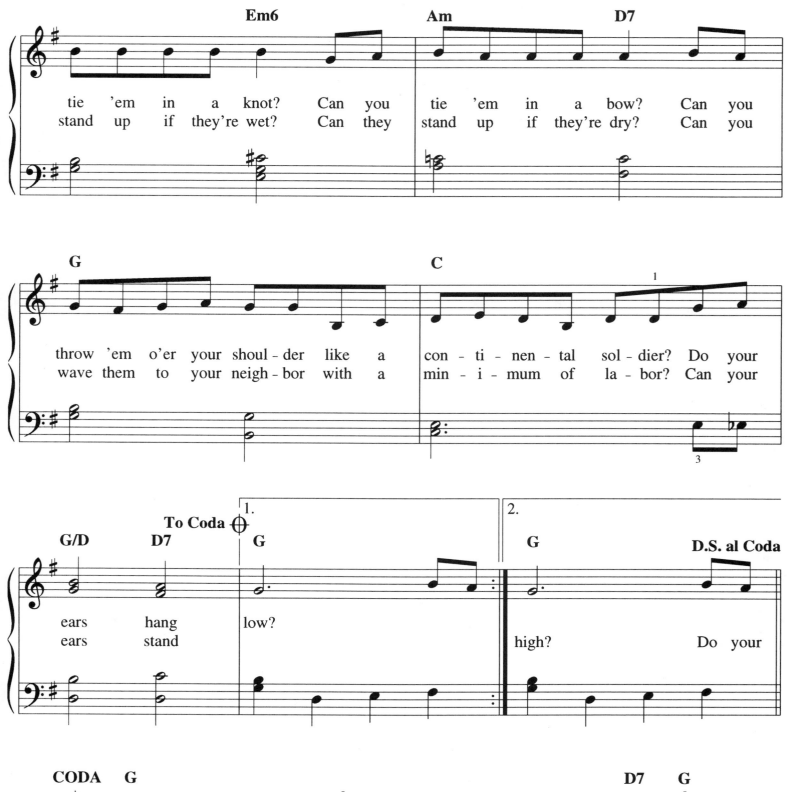

GO THE DISTANCE
from Walt Disney Pictures' HERCULES

Music by ALAN MENKEN
Lyrics by DAVID ZIPPEL

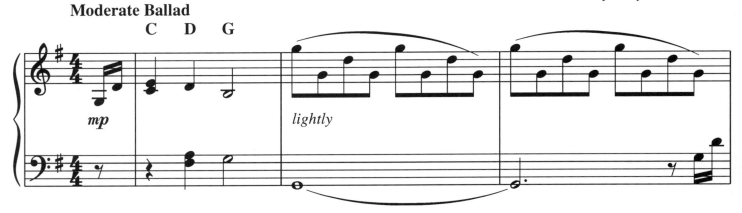

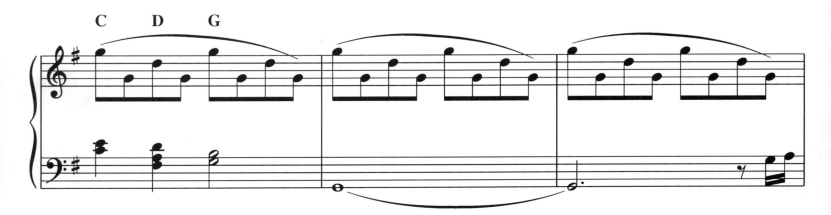

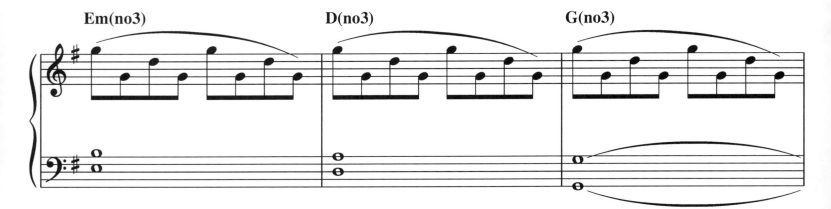

Young Hercules: I have of - ten dreamed of a far - off place where a

great warm wel-come will be wait - ing for me. Where the crowds will cheer when they

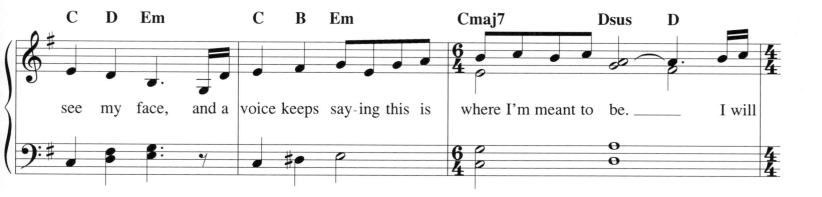

see my face, and a voice keeps say-ing this is where I'm meant to be. _____ I will

find my way. I can go the dis-tance. I'll be there some - day

if I can be strong. I know ev - 'ry mile will be worth my

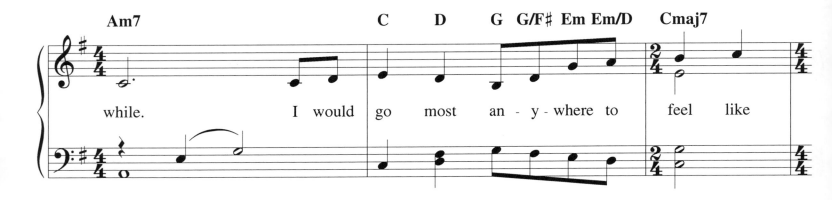

while. I would go most an - y - where to feel like

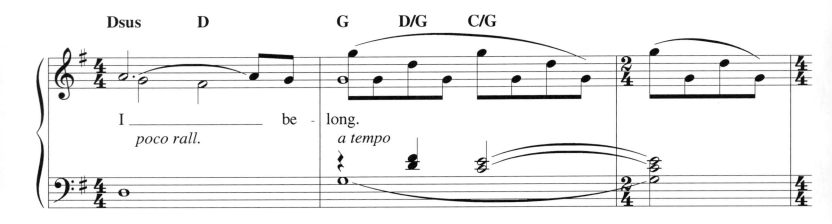

I _____ be - long.

poco rall. *a tempo*

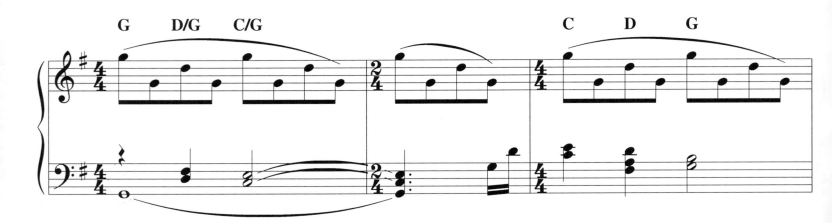

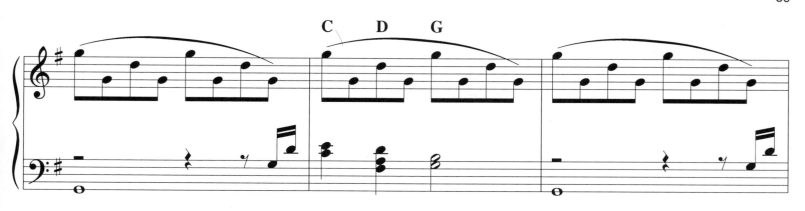

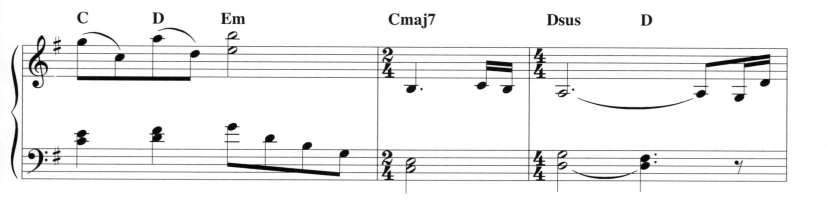

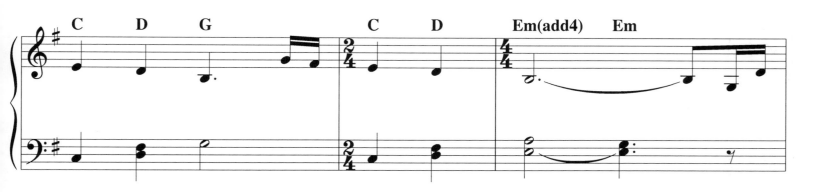

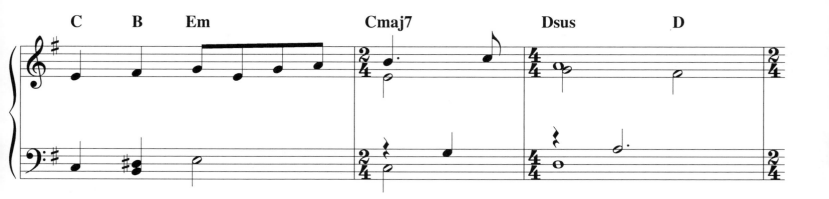

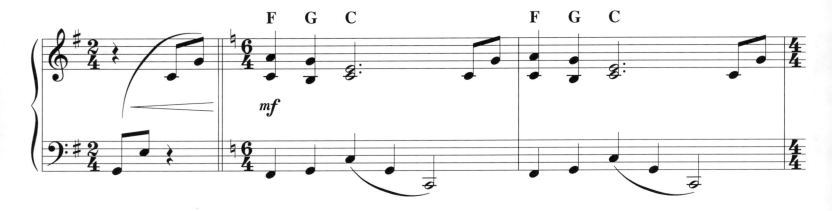

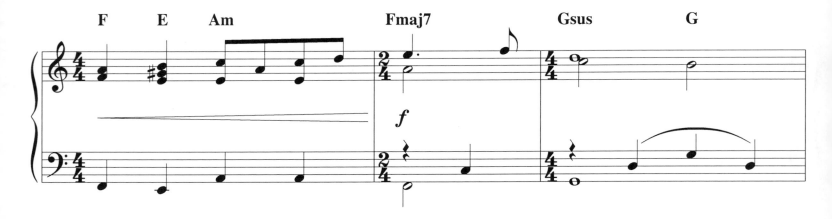

I am on my way. I can go the dis-tance. I don't

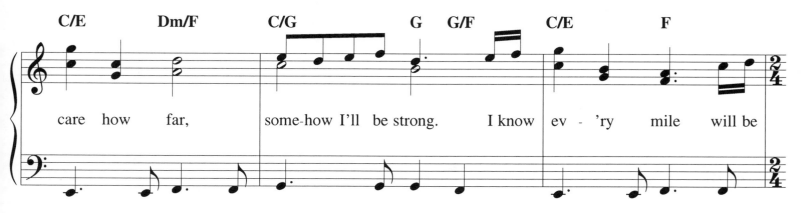

care how far, some-how I'll be strong. I know ev - 'ry mile will be

worth my while. I would go most an - y - where to

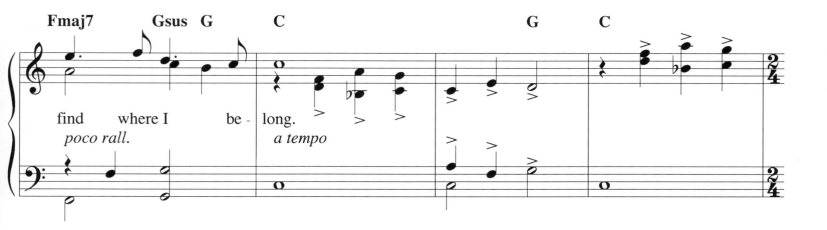

find where I be - long.
poco rall.   *a tempo*

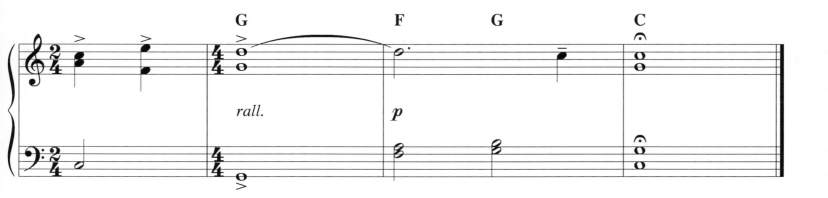

rall.   *p*

GOD HELP THE OUTCASTS

from Walt Disney's THE HUNCHBACK OF NOTRE DAME

Music by ALAN MENKEN
Lyrics by STEPHEN SCHWARTZ

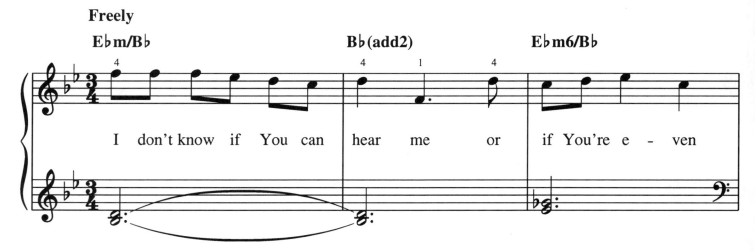

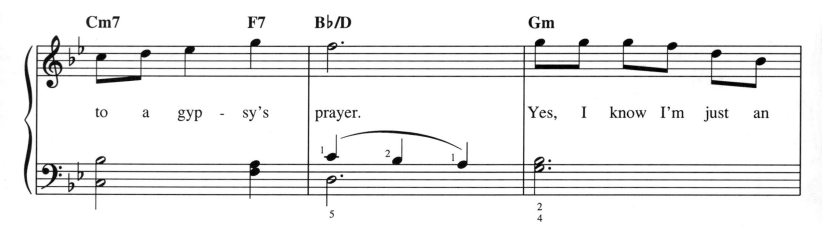

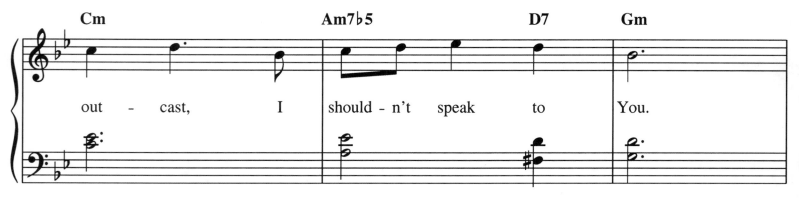

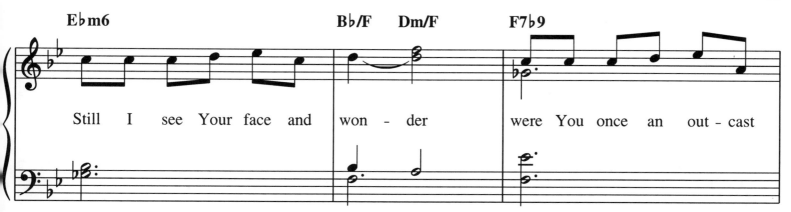

Still I see Your face and won - der were You once an out - cast

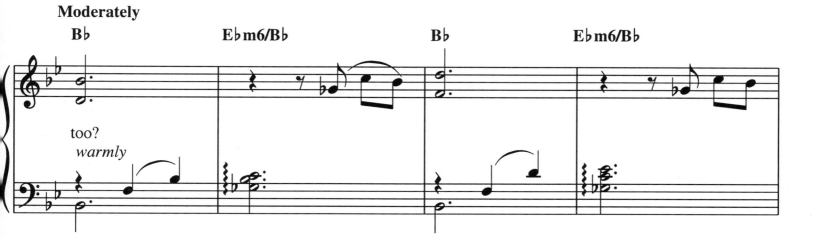

Moderately

too?
warmly

God help the out - casts, hun - gry from birth.

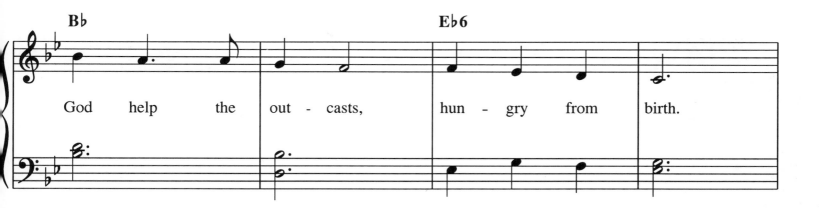

Show them the mer - cy they don't find on

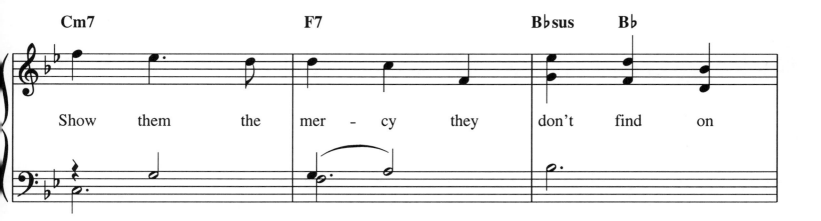

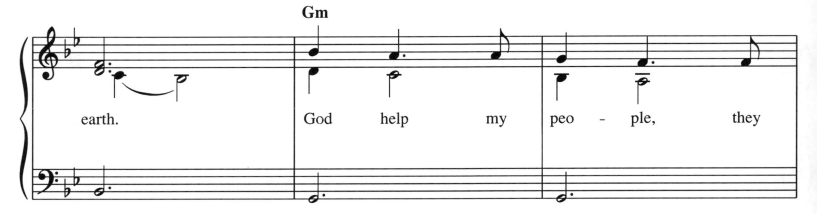

earth.   God   help   my   peo - ple,   they

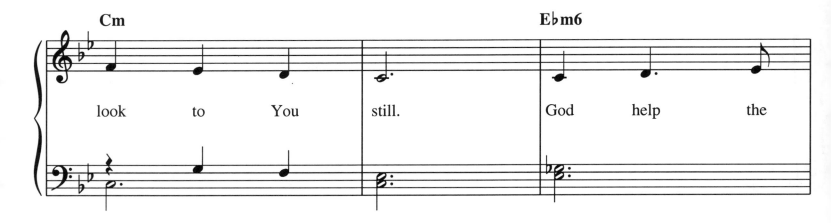

look   to   You   still.   God   help   the

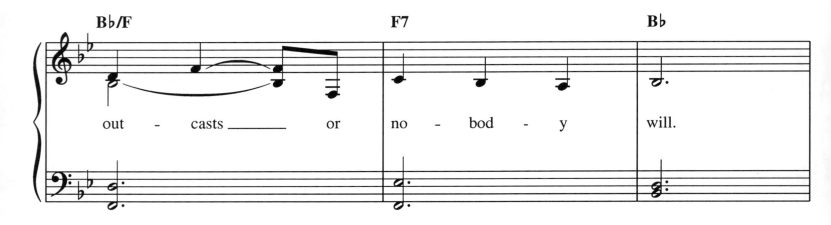

out - casts _____ or   no - bod - y   will.

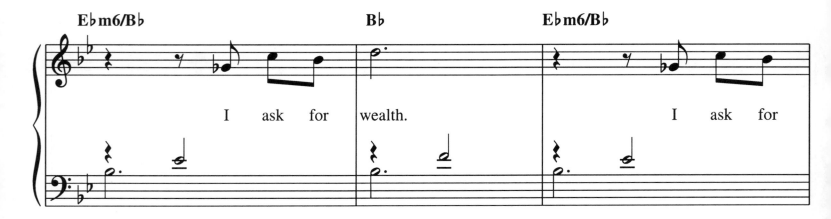

I   ask   for   wealth.   I   ask   for

fame.

Gm   **Gm/F**   **Eb**

I ask for glo - ry to

mf nobly

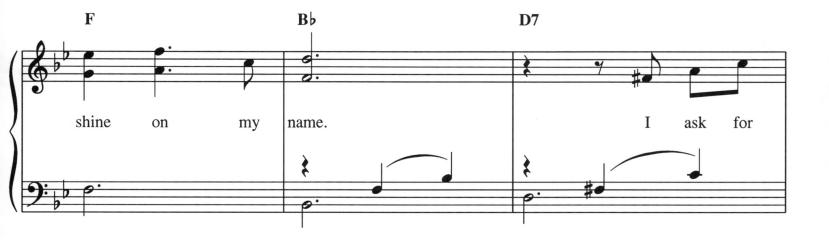

F   **Bb**   **D7**

shine on my name. I ask for

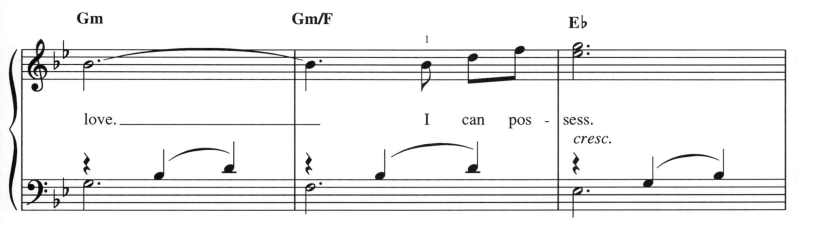

Gm   **Gm/F**   **Eb**

love. _____ I can pos - sess.

cresc.

Gm/D   **Cm7**   **Bb**

I ask for God and His an - gels to

f espr.

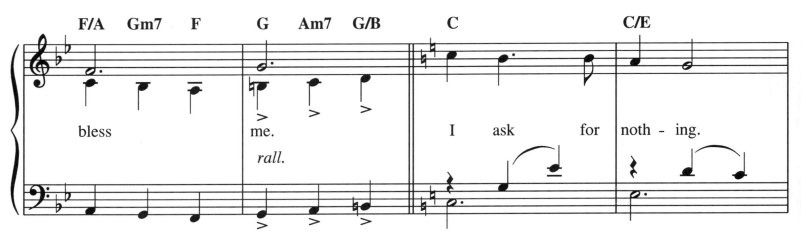

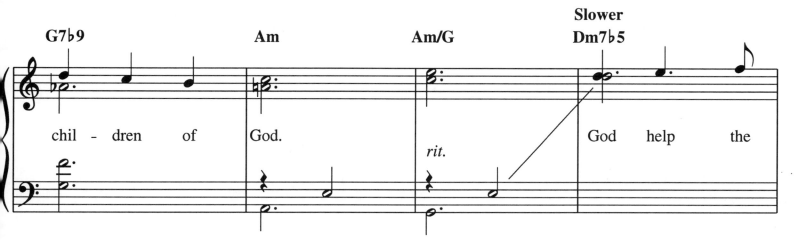

chil - dren of God.   *rit.*   God help the

out - casts   chil - dren of God.

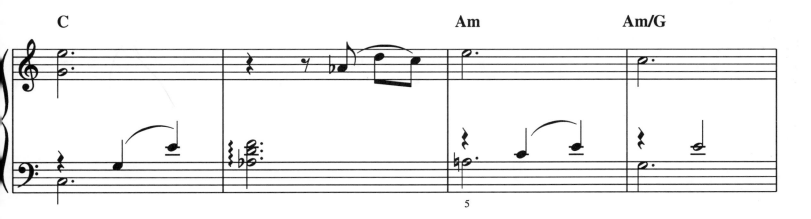

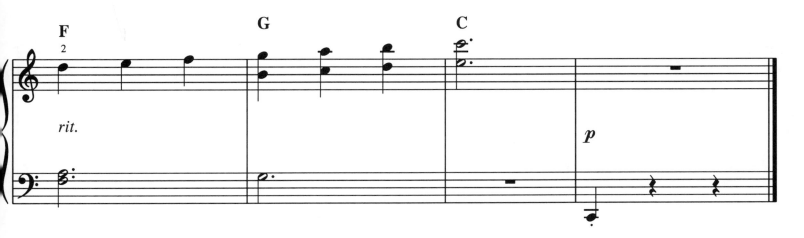

rit.

HOW MUCH IS THAT DOGGIE IN THE WINDOW

Words and Music by
BOB MERRILL

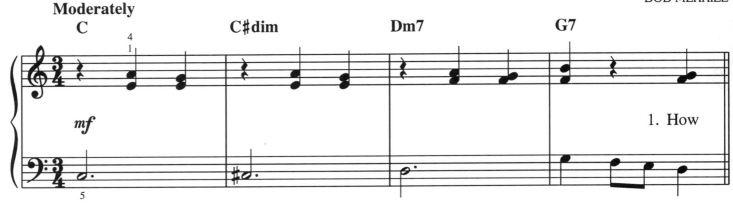

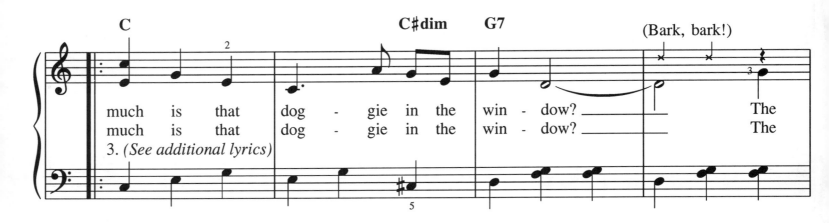

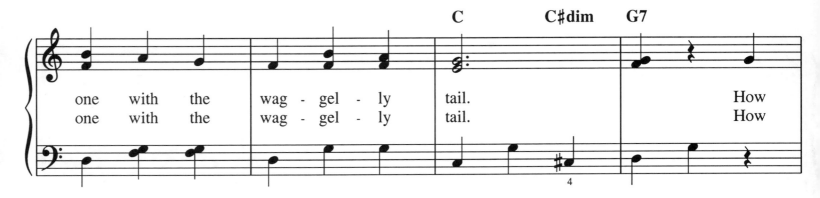

69

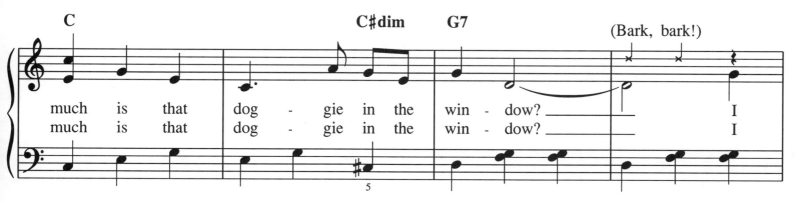

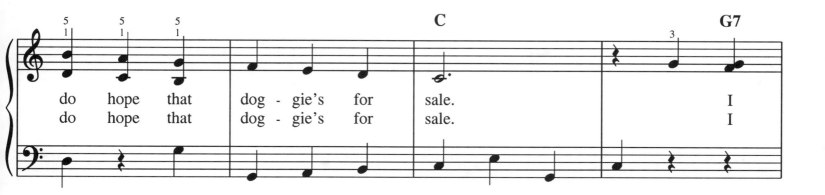

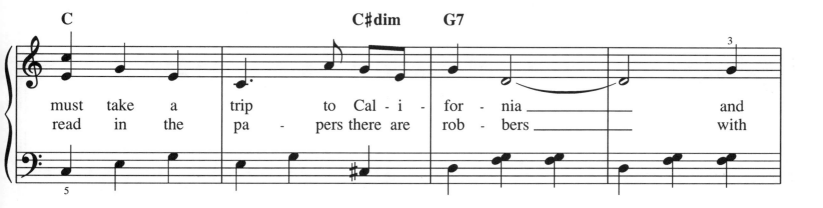

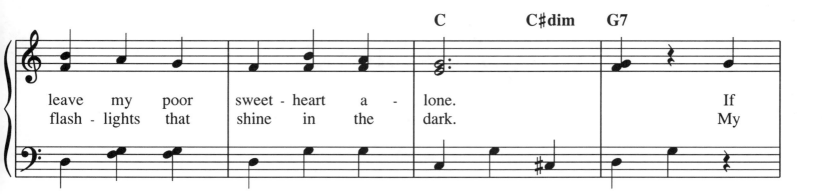

C he has a dog he won't be **C#dim** lone- **G7** some, ___
love needs a dog - gie to pro- tect him ___

___ and the dog - gie will have a good
and ___ scare them a - way with one

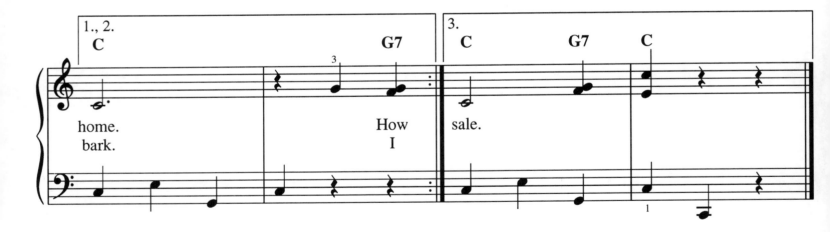

1., 2. **C** home. **G7** How
bark. I
3. **C** sale. **G7** **C**

Additional Lyrics

3. I don't want a bunny or a kitty.
I don't want a parrot that talks,
I don't want a bowl of little fishies;
He can't take a goldfish for walks.
How much is that doggie in the window?
The one with the waggely tail.
How much is that doggie in the window?
I do hope that doggie's for sale.

HAKUNA MATATA

from Walt Disney Pictures' THE LION KING

Music by ELTON JOHN
Lyrics by TIM RICE

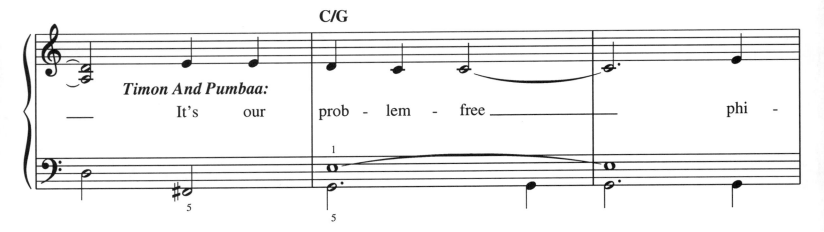

C/G

Timon And Pumbaa:
It's our prob - lem - free _____ phi -

G

lo - so - phy. ___   *Timon:* Ha - ku - na ma - ta - ta. ___

C

rall.

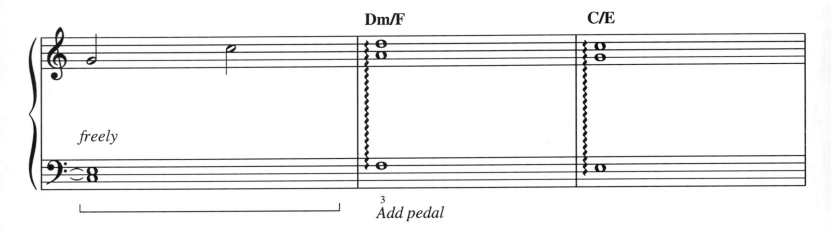

Dm/F   **C/E**

freely

Add pedal

G   **Dm**   **Am**

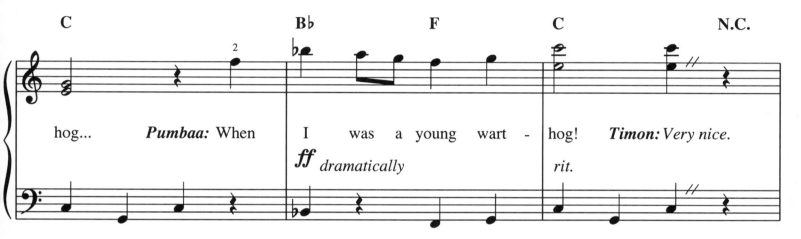

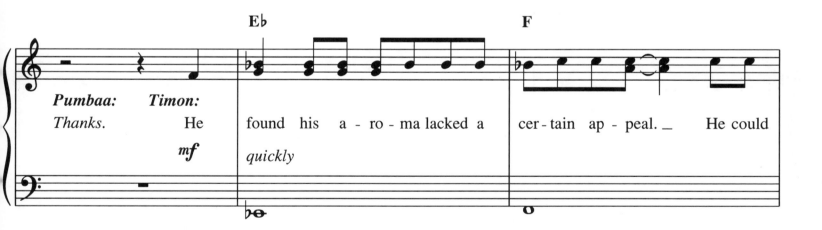

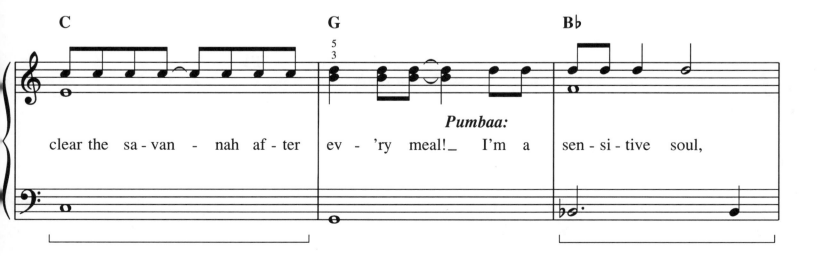

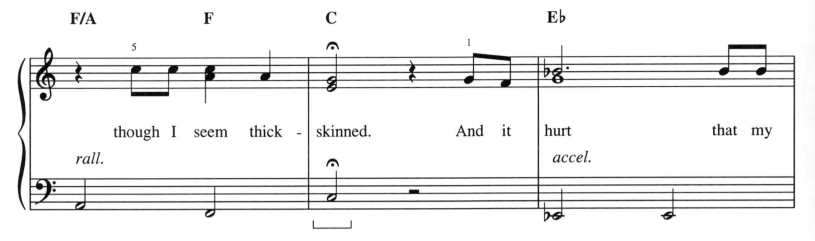

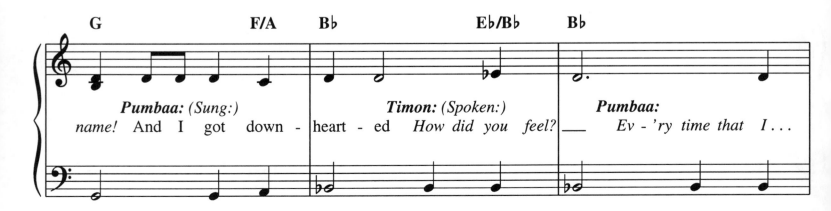

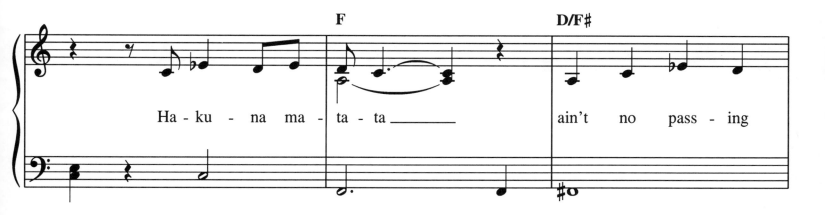

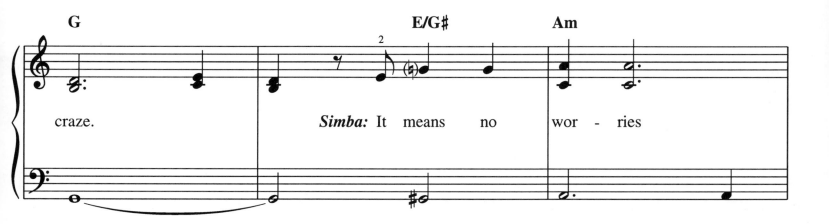

C/E   **F**   **D/F♯**

for   the   rest ___ of your   days. _____   *Timon And Simba:*   It's   our

Timon: Yeah, sing it kid!

C/G   **G**

prob - lem - free _____   *Pumbaa:*   phi - los - o - phy. ____

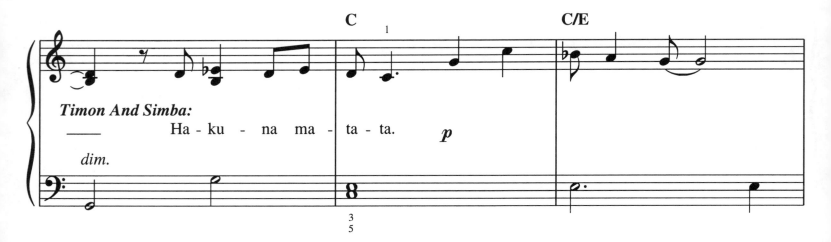

         C   **C/E**

Timon And Simba: ____ Ha - ku - na ma - ta - ta.   *p*

dim.

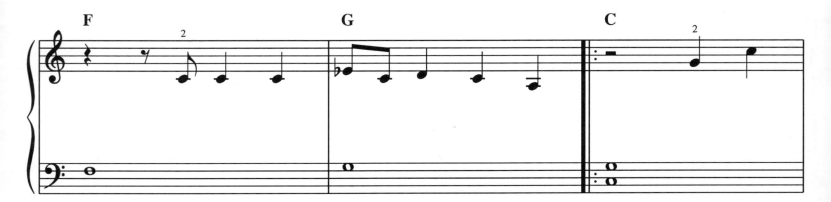

F   **G**   **C**

77

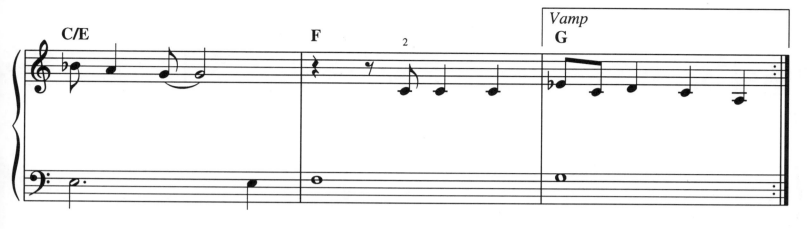

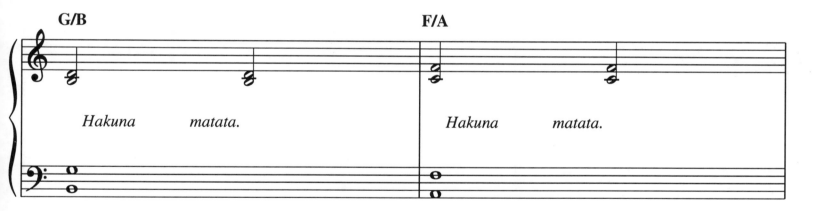

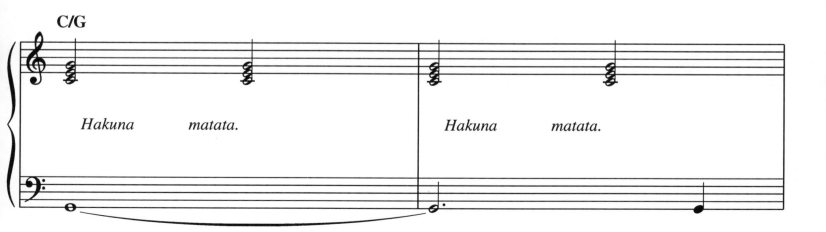

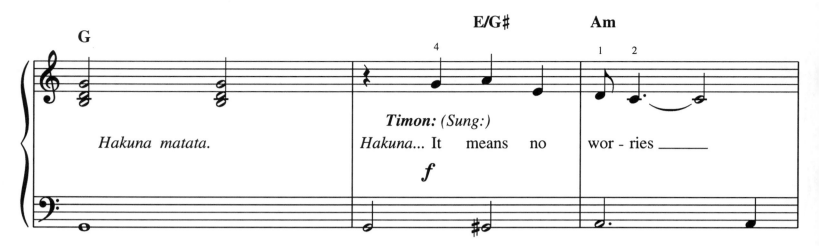

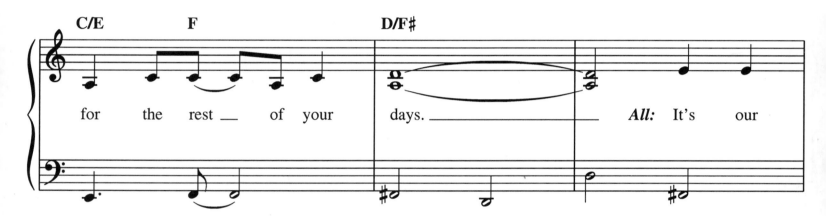

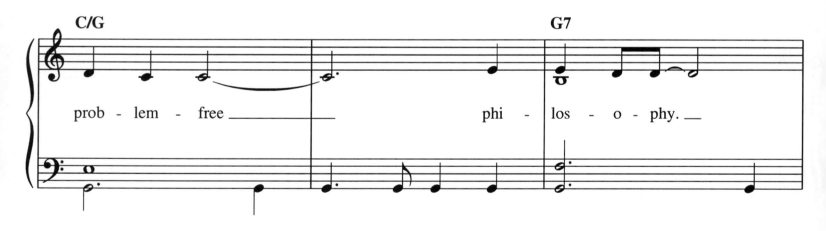

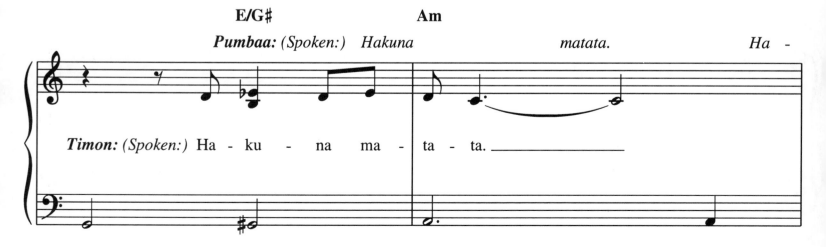

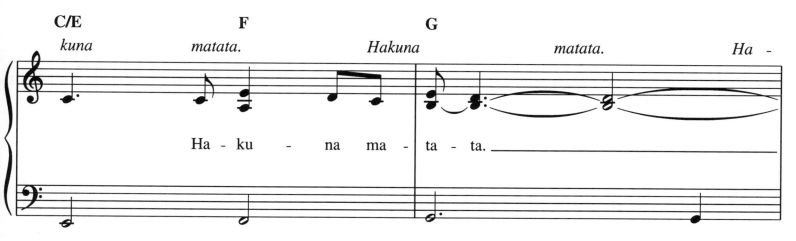

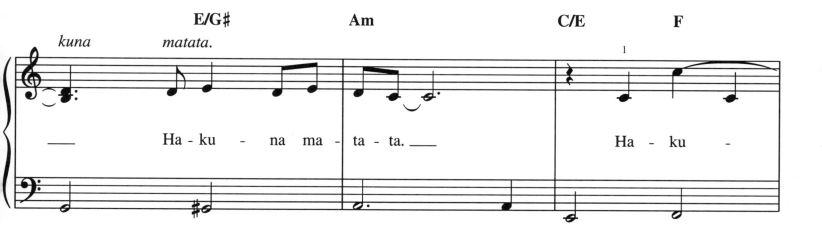

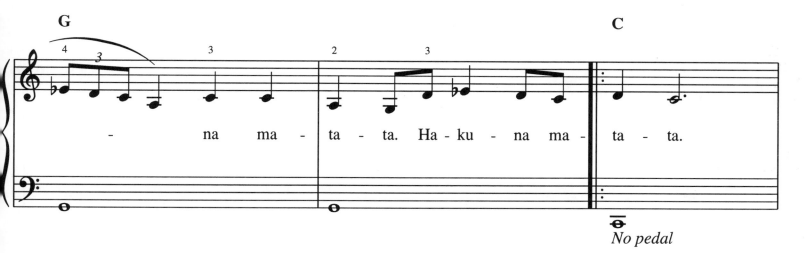

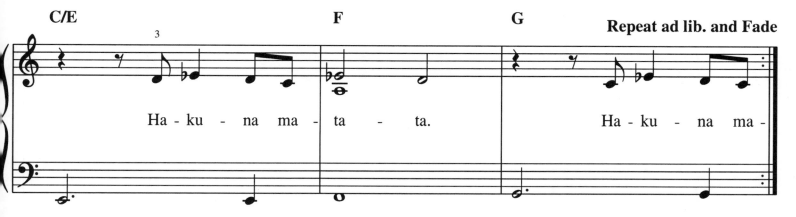

I'M POPEYE THE SAILOR MAN

Theme from the Paramount Cartoon POPEYE THE SAILOR

Words and Music by
SAMMY LERNER

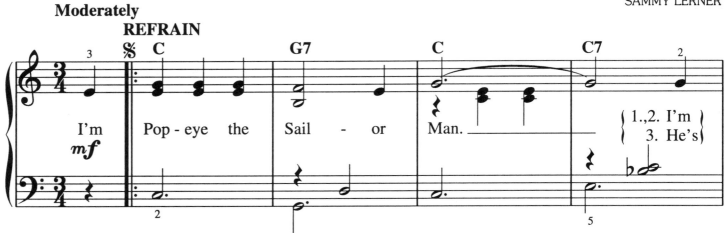

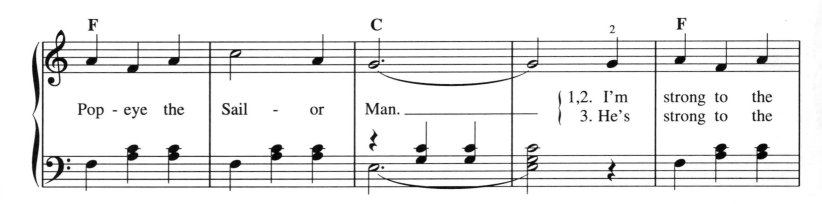

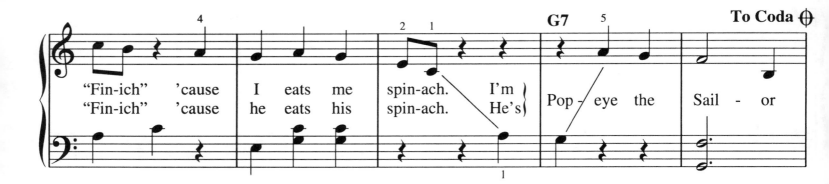

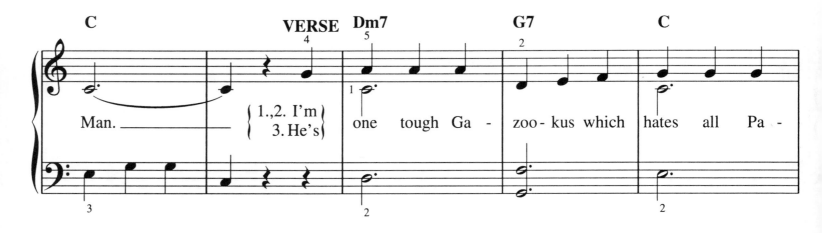

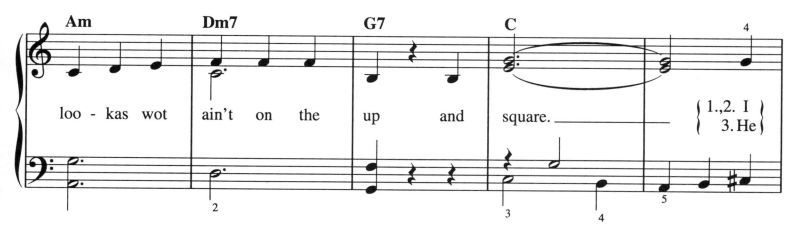

loo-kas wot ain't on the up and square. _____ {1.,2. I / 3. He}

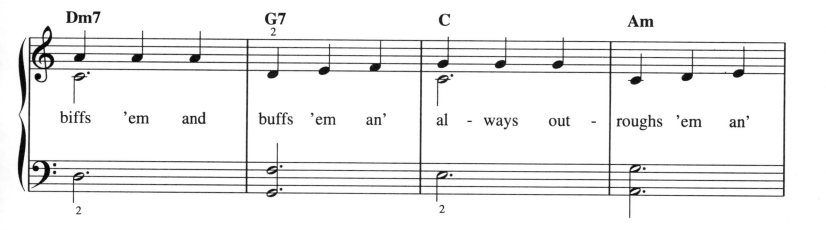

biffs 'em and buffs 'em an' al - ways out - roughs 'em an'

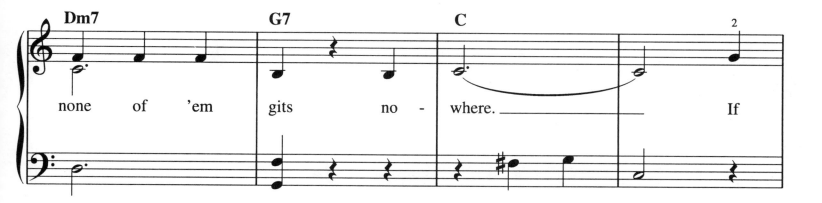

none of 'em gits no - where. _____ If

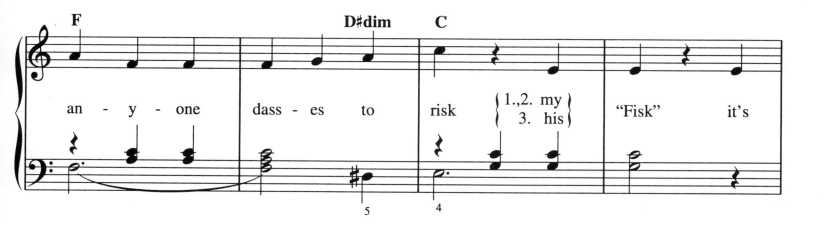

an - y - one dass - es to risk {1.,2. my / 3. his} "Fisk" it's

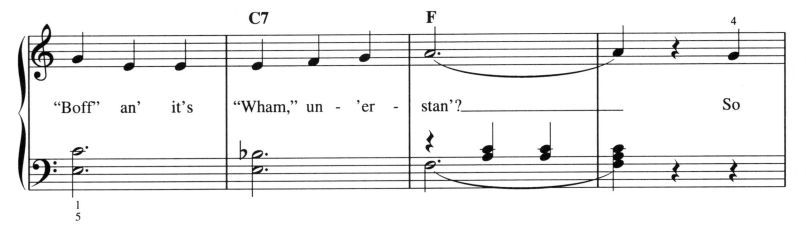

C7 ... **F** ... 4

"Boff" an' it's "Wham," un - 'er - stan'?_____ So

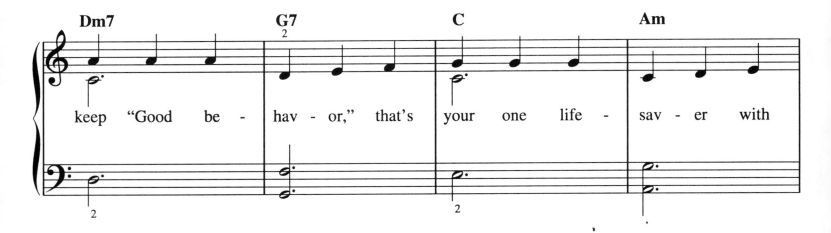

Dm7 ... **G7** ... **C** ... **Am**

keep "Good be - hav - or," that's your one life - sav - er with

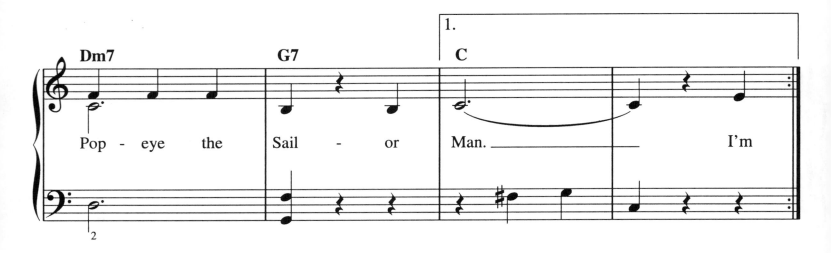

Dm7 ... **G7** ... 1. **C**

Pop - eye the Sail - or Man._____ I'm

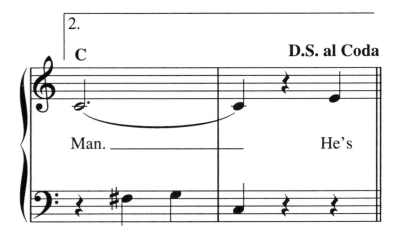

2. **C** ... **D.S. al Coda**

Man._____ He's

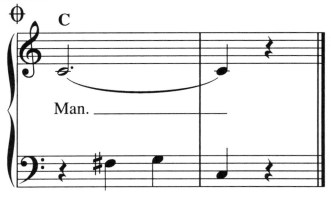

CODA **C**

Man._____

THE HUCKLEBUCK

Lyrics by ROY ALFRED
Music by ANDY GIBSON

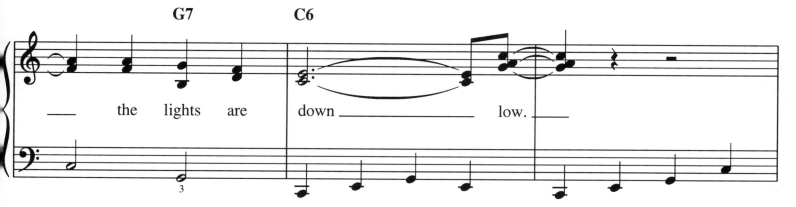

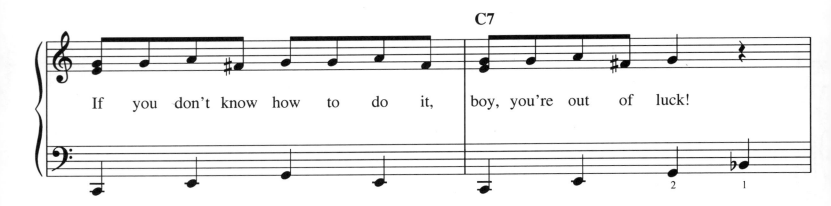

start a lit – tle move – ment in your sac – ro – il – i – ac.

Wig – gle like a snake, wad – dle like a duck.

That's the way you do it when you do the Huck – le – buck.

(Spoken:)
Hey! Not now. I'll tell you when. do the Huck – le – buck.

HUSH, LITTLE BABY

Carolina Folk Lullaby

Tenderly

1. Hush, lit - tle ba - by, don't say a word.
2. If that dia - mond ring is brass,
3.-7. *(See additional lyrics)*

Pa - pa's gon - na buy you a mock - ing - bird, and
Pa - pa's gon - na buy you a look - ing glass, and

if that mock - ing - bird don't sing,
if that look - ing glass should crack,

Pa - pa's gon - na buy you a dia - mond ring.
Pa - pa's gon - na buy you a jump - ing jack.

babe in town.
rit.

Additional Lyrics

3. If that jumping jack won't hop,
   Papa's gonna buy you a lollipop.
   When that lollipop is done,
   Papa's gonna buy you another one.

4. If that lollipop is all eaten up,
   Papa's gonna buy you a real live pup.
   If that puppy dog won't bark,
   Papa's gonna buy you a meadow lark.

5. Hush, little baby, don't say a word.
   Papa's gonna buy you a mockingbird,
   And if that mockingbird don't sing,
   Papa's gonna buy you a diamond ring.

6. If that diamond ring is glass,
   Papa's gonna buy you a cup of brass,
   And from that cup you'll drink your milk,
   And Papa's gonna dress you in the finest silk.

7. Yes, Papa's gonna dress you in the finest silk,
   And Mama's gonna raise you with honey and milk,
   So hush, little baby, sleep safe and sound;
   You're still the sweetest little babe in town.

I LOVE TO LAUGH

from Walt Disney's MARY POPPINS

Words and Music by RICHARD M. SHERMAN
and ROBERT B. SHERMAN

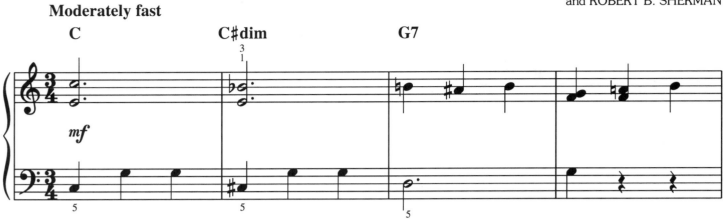

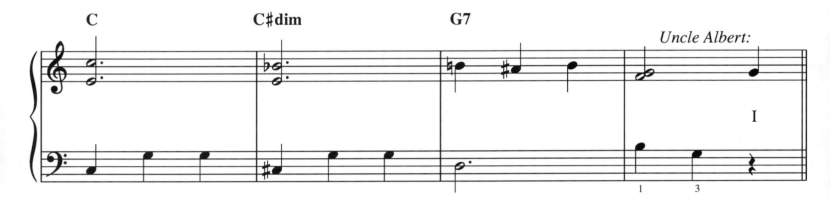

love   to   laugh,   Ha! Ha! Ha!   Ha!

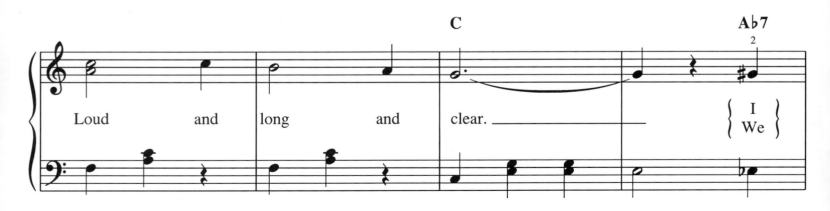

Loud   and   long   and   clear. _____   I / We

love to laugh, Ho! Ho! Ho! Ho!

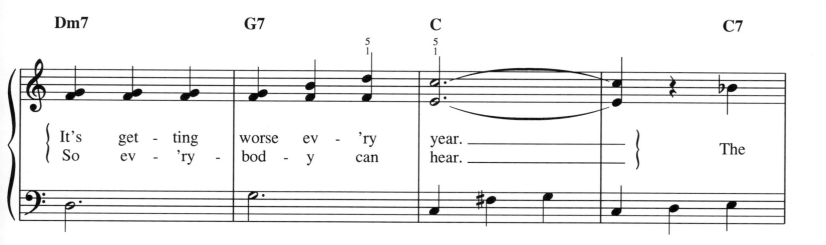

It's get - ting worse ev - 'ry year. _____
So ev - 'ry - bod - y can hear. _____

The

more I laugh, Ha! Ha! Ha! Ha! The

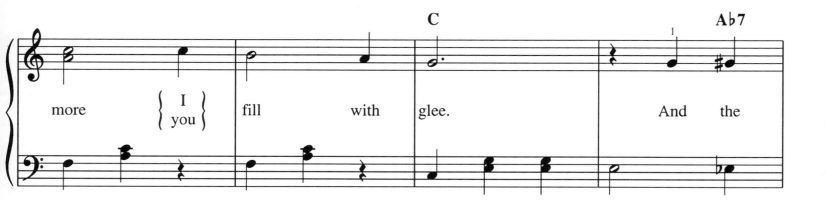

more { I / you } fill with glee. And the

more   the   glee,   He! He! He!   He!   The

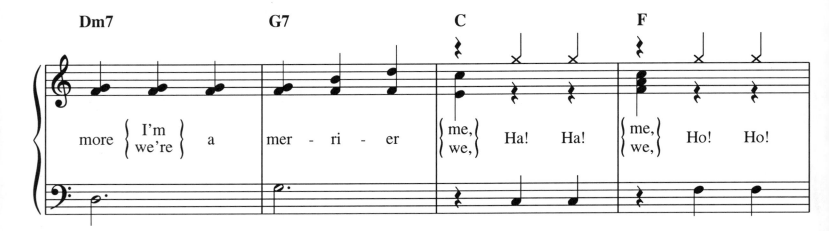

more ⎰ I'm ⎱ a   mer - ri - er   ⎰ me, ⎱ Ha! Ha!   ⎰ me, ⎱ Ho! Ho!
     ⎱ we're ⎰   ⎱ we, ⎰   ⎱ we, ⎰

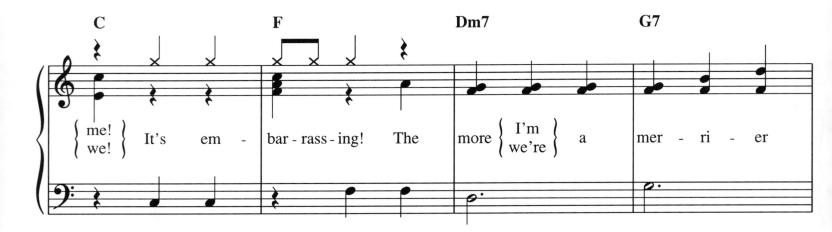

⎰ me! ⎱ It's em - bar - rass - ing!   The   more ⎰ I'm ⎱ a   mer - ri - er
⎱ we! ⎰   ⎱ we're ⎰

Interlude

Fine   *Mary Poppins:*

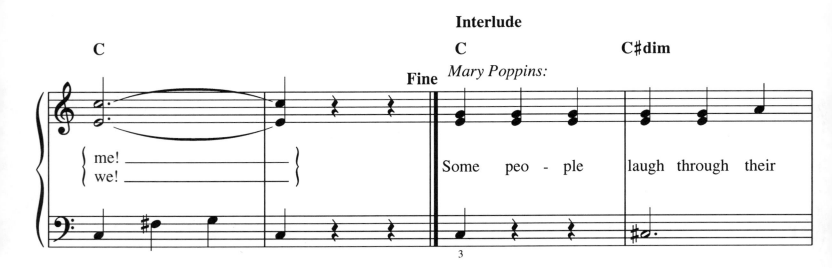

⎰ me! ⎱   Some   peo - ple   laugh through their
⎱ we! ⎰

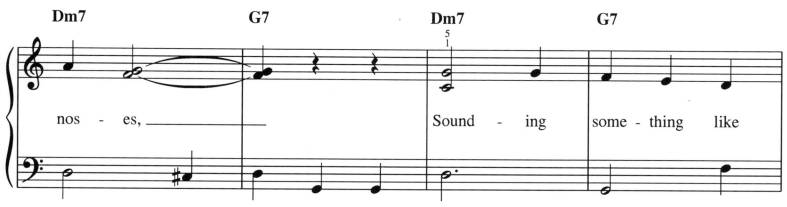

Dm7   **G7**   **Dm7**   **G7**

nos - es, _____   Sound - ing   some - thing   like

C   **C#dim**

this: *(high nasal laughs)*   Some peo - ple   laugh through their

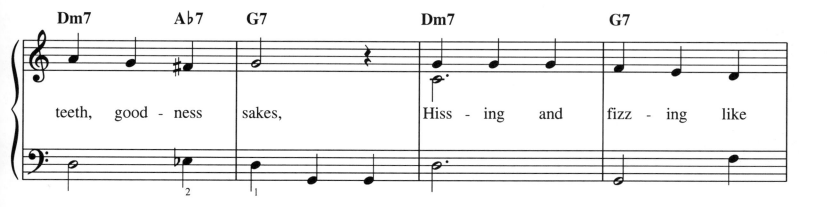

Dm7   **Ab7**   **G7**   **Dm7**   **G7**

teeth, good - ness   sakes,   Hiss - ing and   fizz - ing like

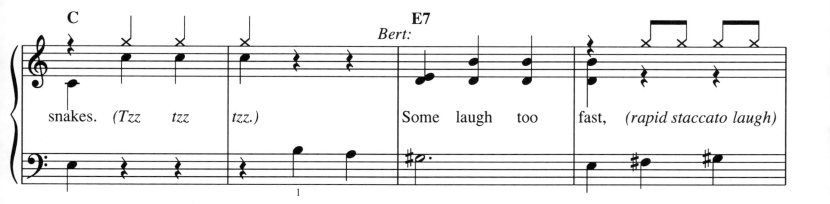

C   **E7**

Bert:

snakes. *(Tzz tzz tzz.)*   Some laugh too   fast, *(rapid staccato laugh)*

some on - ly blast, *(Hah!)* Oth - ers, they twit - ter like

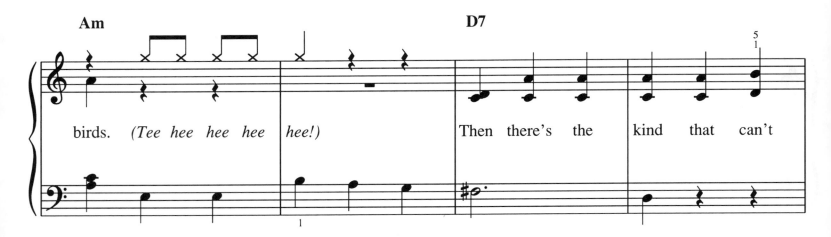

birds. *(Tee hee hee hee hee!)* Then there's the kind that can't

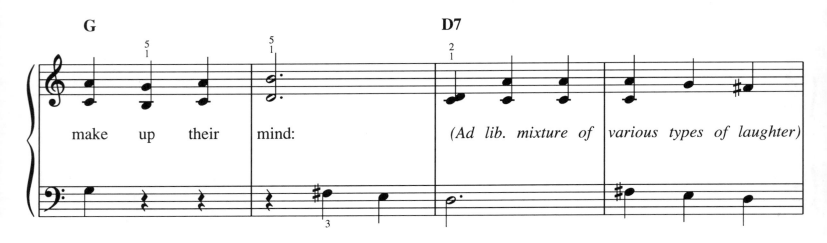

make up their mind: *(Ad lib. mixture of various types of laughter)*

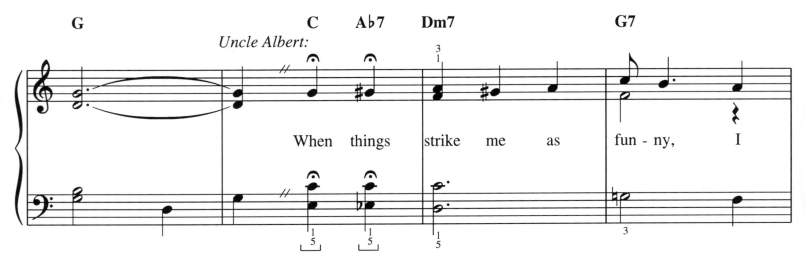

Uncle Albert:

When things strike me as fun - ny, I

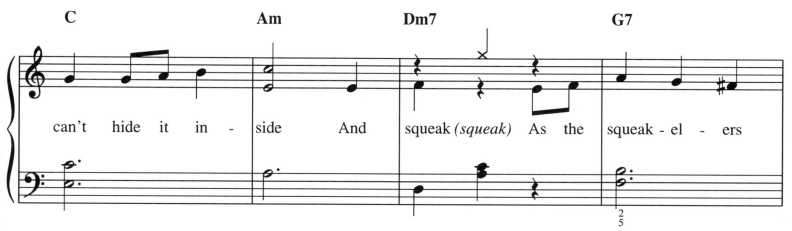

can't hide it in - side And squeak *(squeak)* As the squeak-el - ers

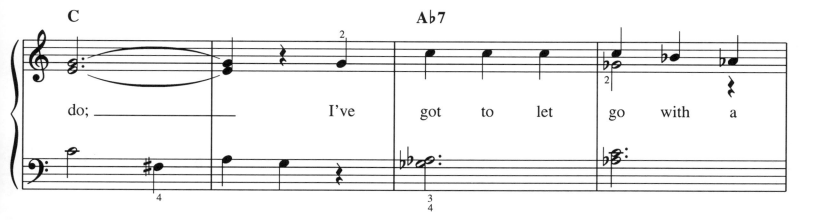

do; _____ I've got to let go with a

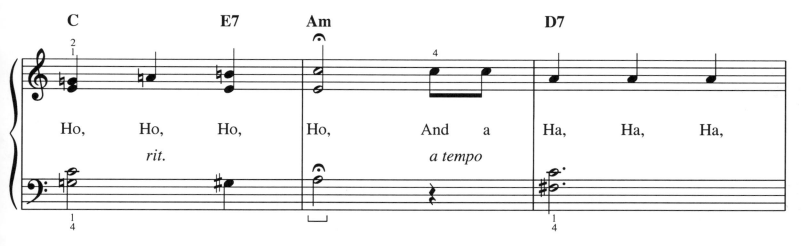

Ho, Ho, Ho, Ho, And a Ha, Ha, Ha,

rit. *a tempo*

D.S. al Fine

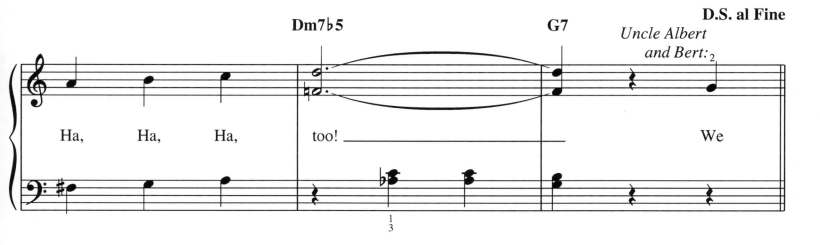

Uncle Albert and Bert:

Ha, Ha, Ha, too! _____ We

(I Scream-You Scream-We All Scream For)

ICE CREAM

Words and Music by HOWARD JOHNSON,
BILLY MOLL and ROBERT KING

95

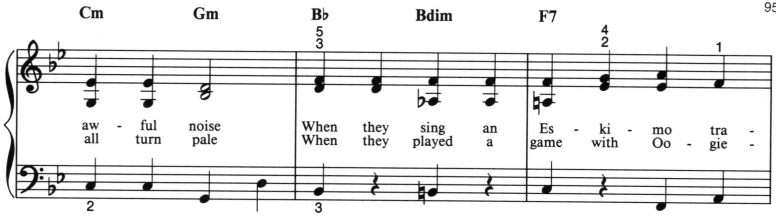

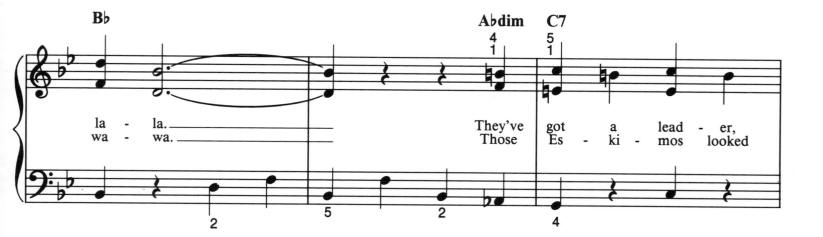

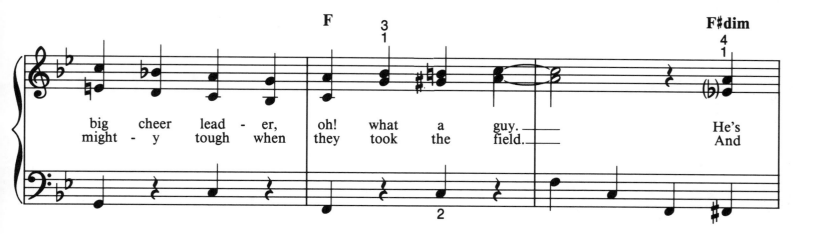

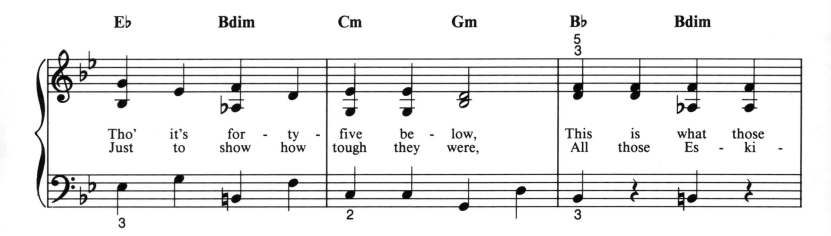

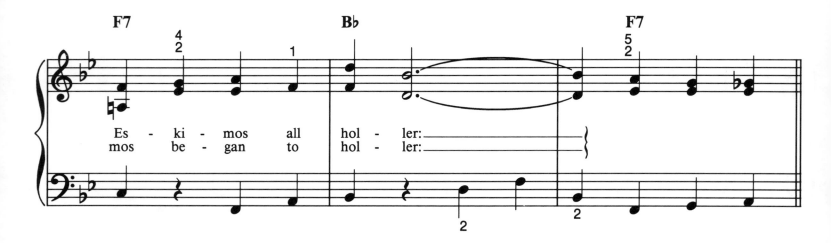

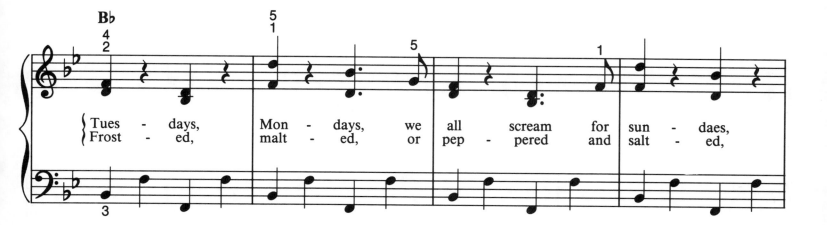

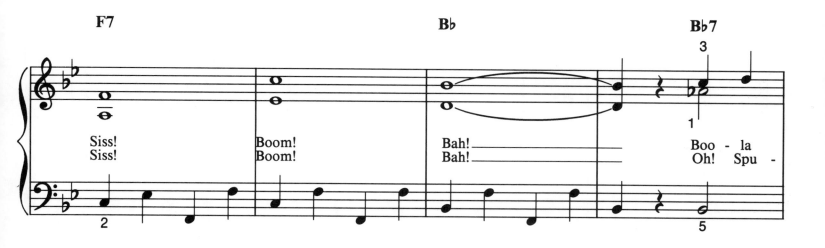

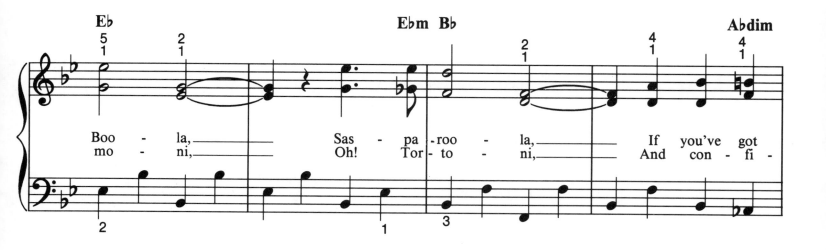

choc - o - let, _____ we'll take va - noo - la.
den - tial - ly, _____ Oh! Oh! Ba - lo - ney. _____

I scream, you scream, we all scream for ice cream,

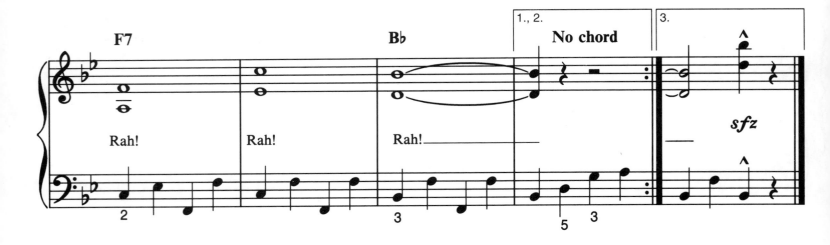

Rah! Rah! Rah! _____

No chord

sfz

Additional Lyrics

3. (Greek)
Alpha, Beta, A frozen tomaytuh,
Yes! Oh! Yes!
Ham and egg-a for Lambda Omega,
S.O.S.
A.B.C. - ses, X.Y.Z. - ses,
But in the winter time, No B. V. D. - ses.
Ketchup, mustard on fresh cherry custard,
Ice cream pi.

I WON'T GROW UP

from PETER PAN

Lyric by CAROLYN LEIGH
Music by MARK CHARLAP

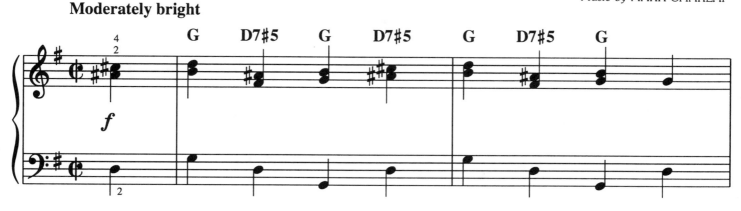

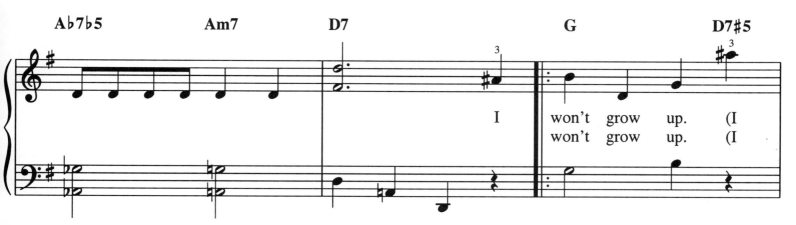

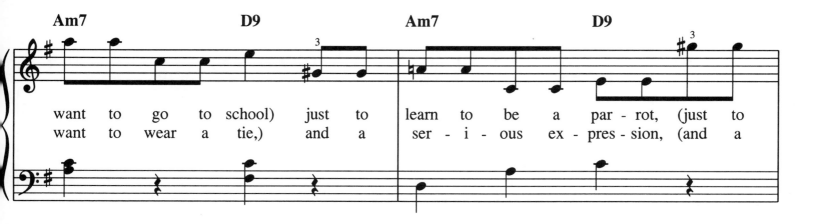

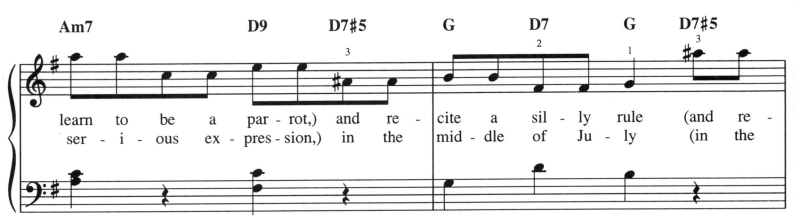

learn to be a par - rot,) and re -
ser - i - ous ex - pres - sion,) in the

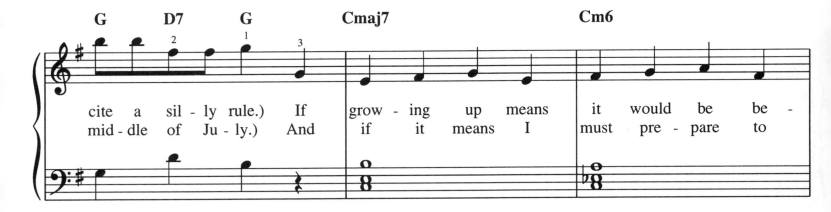

cite a sil - ly rule.) If
mid - dle of Ju - ly.) And

grow - ing up means
if it means I

it would be be -
must pre - pare to

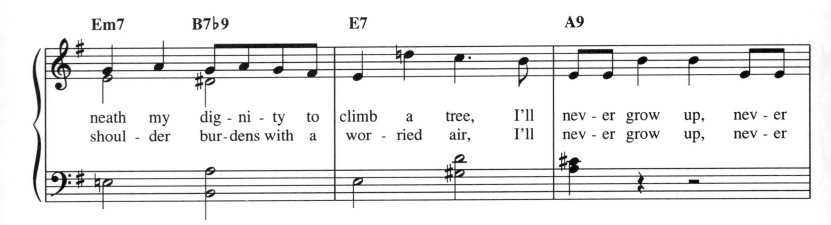

neath my dig - ni - ty to
shoul - der bur - dens with a

climb a tree, I'll
wor - ried air, I'll

nev - er grow up, nev - er
nev - er grow up, nev - er

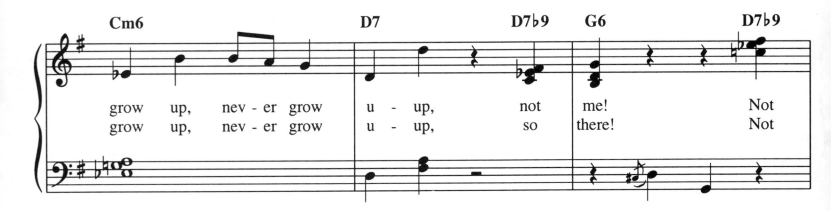

grow up, nev - er grow
grow up, nev - er grow

u - up, not
u - up, so

me! Not
there! Not

I! | Not | me! | | Not | me! | I
I! | Not | | me! | | So

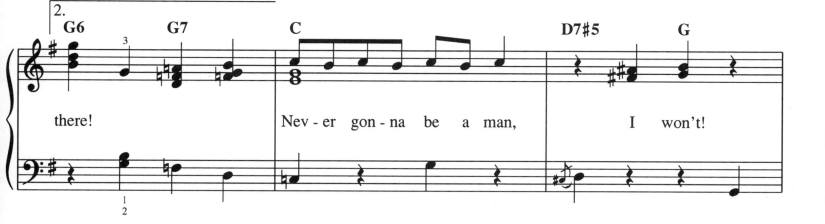

there! | Nev - er gon - na be a man, | I won't!

Like to see some-bod - y try | and make me. | An - y-one who wants to try ___

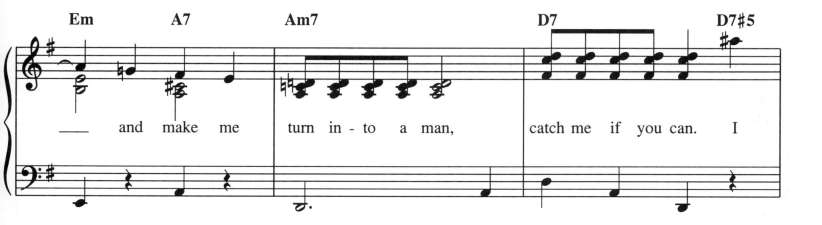

___ and make me | turn in - to a man, | catch me if you can. I

102

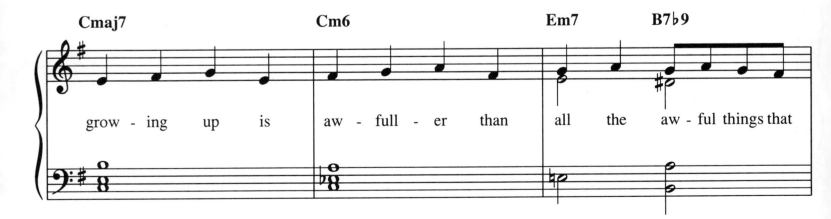

ev - er were. I'll nev - er grow up, nev - er grow up, nev - er grow

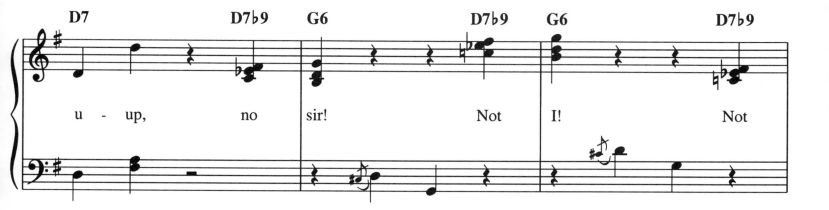

u - up, no sir! Not I! Not

me! No sir! No sir, not I, not

me, I won't, no sir!

I'M LATE
from Walt Disney's ALICE IN WONDERLAND

Words by BOB HILLIARD
Music by SAMMY FAIN

With nervous energy

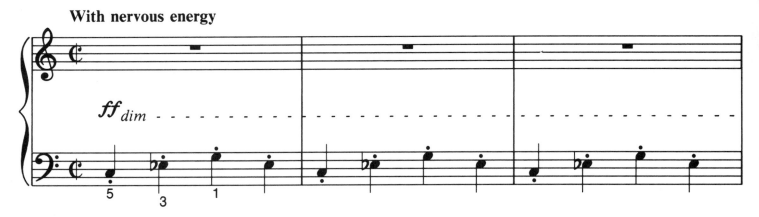

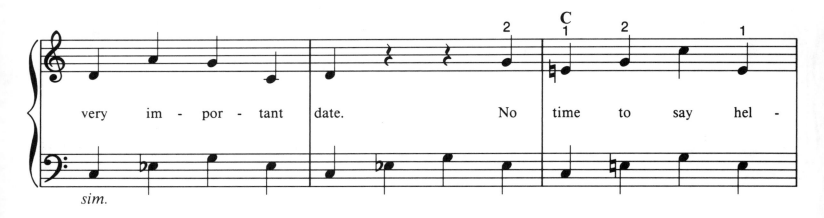

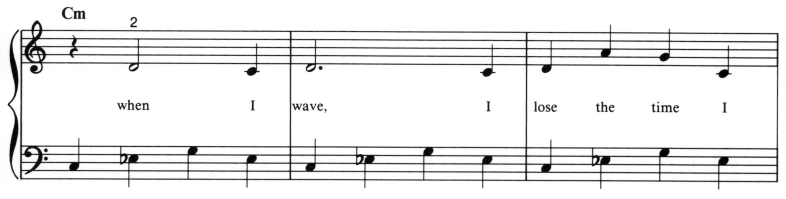

when I wave, I lose the time I

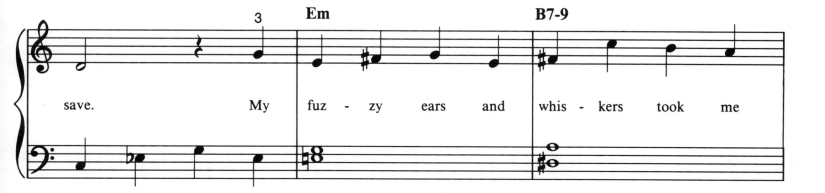

save. My fuz - zy ears and whis - kers took me

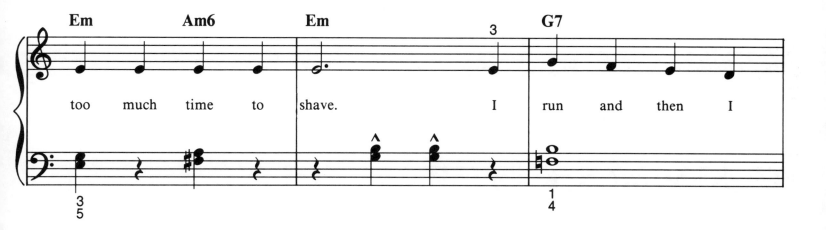

too much time to shave. I run and then I

hop, hop, hop, I wish that I could fly. There's

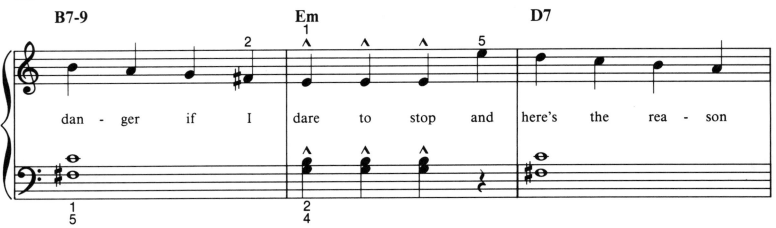

B7-9   **Em**   **D7**

dan - ger if I dare to stop and here's the rea - son

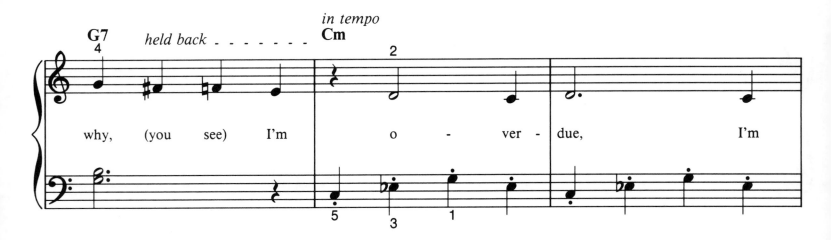

G7   *held back* - - - - - - -   *in tempo*   **Cm**

why, (you see) I'm o - ver - due, I'm

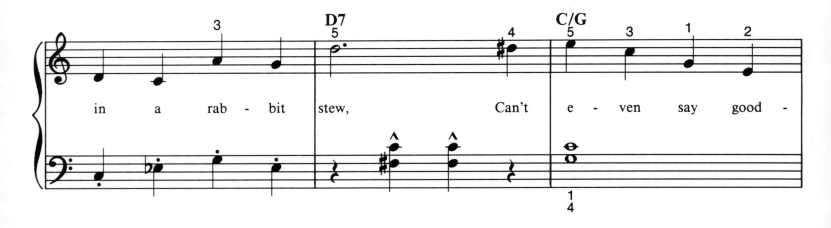

D7   **C/G**

in a rab - bit stew, Can't e - ven say good -

G7   **C**   **F**   **C**

bye, hel - lo, I'm late, I'm late, I'm late!

accel - - - - - - - - - - - - -

KISS THE GIRL
from Walt Disney's THE LITTLE MERMAID

Lyrics by HOWARD ASHMAN
Music by ALAN MENKEN

There you see her

sit-ting there a-cross the way   She don't got a lot to say,

but there's some - thing a - bout her. And you

don't know why, __ but you're dy - ing to try. You wan-na kiss the girl.

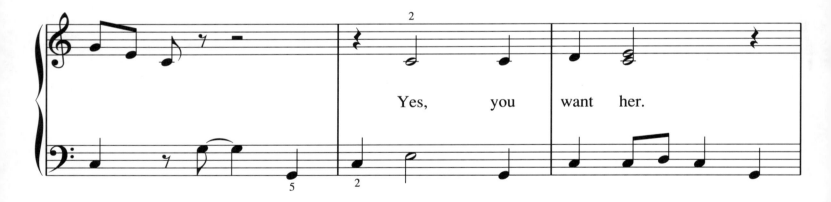

Yes, you want her.

Look at her, you know you do. Pos - si -ble she wants you, too.

There is one way to ask her. It don't

take a word, __ not a sin - gle word, __ go on and kiss the girl.

Sha la la la la la, my oh my, __ Look like the

boy too shy. __ Ain't gon - na kiss the girl. Sha la la la la la,

ain't that sad. __ Ain't it a shame, too bad. __ He gon - na miss the girl. __

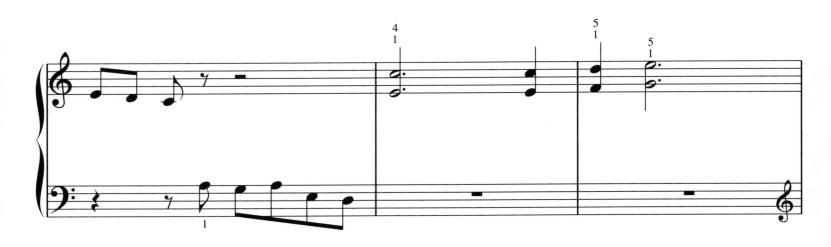

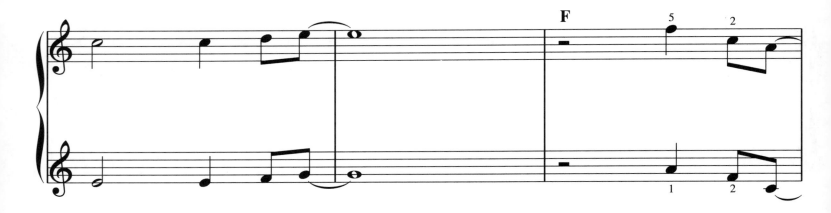

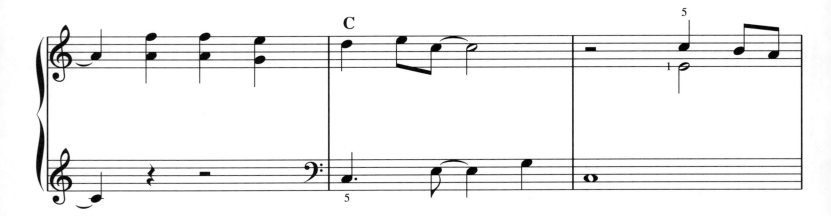

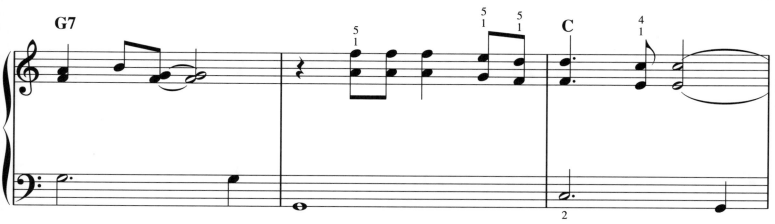

Now's your mo - ment, float-ing in a blue la -

goon. Boy, you bet-ter do it soon, no time will be

bet - ter.
She don't say a word __ and she

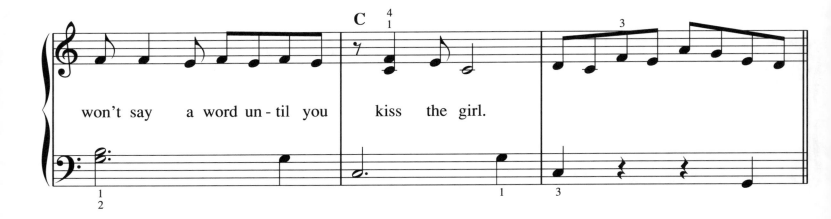

won't say a word un - til you
kiss the girl.

Sha la la la la la, don't be scared. __ You got the mood pre-pared, __ go on and
Sha la la la la la, float a - long. __ And lis - ten to the song, __ the song say

kiss the girl. Sha la la la la la, don't stop now. __ Don't try to
kiss the girl. Sha la la la la the mu - sic play. __ Do what the

IF I NEVER KNEW YOU
(Love Theme from POCAHONTAS)
from Walt Disney's POCAHONTAS

Music by ALAN MENKEN
Lyrics by STEPHEN SCHWARTZ

Moderately

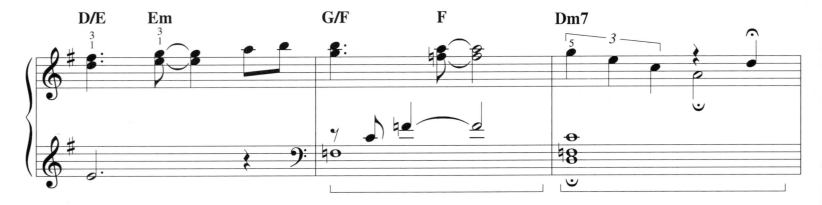

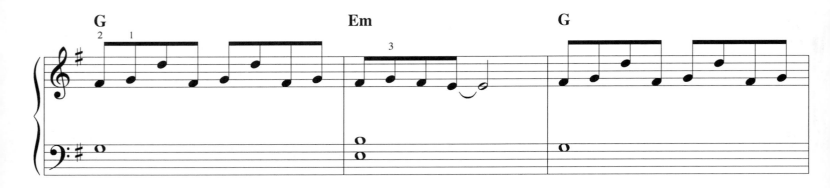

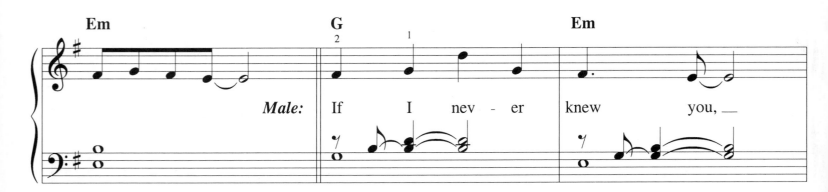

Male: If I nev-er knew you,

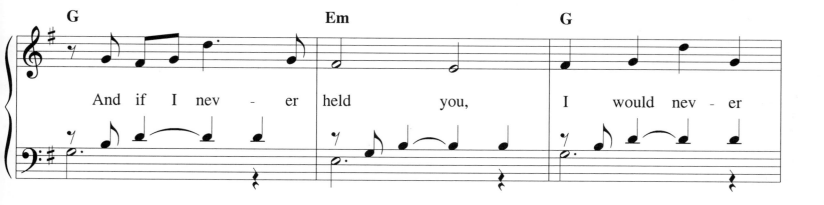

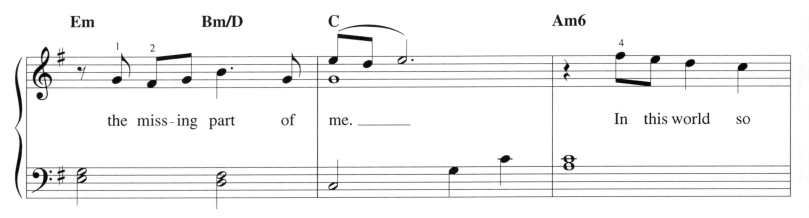

the miss-ing part of me. _____ In this world so

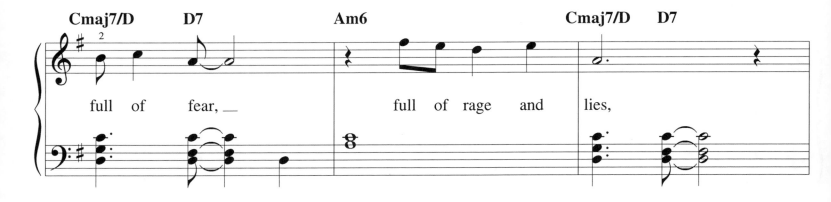

full of fear, ___ full of rage and lies,

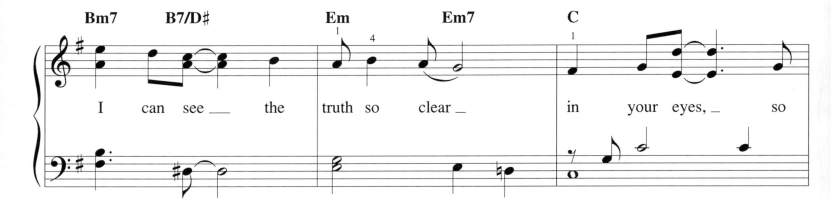

I can see ___ the truth so clear ___ in your eyes, ___ so

dry your eyes. ___ And I'm so grate - ful to you.

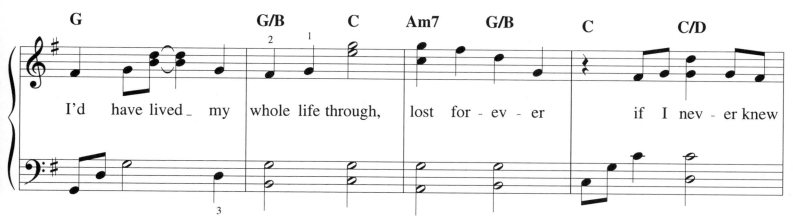

I'd have lived _ my whole life through, lost for - ev - er if I nev - er knew

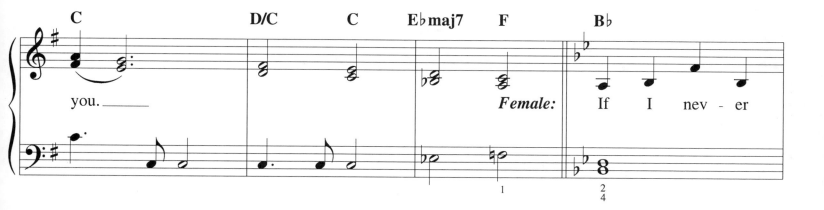

you. _____ *Female:* If I nev - er

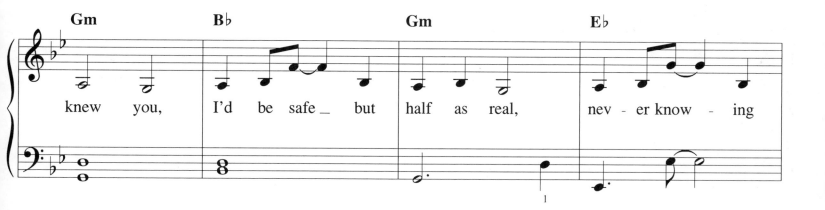

knew you, I'd be safe _ but half as real, nev - er know - ing

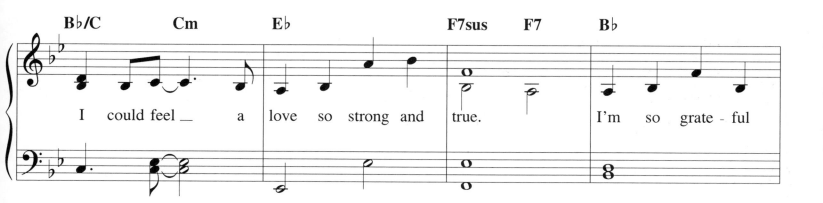

I could feel _ a love so strong and true. I'm so grate - ful

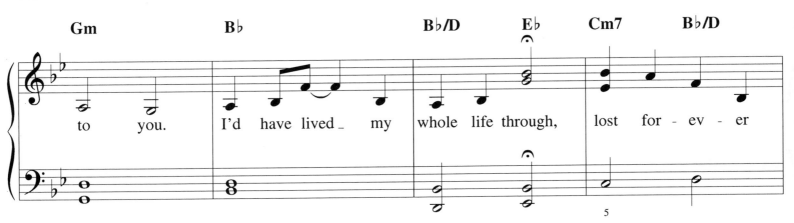

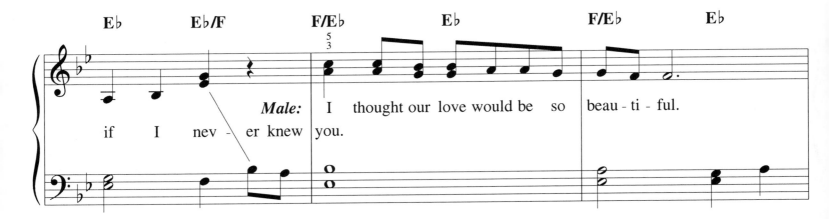

still my heart is say-ing we were right._____ *Female:* Oh._____

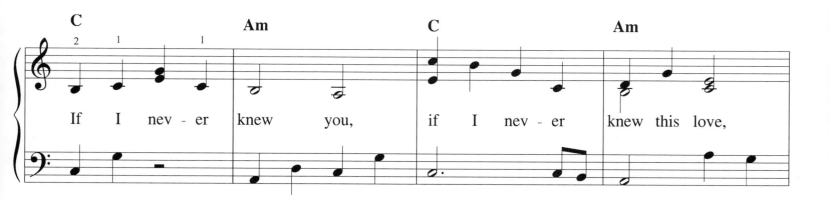

If I nev-er knew you, if I nev-er knew this love,

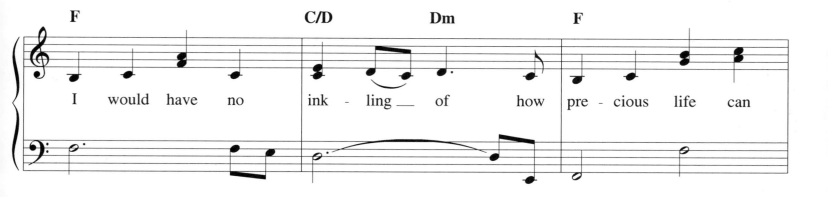

I would have no ink - ling _ of how pre-cious life can

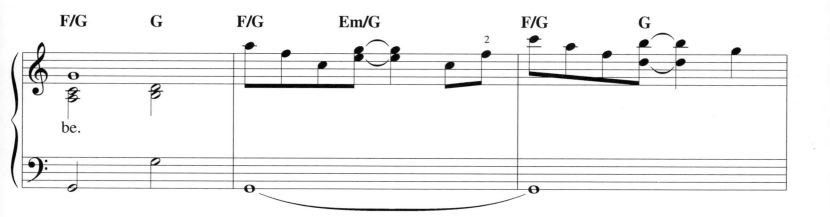

be.

Both: I thought our love would be so beau-ti-ful,

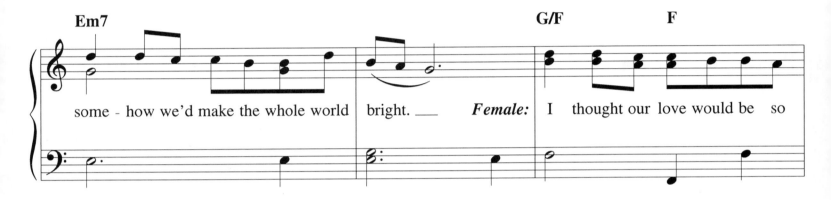

some - how we'd make the whole world bright. ___ **Female:** I thought our love would be so

beau-ti-ful, we'd turn the dark-ness in - to light. _____ **Both:** And

still my heart is say-ing we were right. ___ **Male:** We were right. And

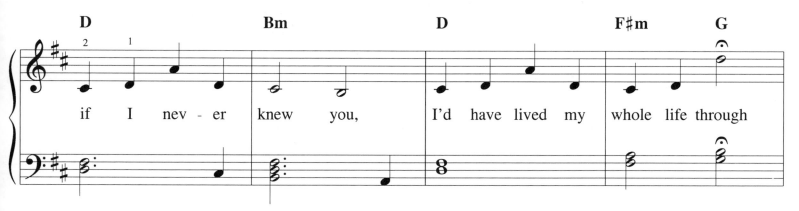

if I nev-er knew you, I'd have lived my whole life through

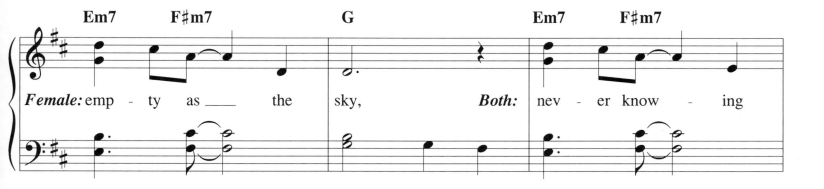

Female: emp - ty as ____ the sky, ***Both:*** nev - er know - ing

why, ____ lost for-ev - er if I nev-er knew you.

a tempo

rit.

JUST AROUND THE RIVERBEND

from Walt Disney's POCAHONTAS

Music by ALAN MENKEN
Lyrics by STEPHEN SCHWARTZ

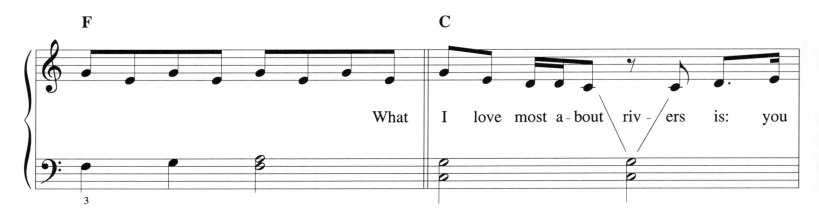

What I love most a-bout riv-ers is: you

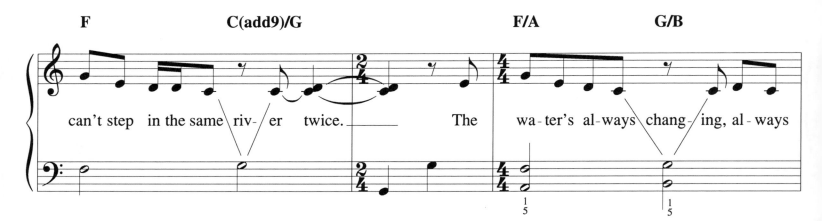

can't step in the same riv-er twice. ___ The wa-ter's al-ways chang-ing, al-ways

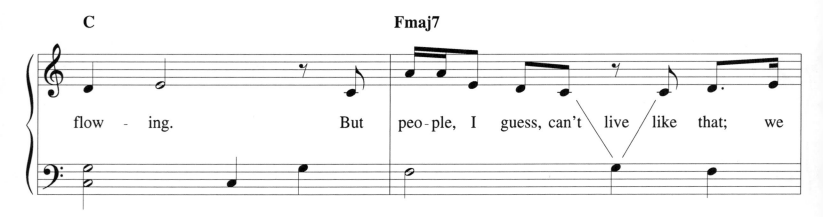

flow - ing. But peo-ple, I guess, can't live like that; we

all must pay a price: To be safe we lose our chance of ev - er

know - ing _____ what's a-round the riv - er - bend, _____ wait - ing

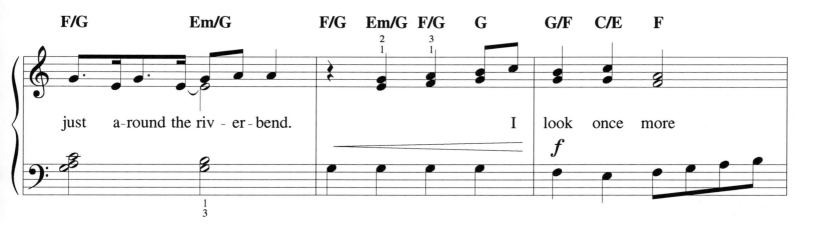

just a-round the riv - er-bend. I look once more

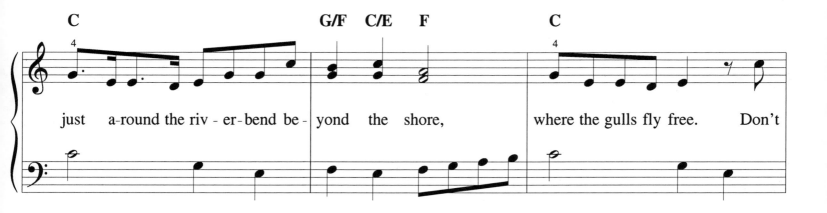

just a-round the riv - er-bend be - yond the shore, where the gulls fly free. Don't

know what for, what I dream the day might send just a-round the riv-er bend

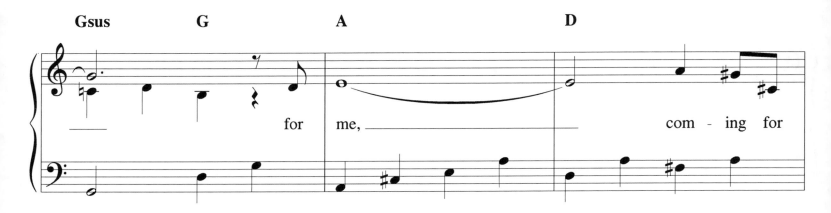

for me, com-ing for

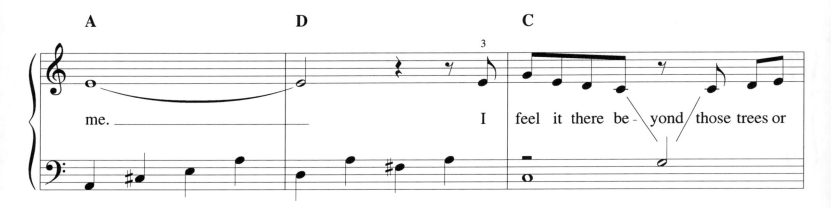

me. I feel it there be-yond those trees or

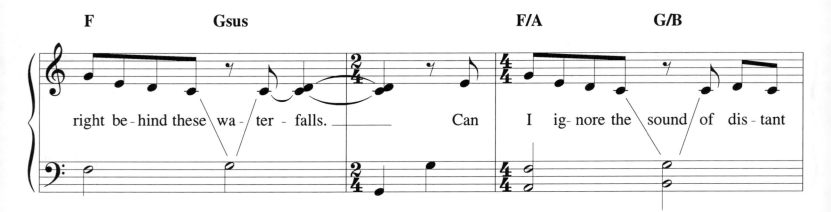

right be-hind these wa-ter-falls. Can I ig-nore the sound of dis-tant

C   **Fmaj7**   **G/A**   **Am**

drum - ming   for a hand - some stur - dy hus - band who builds hand - some stur - dy walls   and

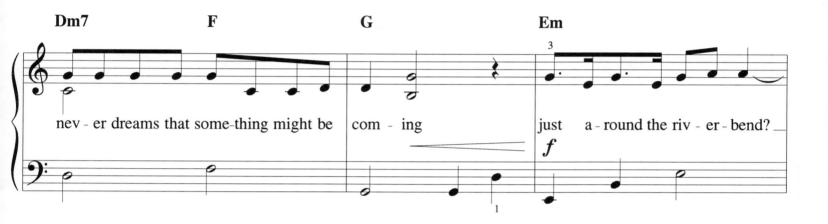

Dm7   **F**   **G**   **Em**

nev - er dreams that some-thing might be com - ing   just   a - round the riv - er - bend? __

f

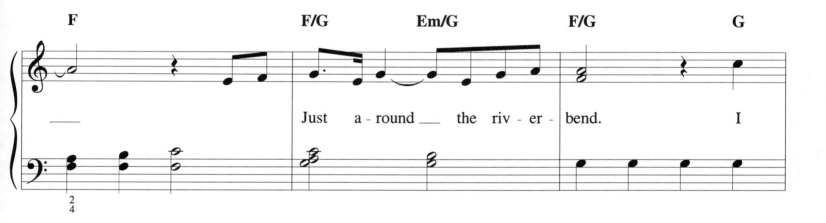

F   **F/G**   **Em/G**   **F/G**   **G**

Just   a - round __ the riv - er - bend.   I

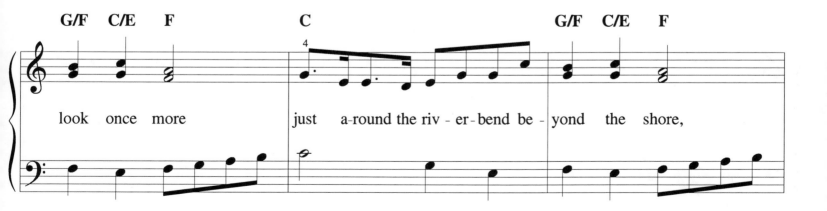

G/F C/E   F   **C**   **G/F C/E   F**

look once more   just   a - round the riv - er - bend be - yond   the   shore,

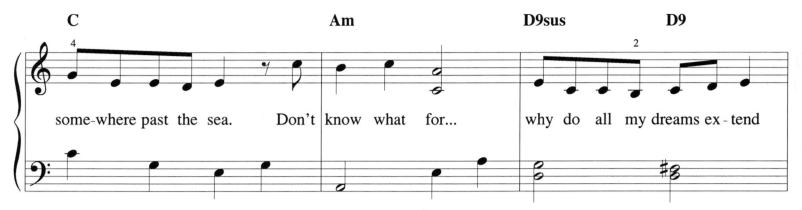

C   **Am**   **D9sus**   **D9**

some-where past the sea.   Don't know what for...   why do all my dreams ex-tend

F/G   **F+/G**   **Dm/G**

just a-round the riv - er - bend?___   Just a - round ___ the riv - er -

Slowly
F(add9)

bend.   Should I choose the smooth-est course
rit.   *p*

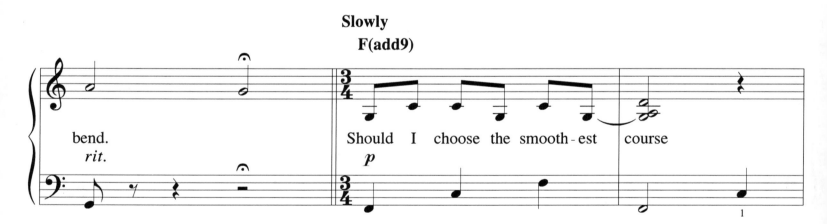

C/E   **F(add9)**   **F/A**

stead - y as the beat - ing drum?   Should I mar - ry Ko - co -

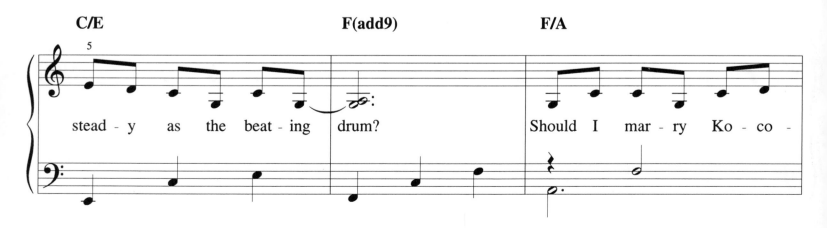

G/B   C   F(add9)

um? _____ Is all my dream-ing at an end? _____ Or

F   G/A   Am   G/A   Am

do you still wait for me, ___ Dream Giv - er _____

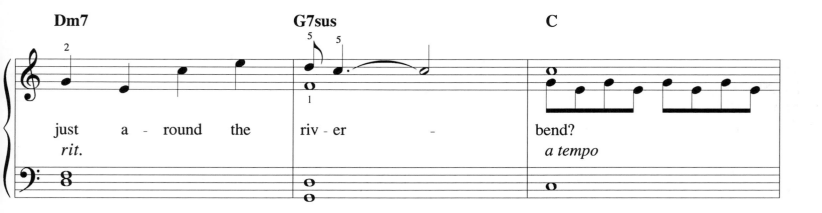

Dm7   G7sus   C

just a - round the riv - er - bend?

rit.   *a tempo*

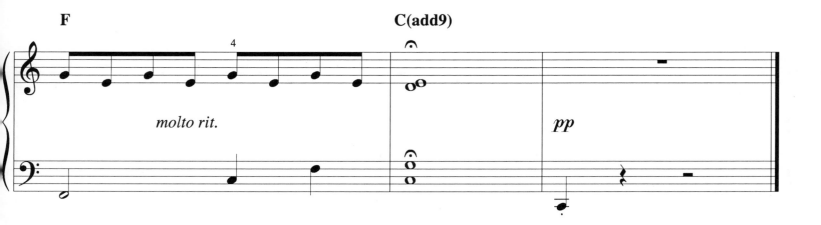

F   C(add9)

molto rit.   *pp*

KUM BA YAH

Traditional

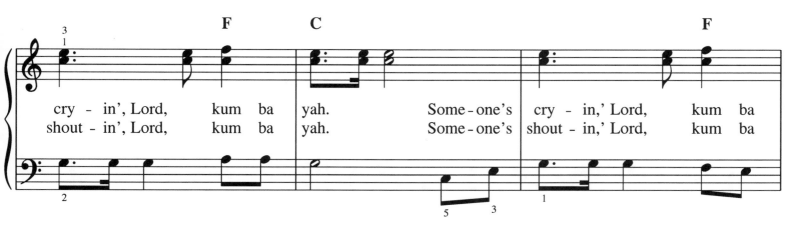

cry - in', Lord, kum ba yah. Some-one's cry - in,' Lord, kum ba
shout - in', Lord, kum ba yah. Some-one's shout - in,' Lord, kum ba

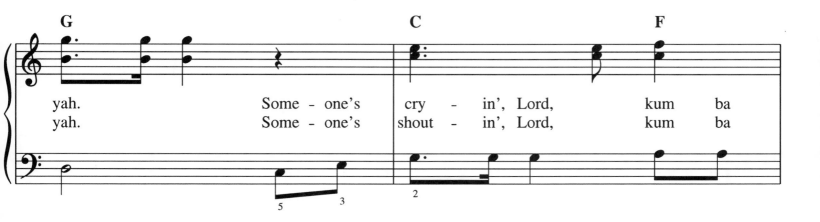

yah. Some - one's cry - in', Lord, kum ba
yah. Some - one's shout - in', Lord, kum ba

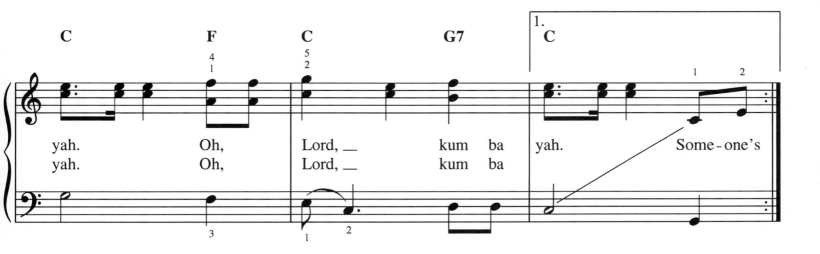

yah. Oh, Lord, __ kum ba yah. Some-one's
yah. Oh, Lord, __ kum ba

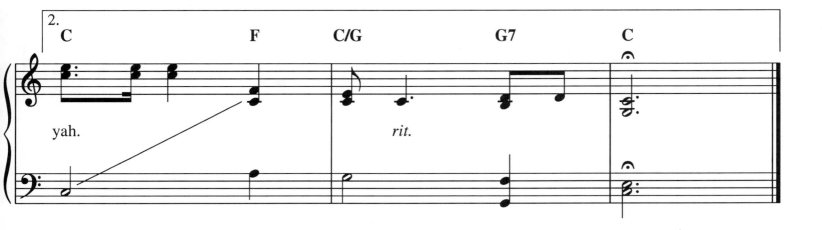

yah.

rit.

LITTLE BUNNY FOO FOO

Traditional

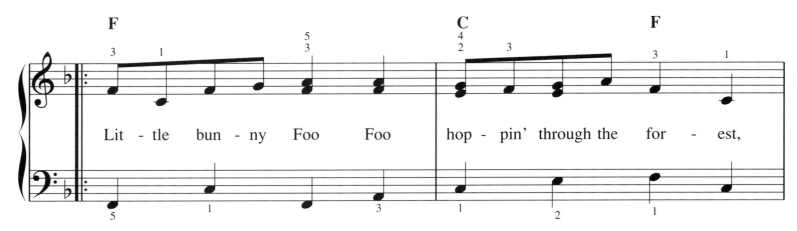

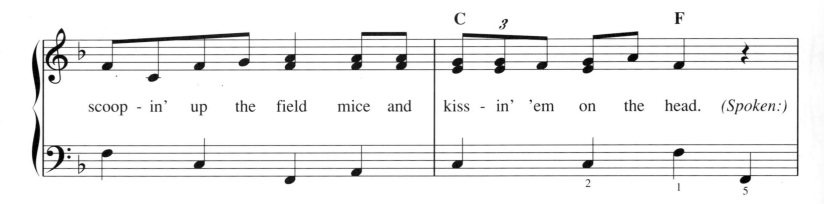

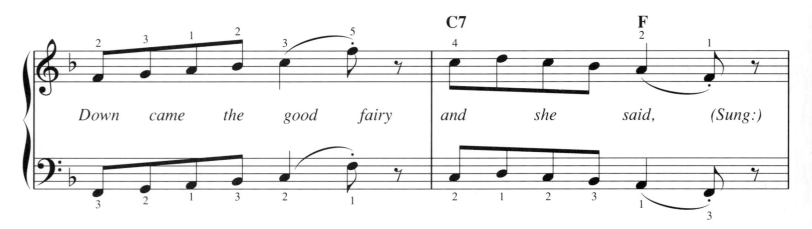

(Sung:) Lit - tle bun -ny Foo Foo I don't want to see you scoop-in' up the field mice and

kiss - in' 'em on the head. (Spoken:) I'll give you { three / two more / one more } { chances / chances / chance } and if you don't

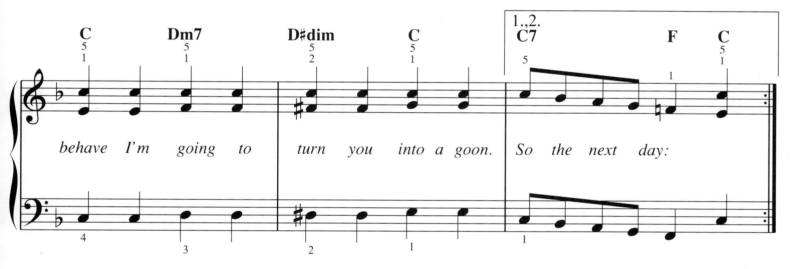

behave I'm going to turn you into a goon. So the next day:

So the next day: (Sung:) 4. Lit-tle bun - ny Foo Foo hop - pin' through the for - est,

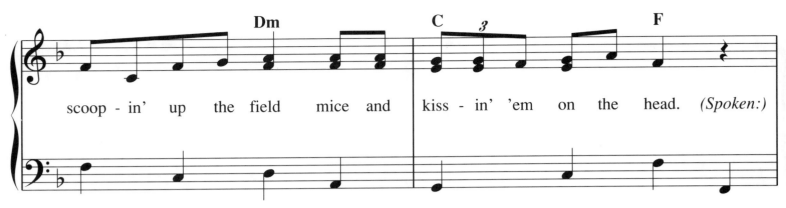

scoop - in' up the field mice and kiss - in' 'em on the head. *(Spoken:)*

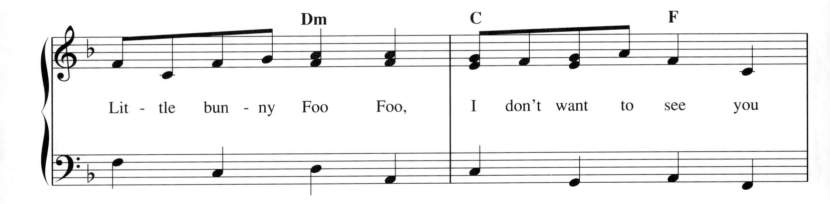

Down came the good fairy and she said: (Sung:)

Lit - tle bun - ny Foo Foo, I don't want to see you

scoop - in' up the field mice and kiss - in' 'em on the head. *(Spoken:)*

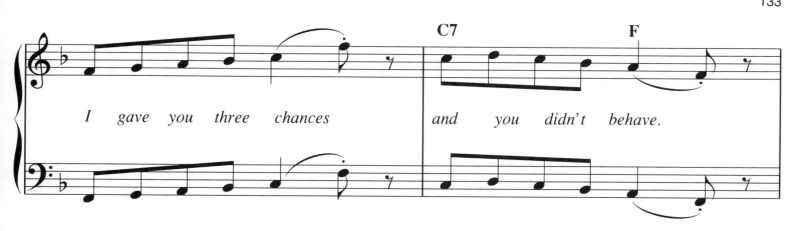

I gave you three chances and you didn't behave.

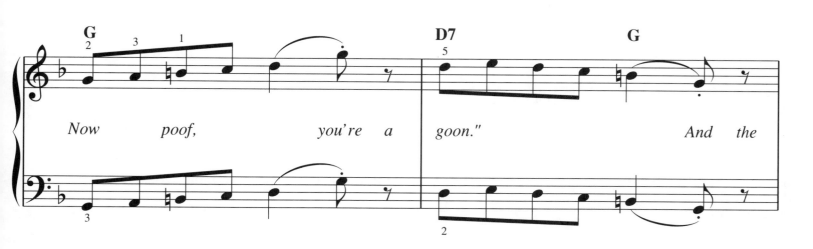

Now poof, you're a goon." And the

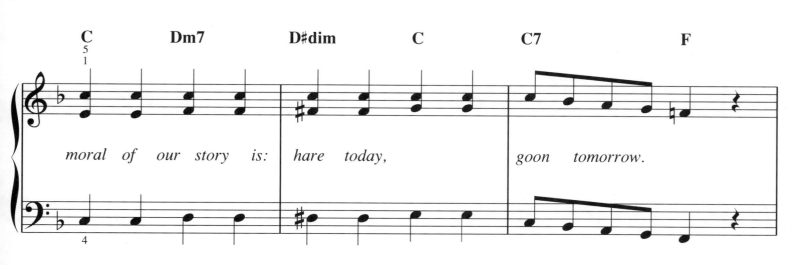

moral of our story is: hare today, goon tomorrow.

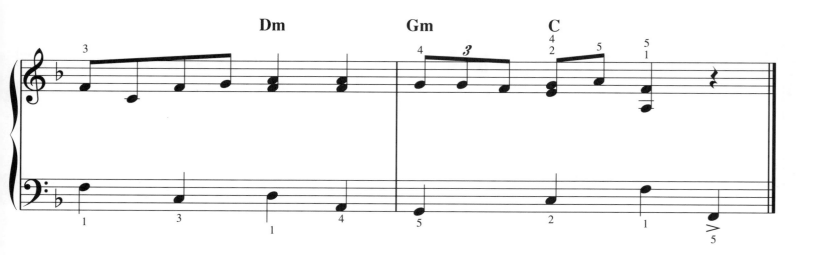

LITTLE PEOPLE
from LES MISÉRABLES

Music by CLAUDE-MICHEL SCHÖNBERG
Original Text by ALAIN BOUBLIL and JEAN-MARC NATEL
Lyrics by HERBERT KRETZMER

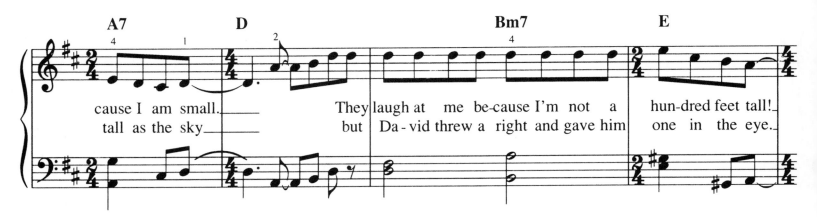

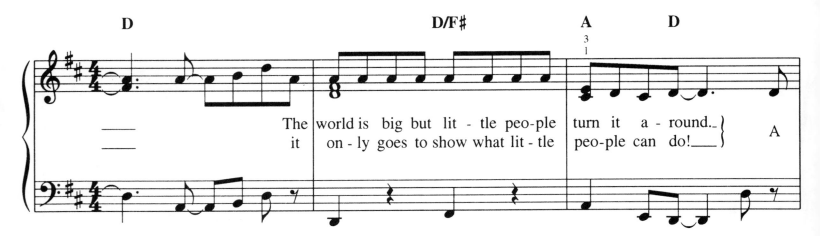

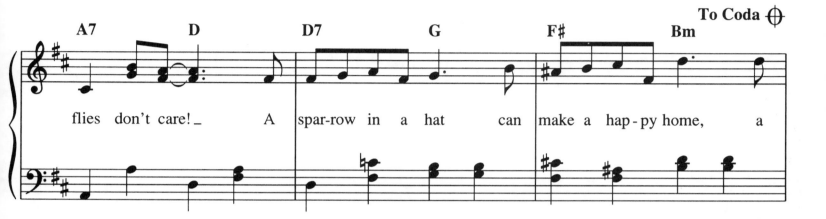

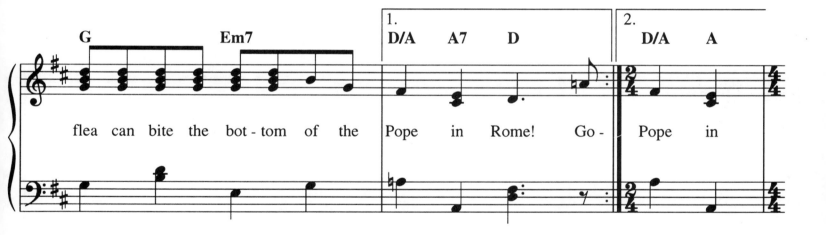

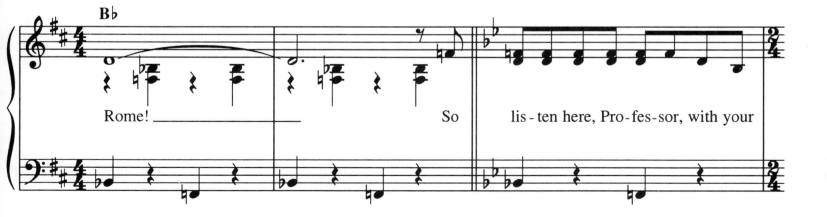

head in the cloud. ___ it's of-ten kind of use-ful to get

lost in a crowd. ___ So keep your u - ni - ver - si - ties, I

don't give a damn. ___ for bet - ter or for worse it is the

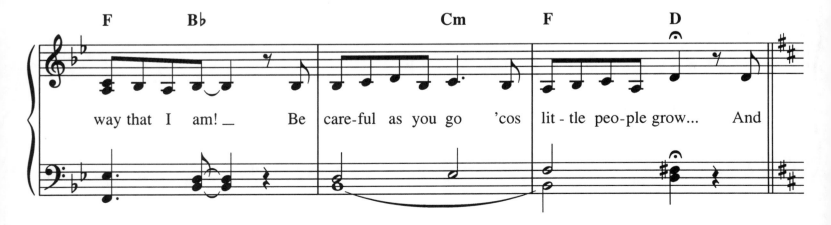

way that I am! _ Be care-ful as you go 'cos lit - tle peo-ple grow... And

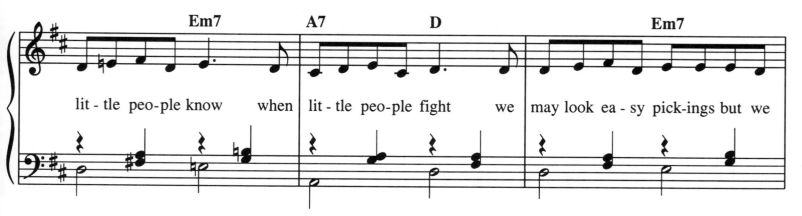

lit - tle peo-ple know when lit - tle peo-ple fight we may look ea - sy pick-ings but we

got some bite! So nev-er kick a dog be-cause it's just a pup. You bet-ter run for cov-er when the

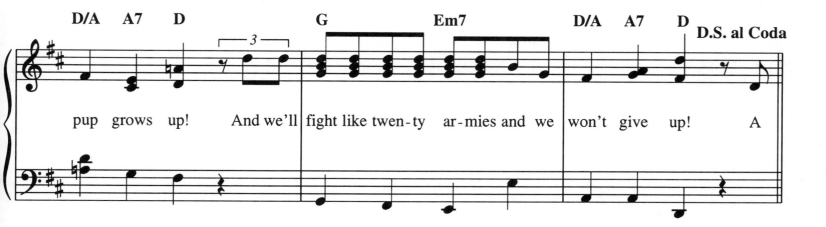

pup grows up! And we'll fight like twen-ty ar-mies and we won't give up! A

D.S. al Coda

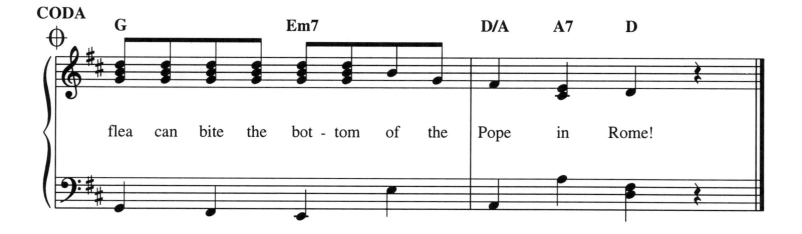

CODA

flea can bite the bot - tom of the Pope in Rome!

THE LONELY GOATHERD

from THE SOUND OF MUSIC

Lyrics by OSCAR HAMMERSTEIN II
Music by RICHARD RODGERS

Brightly

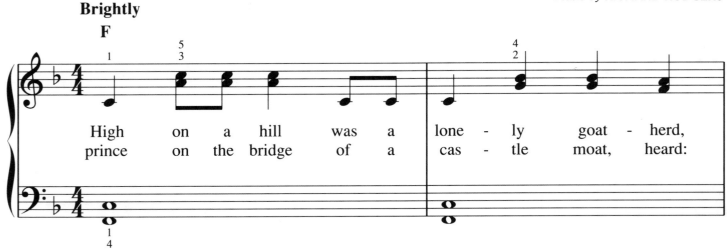

High on a hill was a lone - ly goat - herd,
prince on the bridge of a cas - tle moat, heard:

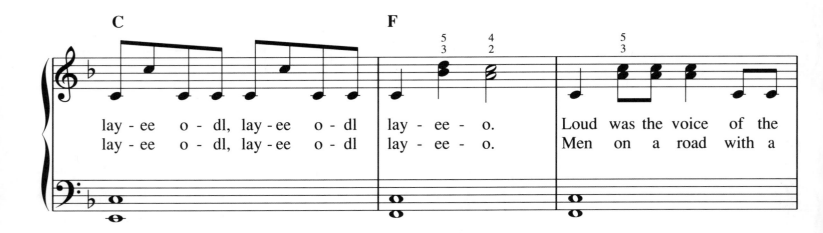

lay - ee o - dl, lay - ee o - dl lay - ee - o. Loud was the voice of the
lay - ee o - dl, lay - ee o - dl lay - ee - o. Men on a road with a

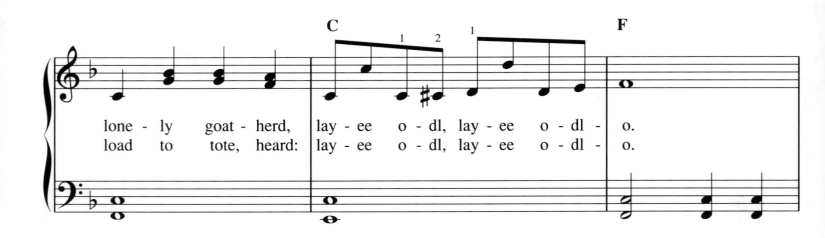

lone - ly goat - herd, lay - ee o - dl, lay - ee o - dl - o.
load to tote, heard: lay - ee o - dl, lay - ee o - dl - o.

Folks in a town that was quite re - mote, heard: lay - ee o - dl, lay - ee o - dl
Men in the midst of a ta - ble d'hôte heard: lay - ee o - dl, lay - ee o - dl

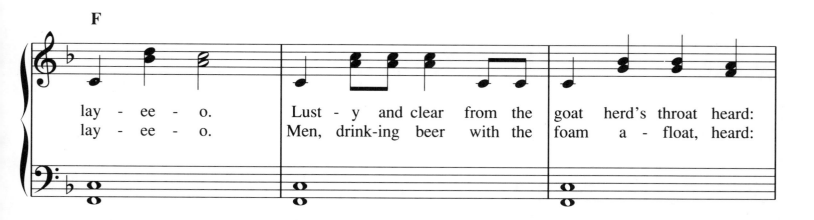

lay - ee - o. Lust - y and clear from the goat herd's throat heard:
lay - ee - o. Men, drink-ing beer with the foam a - float, heard:

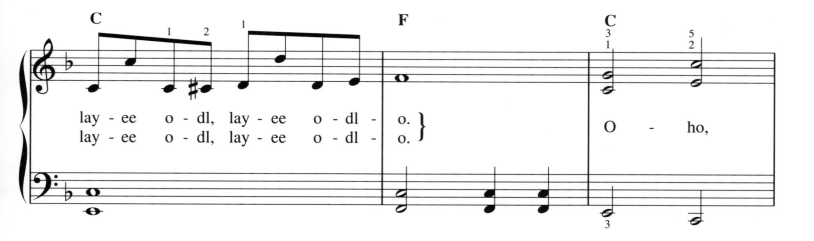

lay - ee o - dl, lay - ee o - dl - o. } O - ho,
lay - ee o - dl, lay - ee o - dl - o. }

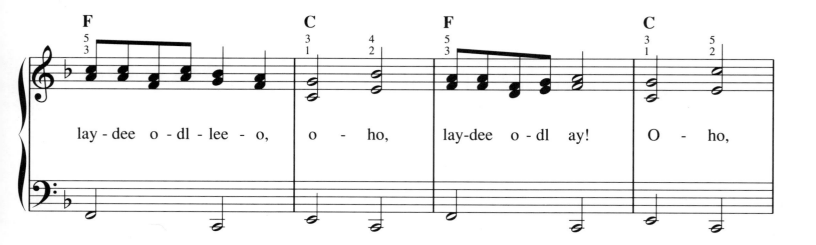

lay - dee o - dl - lee - o, o - ho, lay-dee o - dl ay! O - ho,

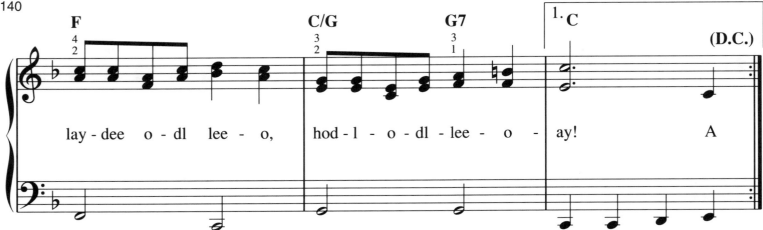

lay - dee o - dl lee - o,   hod - l - o - dl - lee - o - ay!   A

ay!   One lit - tle girl, in a pale pink coat, heard:

Soon her ma - ma with a gleam - ing gloat, heard:

lay - ee o - dl, lay - ee o - dl lay - ee - o. She yo - deled back to the

lay - ee o - dl, lay - ee o - dl lay - ee - o. What a du - et for a

lone - ly goat - herd: lay - ee o - dl, lay - ee o - dl - o.

girl and goat - herd: lay - ee o - dl, lay - ee o - dl - o.

O - ho, lay-dee o - dl lee - o, o - ho, lay-dee o - dl ay!

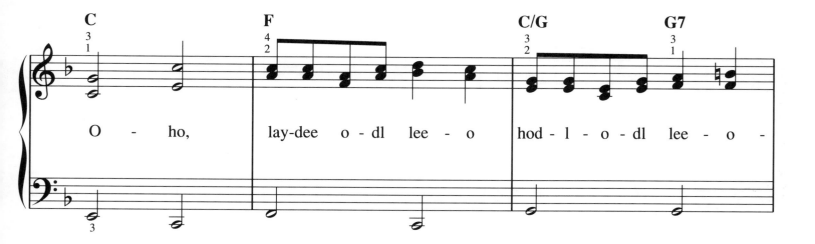

O - ho, lay-dee o - dl lee - o hod - l - o - dl lee - o -

ay! Hap - py are they, lay - ee o lay - ee lee - o!

O lay - lee o lay - lee lay - ee - o. Soon the du - et will be -

142

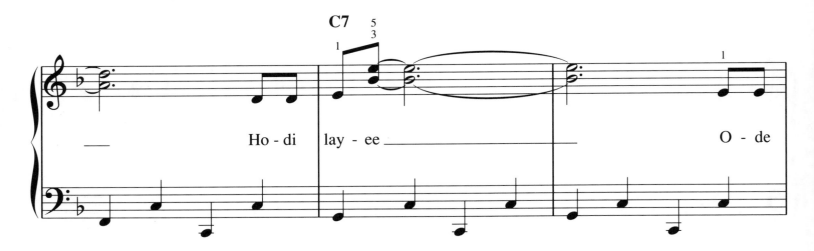

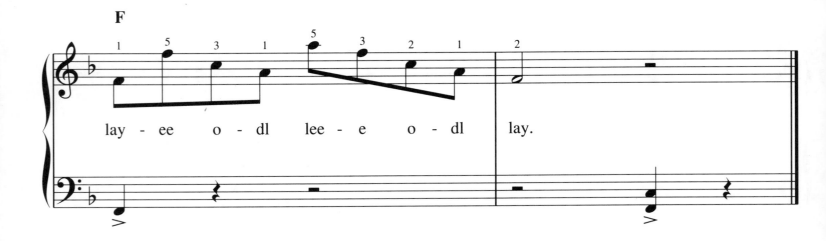

MAH-NA MAH-NA

By PIERO UMILIANI

Moderately bright

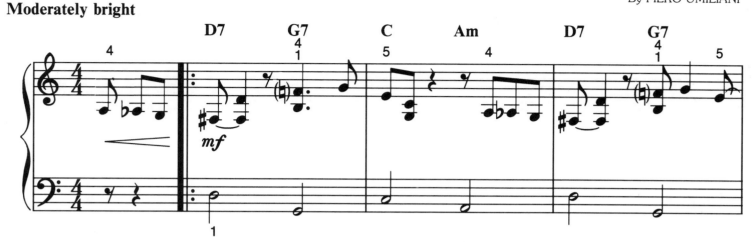

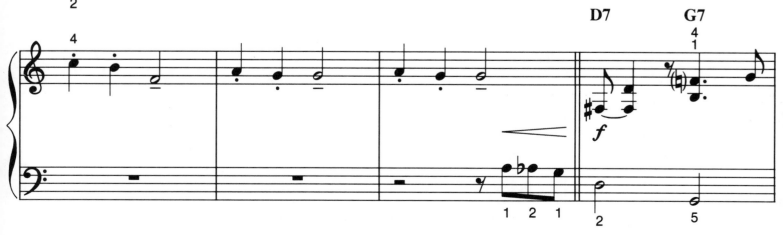

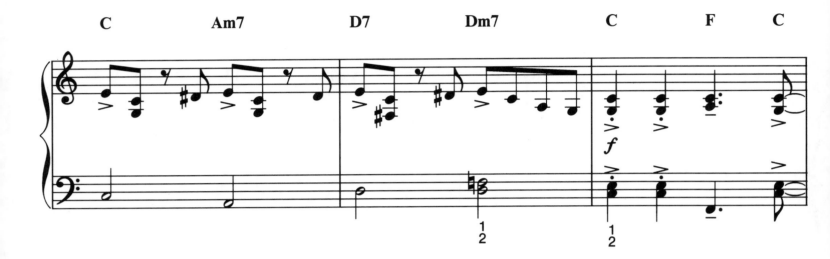

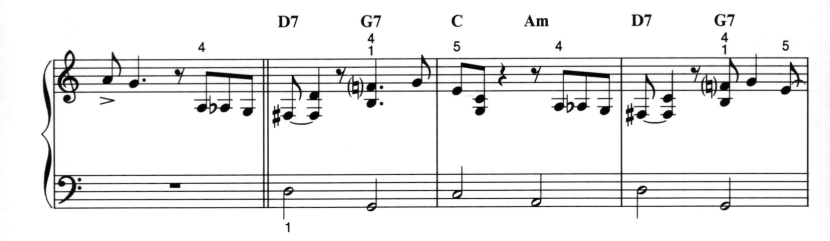

145

THE MAN ON THE FLYING TRAPEZE

Words by GEORGE LEYBOURNE
Music by ALFRED LEE

Moderate Waltz

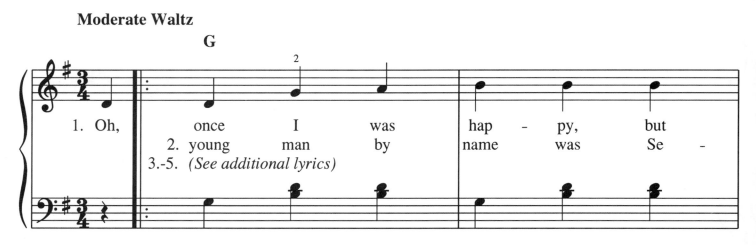

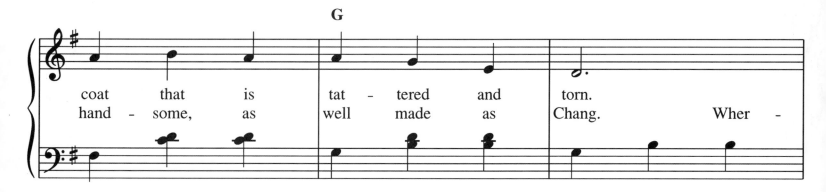

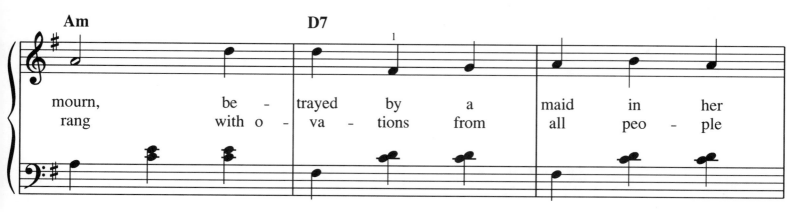

Am   **D7**

mourn,   be - trayed   by   a   maid   in   her
rang   with o - va - tions a   from   all   peo - ple

G   **Em**

teens.   Oh, the   girl   that   I
there.   He'd   smile   from   the

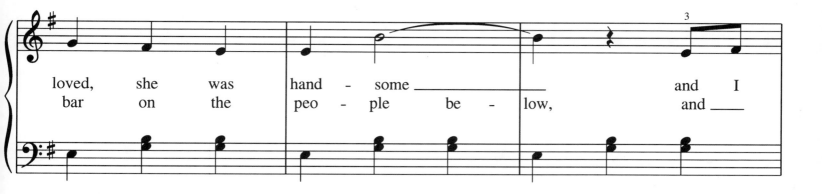

loved,   she   was   hand - some   and   I
bar   on   was   the   peo - ple   be - low,   and

B

tried   all   I   knew   her   to   please, ____
one   night   he   smiled   on   my   love. ____

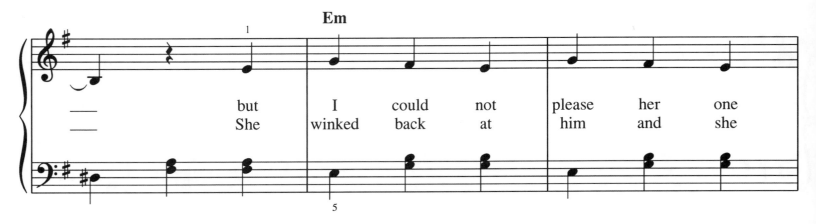

but I could not please her one
She winked back at him and she

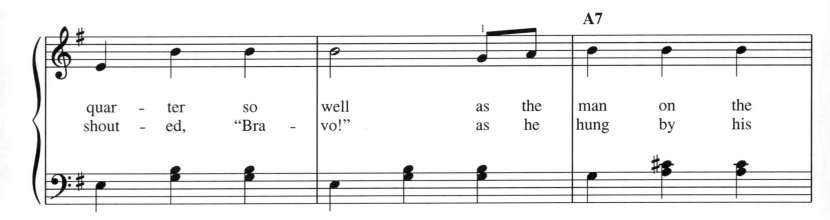

quar - ter so well as the man on the
shout - ed, "Bra - vo!" as he hung by his

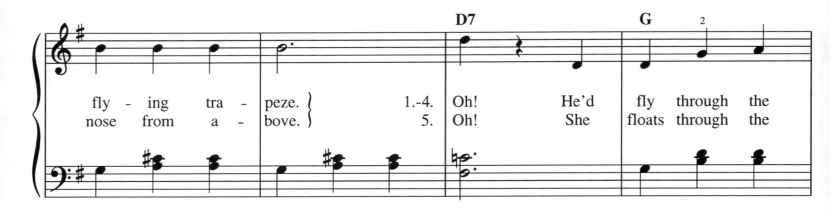

fly - ing tra - peze. 1.-4. Oh! He'd fly through the
nose from a - bove. 5. Oh! She floats through the

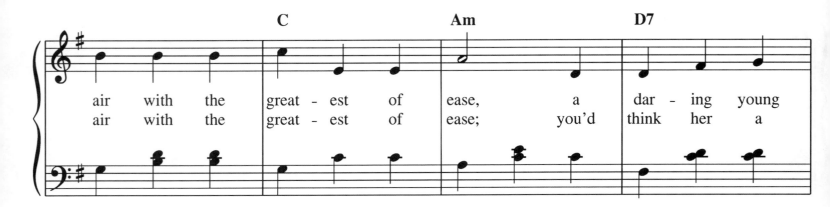

air with the great - est of ease, a dar - ing young
air with the great - est of ease; you'd think her a

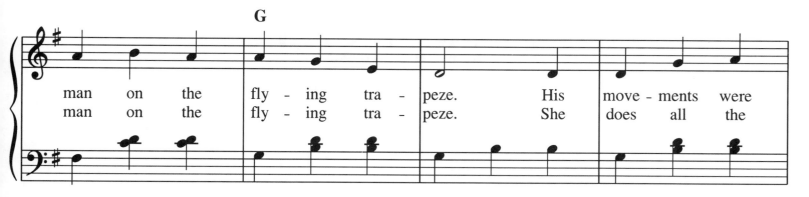

G

man on the fly - ing tra - peze. His move - ments were
man on the fly - ing tra - peze. She does all the

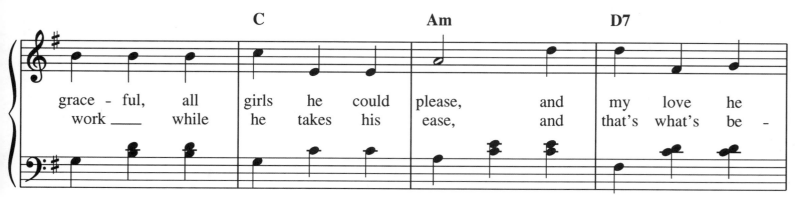

C   **Am**   **D7**

grace - ful, all girls he could please, and my love he
work ___ while he takes his ease, and that's what's be -

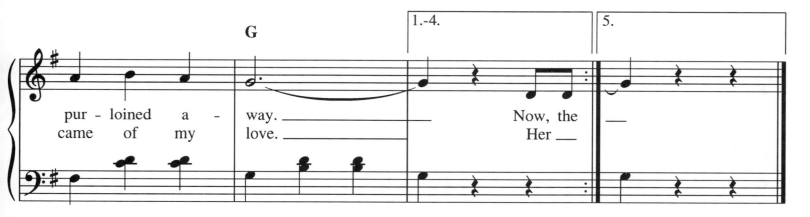

G   1.-4.   5.

pur - loined a - way. ___ Now, the ___
came of my love. ___ Her ___

Additional Lyrics

3. Her father and mother were both on my side
   And tried very hard to make her my bride.
   Her father, he sighed, and her mother, she cried
   To see her throw herself away.
   'Twas all no avail, she went there ev'ry night
   And threw her bouquets on the stage,
   Which caused him to meet her; how he ran me down,
   To tell it would take a whole page.

4. One night I as usual went to her dear home,
   And found there her mother and father alone.
   I asked for my love, and soon 'twas made known,
   To my horror, that she'd run away.
   She packed up her boxes and eloped in the night
   With him, with the greatest of ease.
   From two stories high he had lowered her down
   To the ground on his flying trapeze.

5. Some months after that I went into a hall;
   To my surprise I found there on the wall
   A bill in red letters which did my heart gall,
   That she was appearing with him.
   He'd taught her gymnastics and dressed her in tights
   To help him live at ease.
   He'd made her assume a masculine name,
   And now she goes on the trapeze.

THE MARCH OF
THE SIAMESE CHILDREN

from THE KING AND I

Music by RICHARD RODGERS

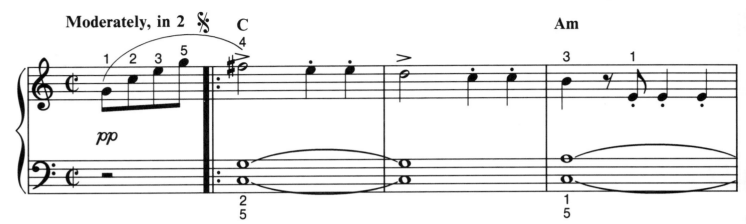

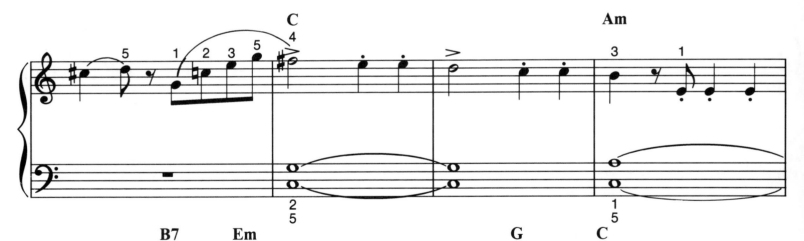

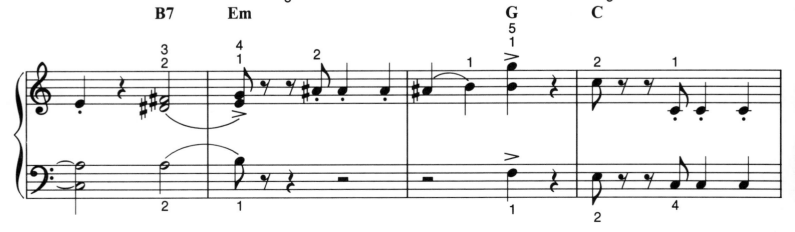

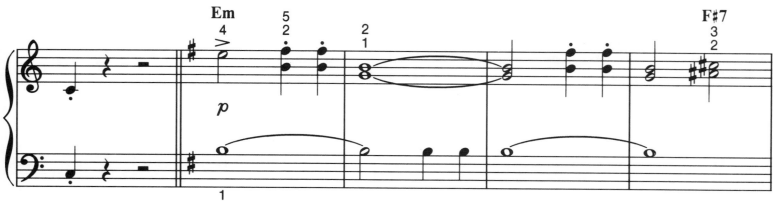

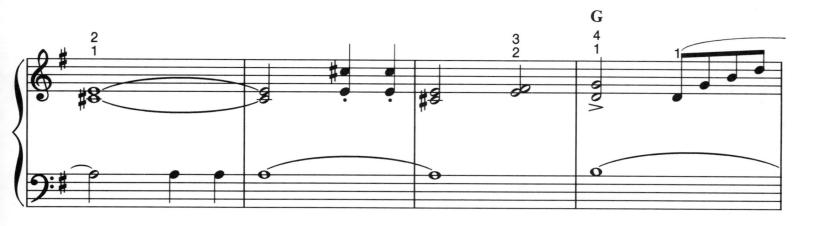

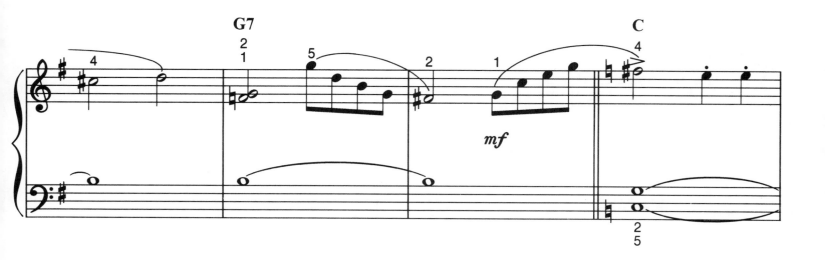

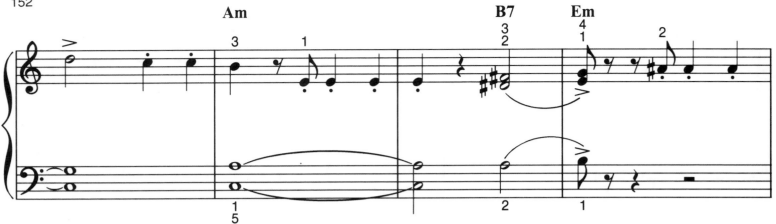

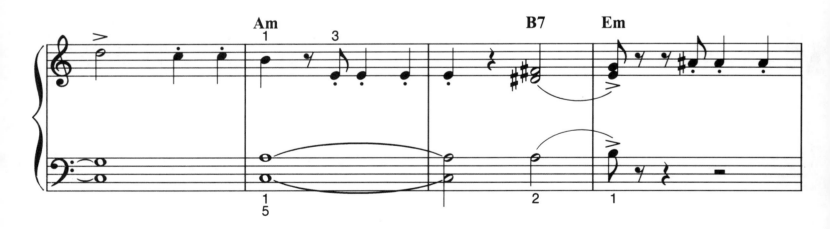

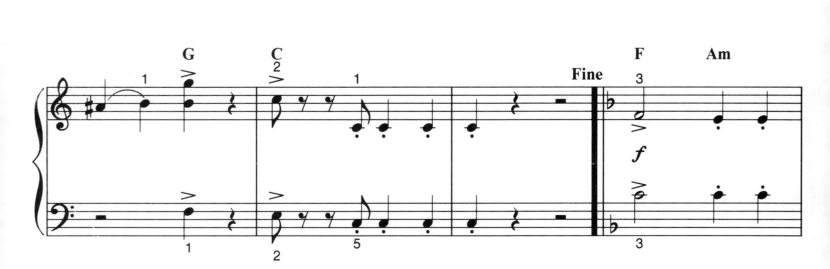

153

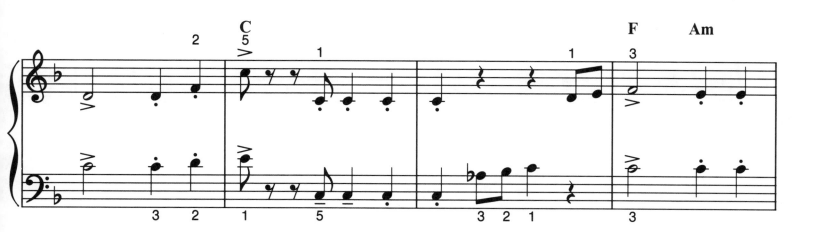

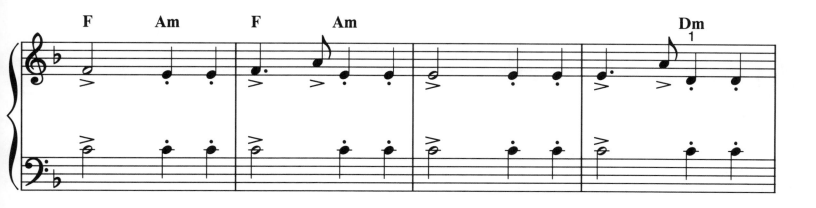

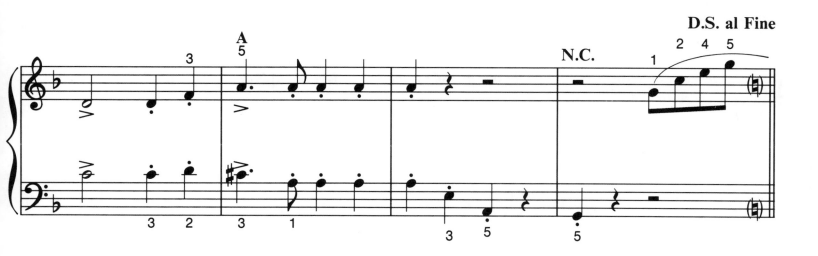

MONSTER MASH

Words and Music by BOBBY PICKETT
and LEONARD CAPIZZI

Medium Rock beat

(Spoken:) 1. I was working in the lab late one night,
2,3,4,5,6. (See additional lyrics) when my eyes beheld

an eerie sight, for my monster from his slab began to rise, and

155

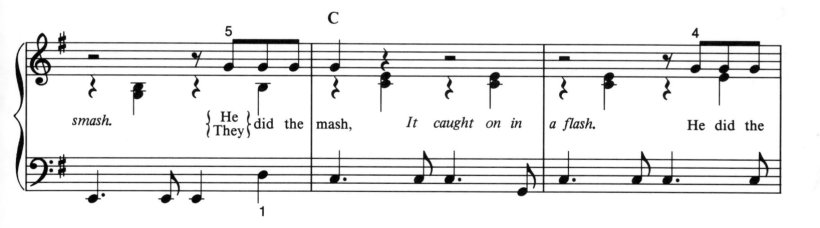

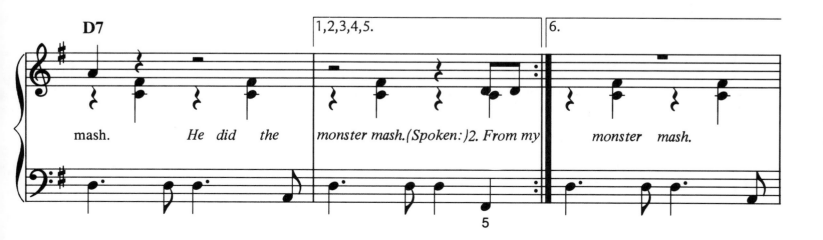

Additional Lyrics

2. From my laboratory in the castle east.
   To the master bedroom where the vampires feast.
   The ghouls all came from their humble abodes
   To catch a jolt from my electrodes.
   Chorus:

3. The zombies were having fun,
   The party had just begun.
   The guests included Wolf-man,
   Dracula, and his son.

4. The scene was rockin'; all were digging the sounds,
   Igor on chains, backed by his baying hounds.
   The coffin-bangers were about to arrive
   With their vocal group "The Crypt-Kicker Five"
   Chorus:

5. Out from his coffin, Drac's voice did ring;
   Seems he was troubled by just one thing.
   He opened the lid and shook his fist,
   And said, "Whatever happened to my Transylvanian twist?"
   Chorus:

6. Now everything's cool, Drac's part of the band
   And my monster mash is the hit of the land.
   For you, the living, this mash was meant too,
   When you get to my door, tell them Boris sent you. (till fade)
   Chorus:

MAYBE
from the Musical Production ANNIE

Lyric by MARTIN CHARNIN
Music by CHARLES STROUSE

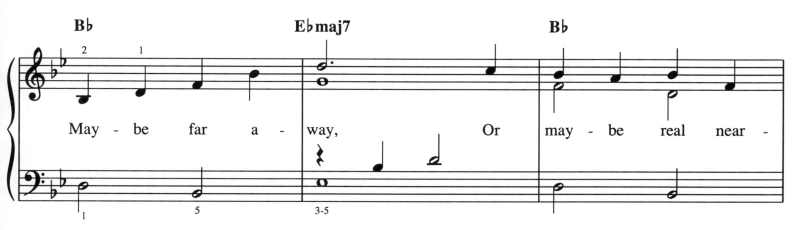

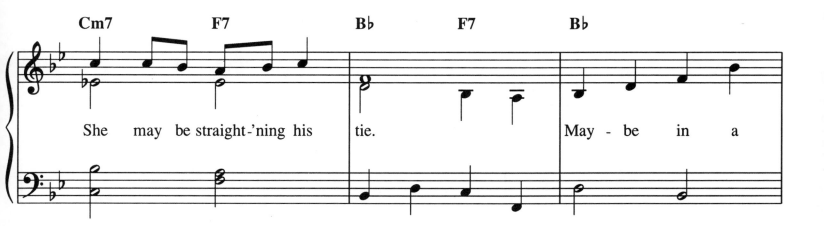

158

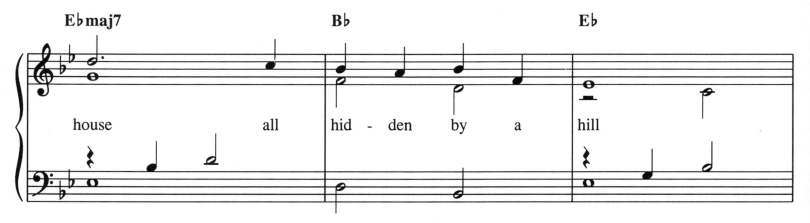

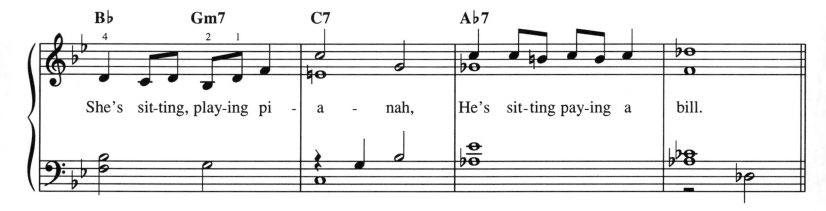

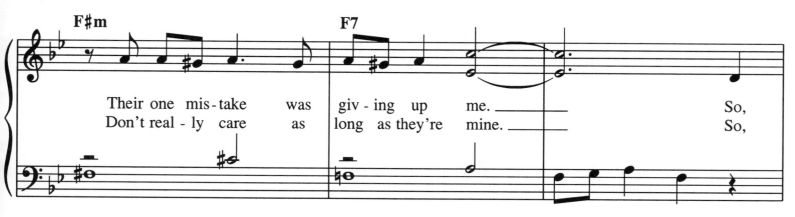

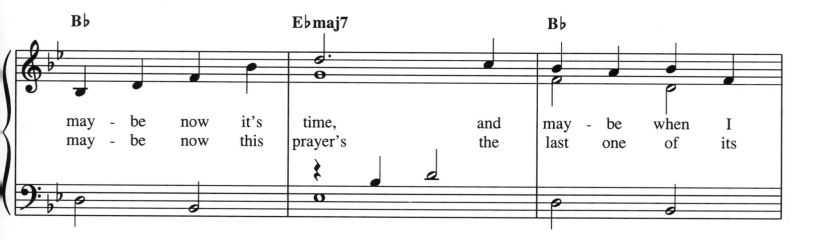

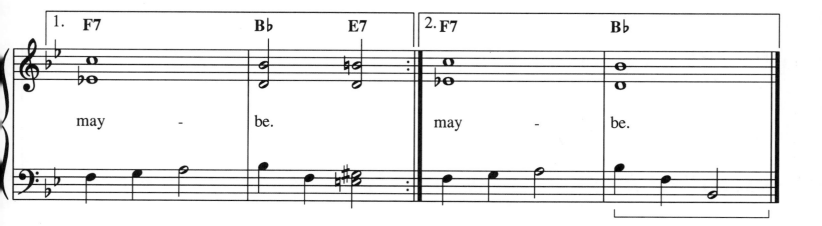

MY FAVORITE THINGS
from THE SOUND OF MUSIC

Lyrics by OSCAR HAMMERSTEIN II
Music by RICHARD RODGERS

Brightly

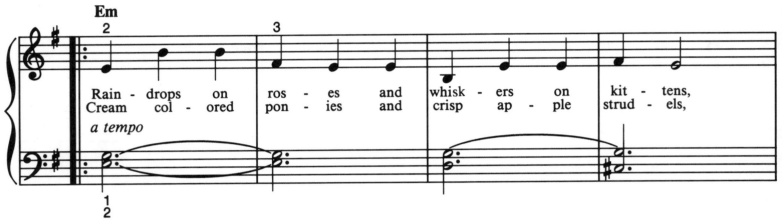

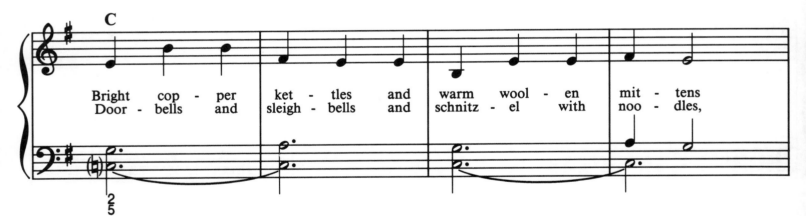

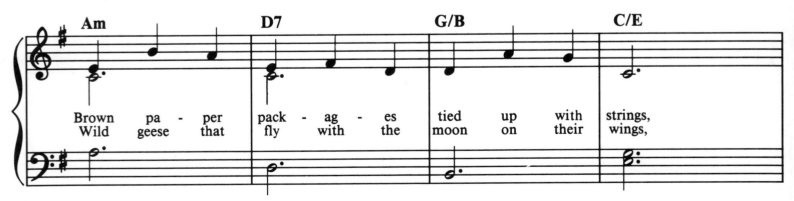

G/D **C** **F#m7♭5** **B7**

These are a few of my fa - vor - ite things.
These are a few of my fa - vor - ite things.

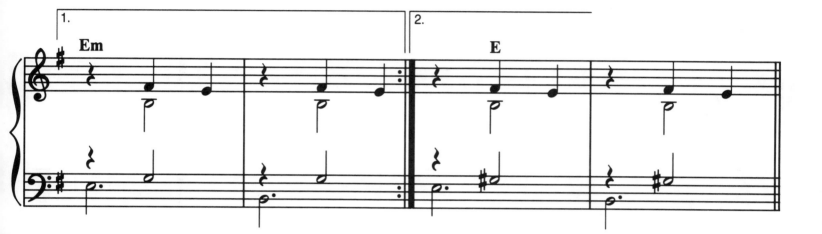

1. **Em** **2.** **E**

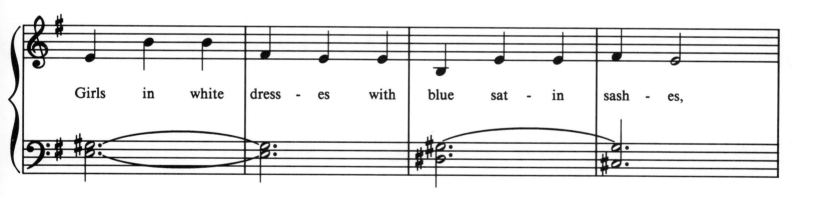

Girls in white dress - es with blue sat - in sash - es,

A/C#

Snow - flakes that stay on my nose and eye - lash - es,

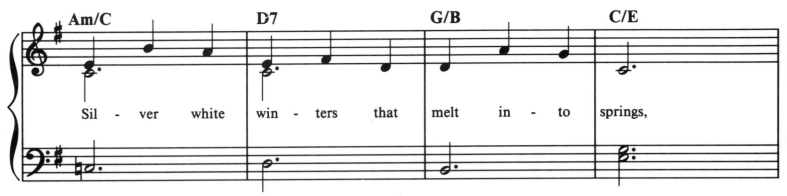

Sil - ver white win - ters that melt in - to springs,

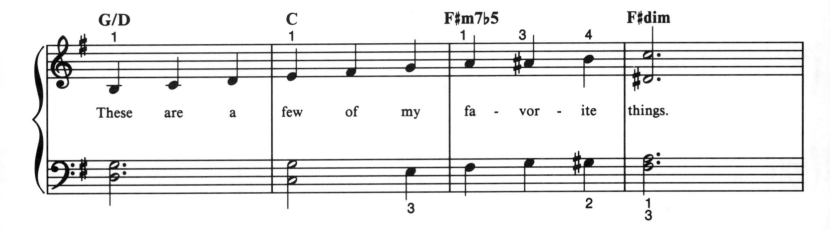

These are a few of my fa - vor - ite things.

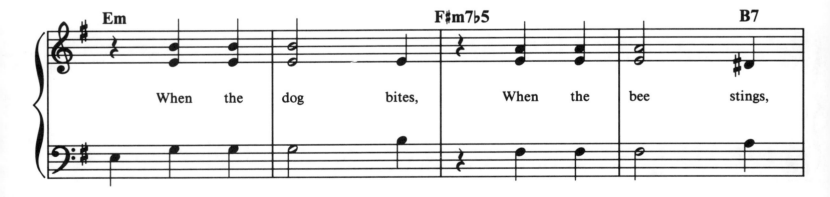

When the dog bites, When the bee stings,

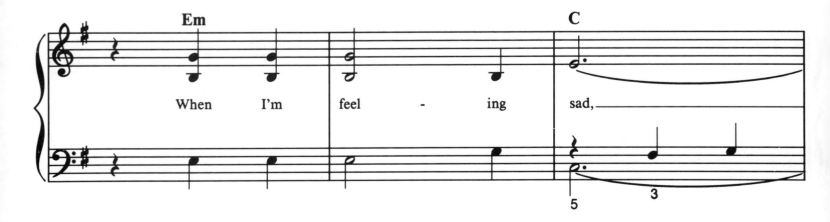

When I'm feel - ing sad,

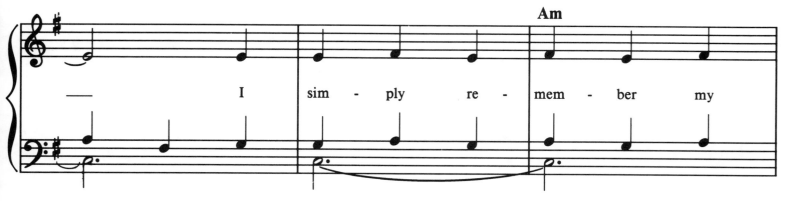

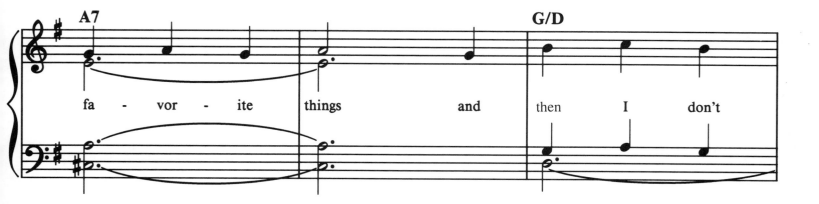

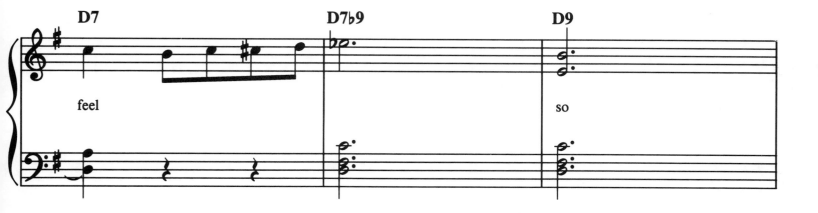

NEVER SMILE AT A CROCODILE

from Walt Disney's PETER PAN

Words by JACK LAWRENCE
Music by FRANK CHURCHILL

Moderately slow (Allegretto)

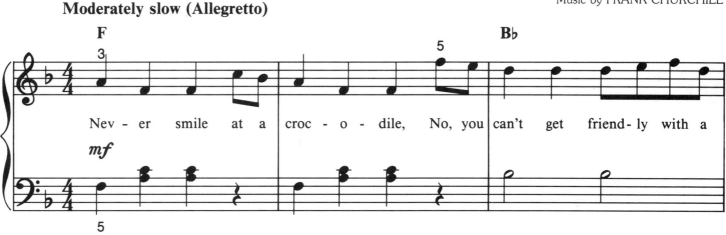

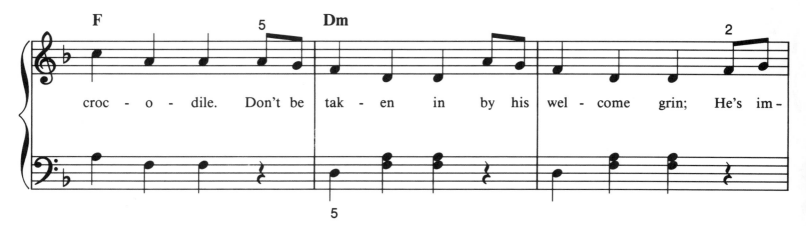

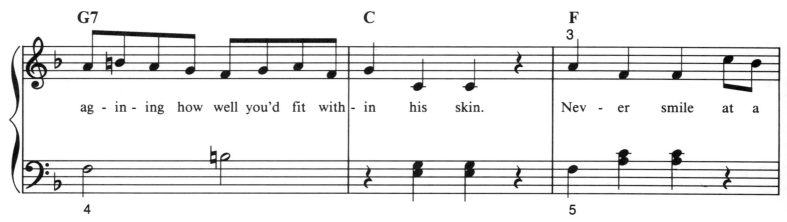

run, walk a - way; Say "Good-night" not "Good day."
rude, nev - er mock; Throw a kiss, not a rock.
Clear the aisle and nev- er smile at Mis- ter

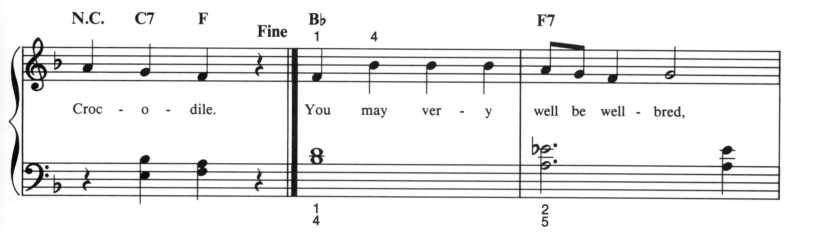

Croc - o - dile. | You may ver - y | well be well - bred,

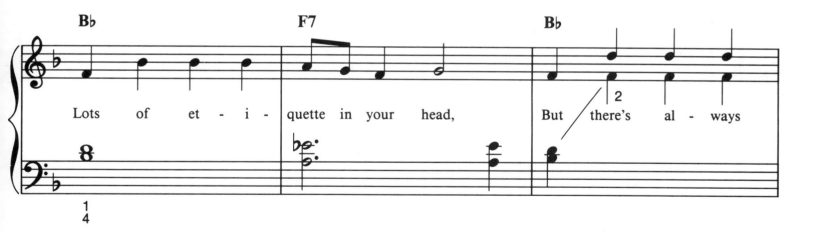

Lots of et - i - quette in your head, | But there's al - ways

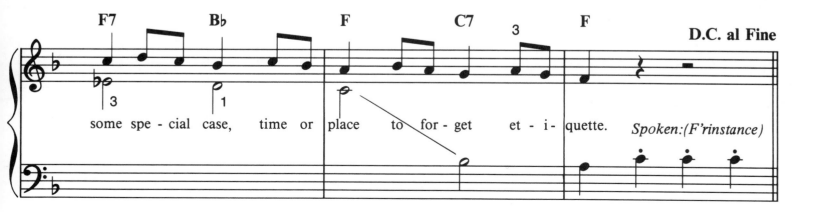

some spe - cial case, time or place to for- get et - i- quette. *Spoken:(F'rinstance)*

ON TOP OF SPAGHETTI

Words and Music by
TOM GLAZER

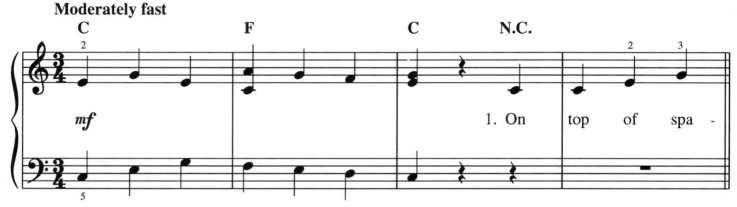

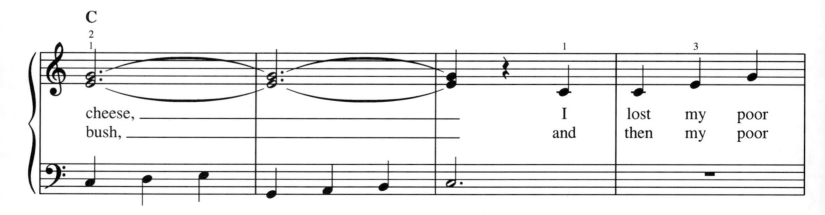

G7

meat - ball _____   when some - bod - y
meat - ball _____   was noth - ing but

C   **F**   **C**   **N.C.**

sneezed.   It rolled off the
mush.   The mush was as

F   **G7**

ta - ble _____   and on - to the
tast - y _____   as tast - y could

C

floor, _____   and then my poor
be, _____   and ear - ly next

meat - ball _____ rolled out of the
sum - mer, _____ it grew in - to a

1., 2.

door. It rolled in the
tree. The tree was all

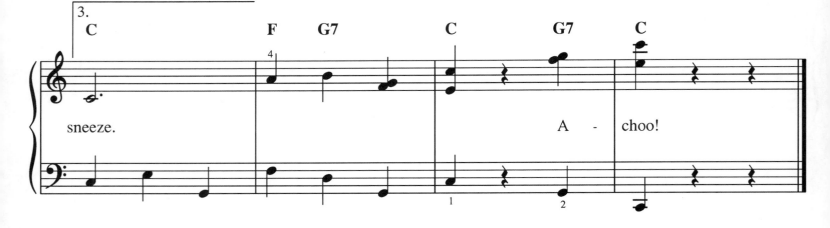

3.

sneeze. A - choo!

Additional Lyrics

3. The tree was all covered with beautiful moss;
   It grew lovely meatballs and tomato sauce.
   So if you eat spaghetti all covered with cheese,
   Hold on to your meatballs and don't ever sneeze.

ONE SMALL VOICE

from the Television Series SESAME STREET

Words and Music by
JEFF MOSS

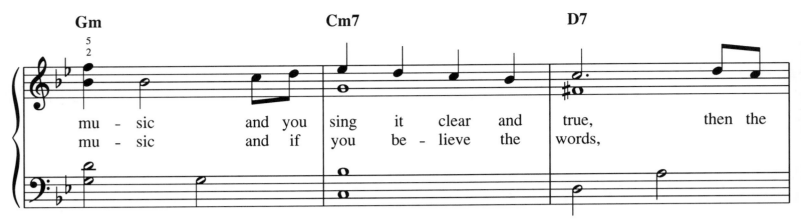

mu - sic and you sing it clear and true, then the
mu - sic and if you be - lieve the words,

world can sing with you. _____
sing and you'll be heard. _____

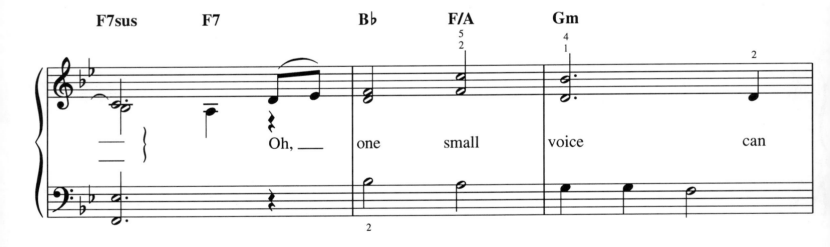

Oh, ___ one small voice can

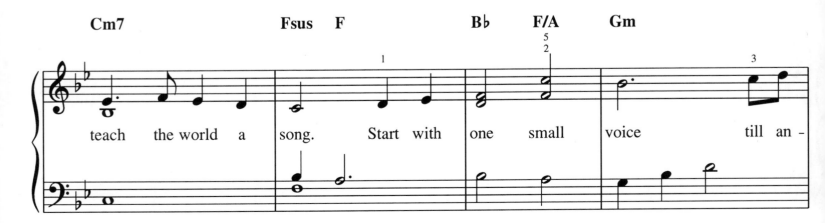

teach the world a song. Start with one small voice till an -

oth - er joins a - long,   and you'll   feel   the   mu - sic   grow - ing

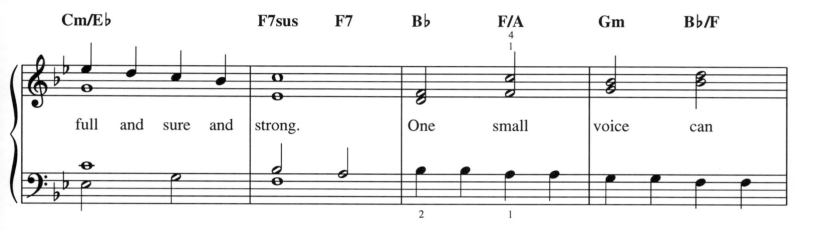

full and sure and strong.   One   small   voice   can

teach   the world   a   song.

song.   rit.

PART OF YOUR WORLD
from Walt Disney's THE LITTLE MERMAID

Lyrics by HOWARD ASHMAN
Music by ALAN MENKEN

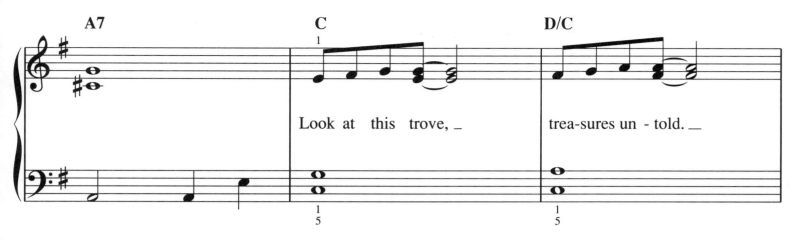

Look at this trove, _ trea-sures un - told. _

How man-y won - ders can one cav-ern hold? Look-ing a - round _ here you'd

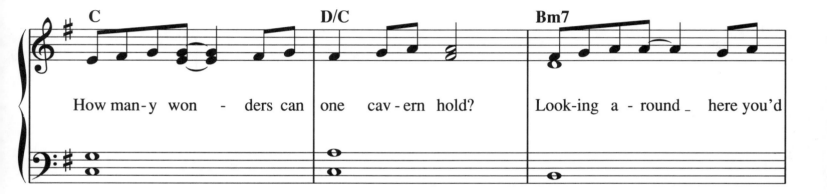

think, sure, she's got ev - 'ry-thing. _ I've got

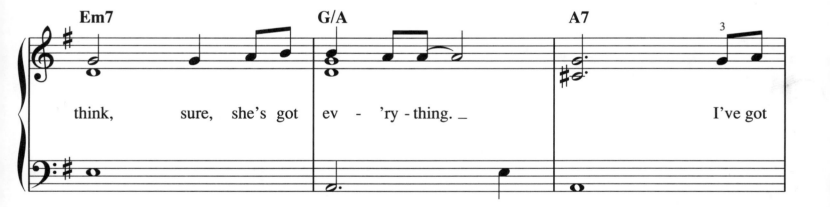

gad - gets and giz - mos a - plen-ty. _____ I've got who - zits and what - zits ga -

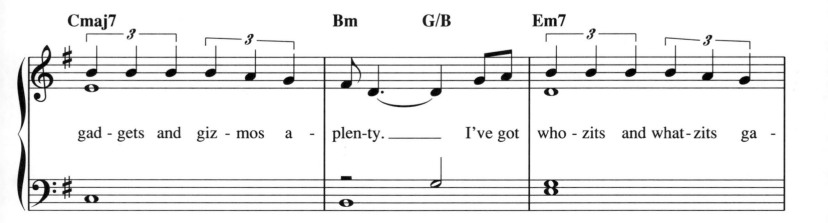

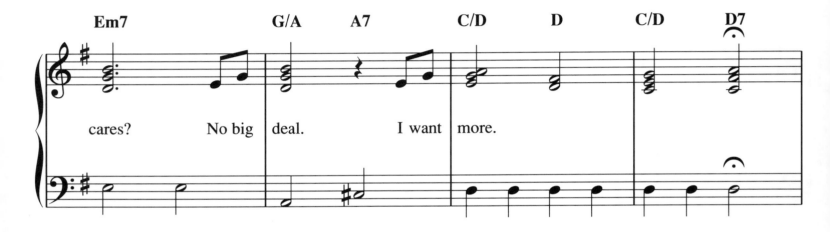

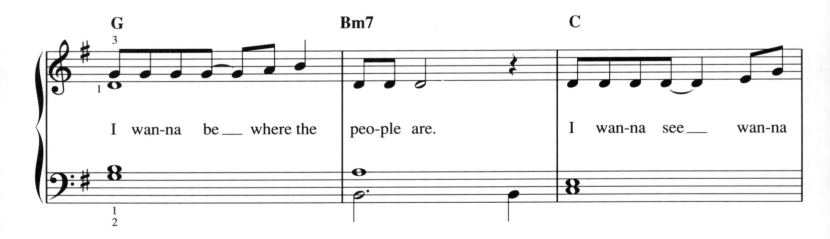

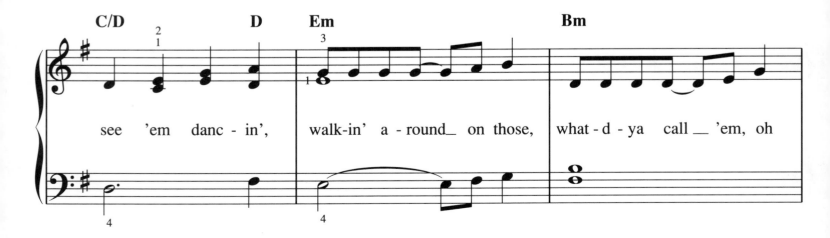

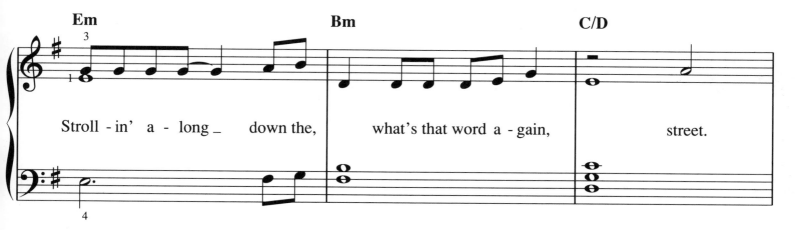

stay all day in the sun. Wan - der - in' free, wish I could

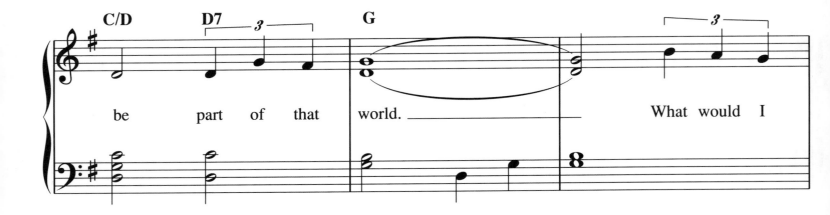

be part of that world. _____ What would I

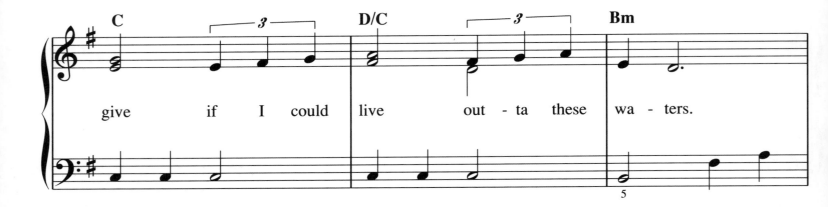

give if I could live out - ta these wa - ters.

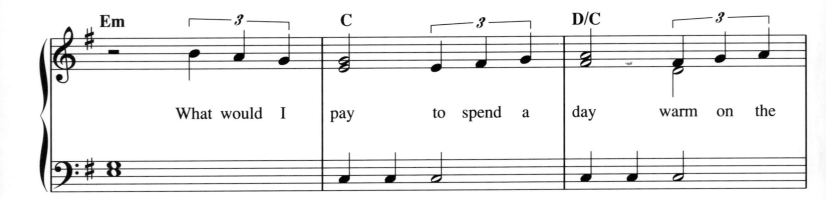

What would I pay to spend a day warm on the

sand. Bet - cha on land they un - der -

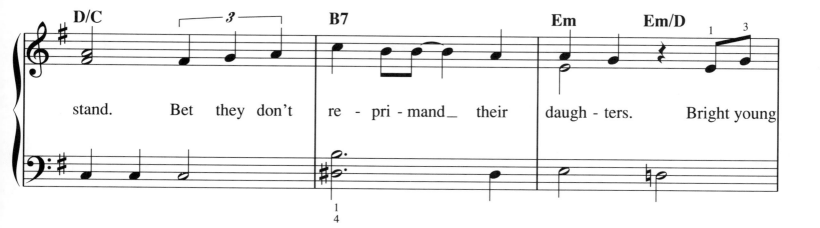

stand. Bet they don't re - pri - mand__ their daugh - ters. Bright young

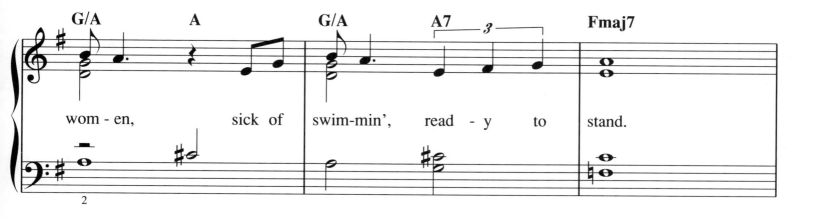

wom - en, sick of swim-min', read - y to stand.

And read - y to know__ what the peo - ple __ know.

Ask 'em my ques - tions and get some an - swers. What's a fire _____ and

why does it, what's the word, burn. When's it my

turn? Would-n't I love, love to ex - plore that shore up a -

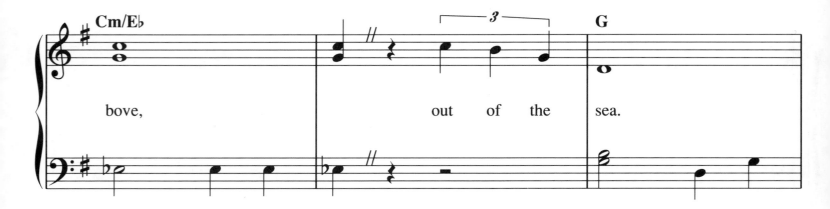

bove, out of the sea.

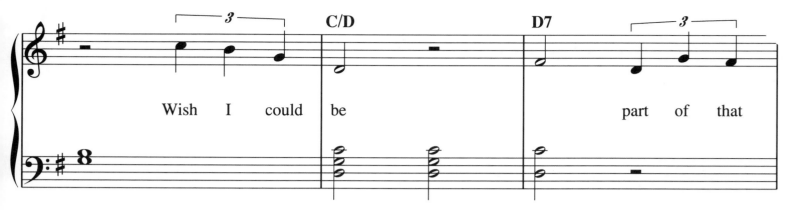

Wish I could be part of that

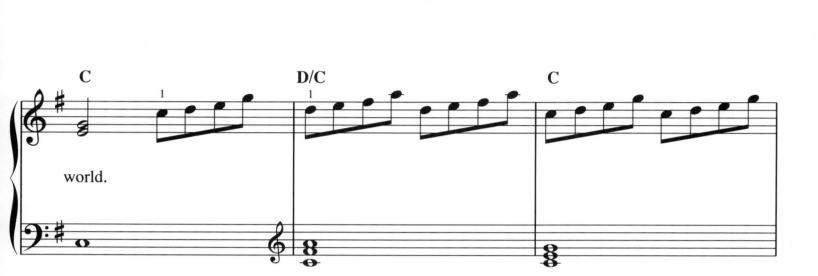

world.

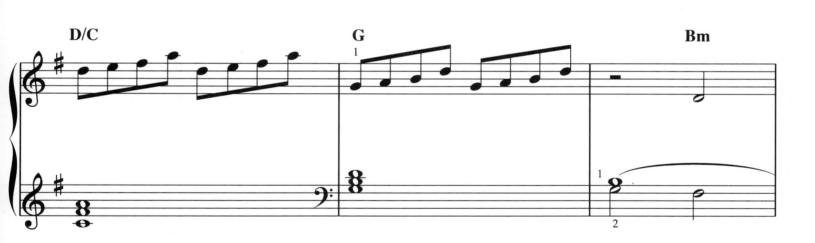

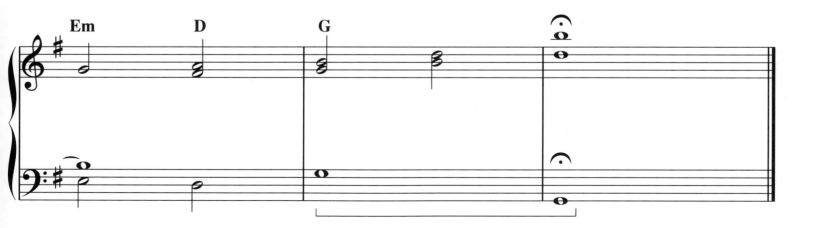

PEANUT SAT ON A RAILROAD TRACK

Traditional

(like a locomotive)

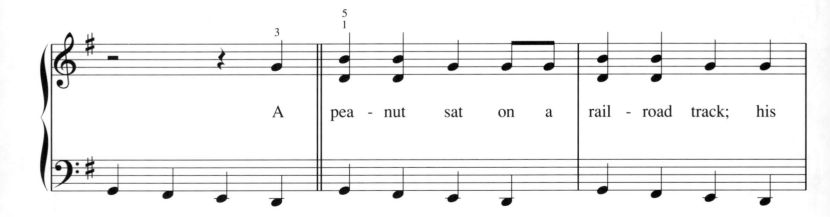

A pea - nut sat on a rail - road track; his

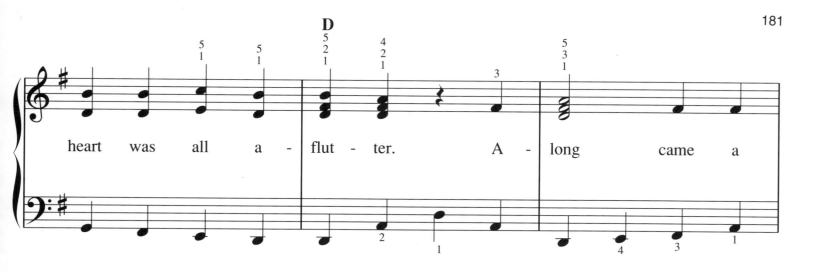

heart was all a - flut - ter. A - long came a

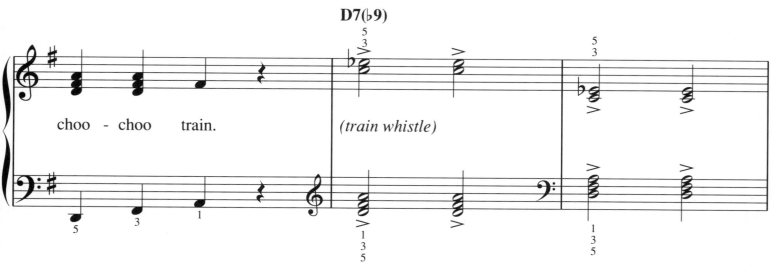

choo - choo train. *(train whistle)*

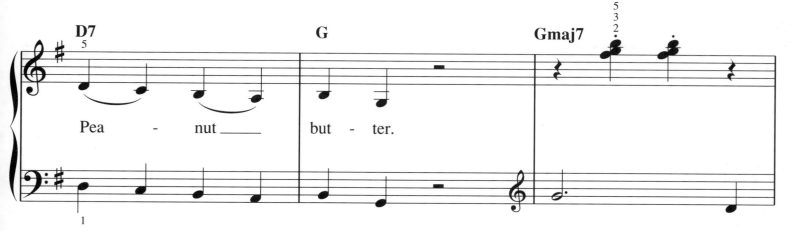

Pea - nut _____ but - ter.

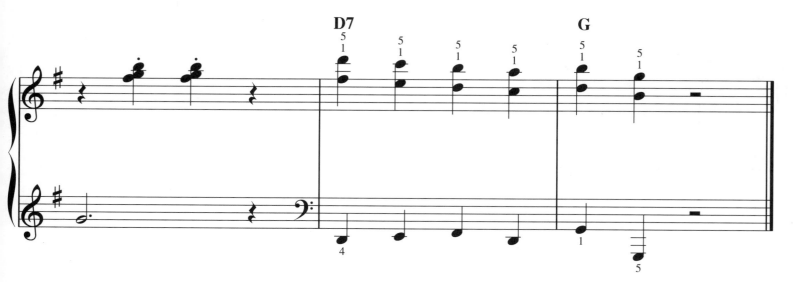

PURPLE PEOPLE EATER

Words and Music by
SHEB WOOLEY

Bright Rock

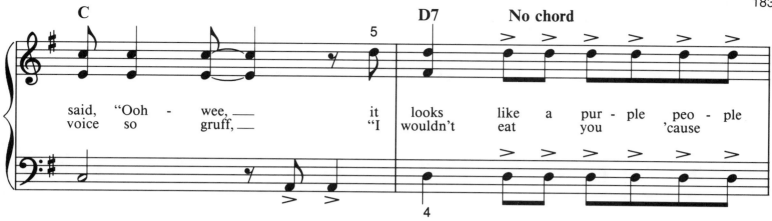

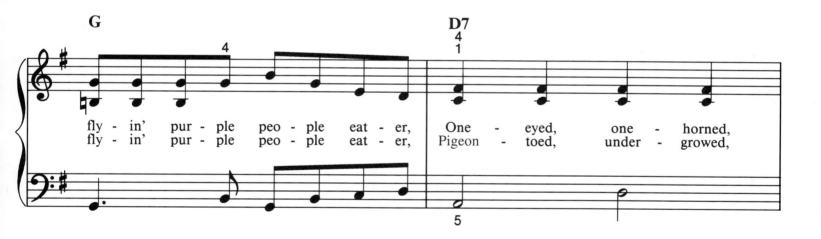

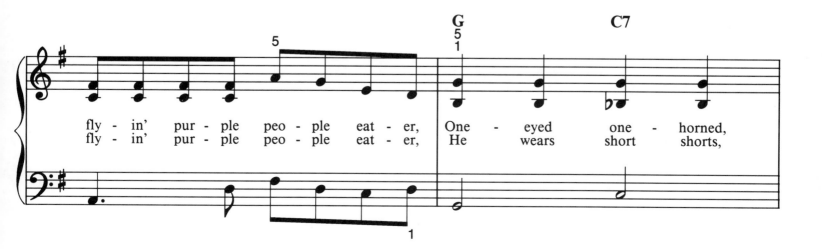

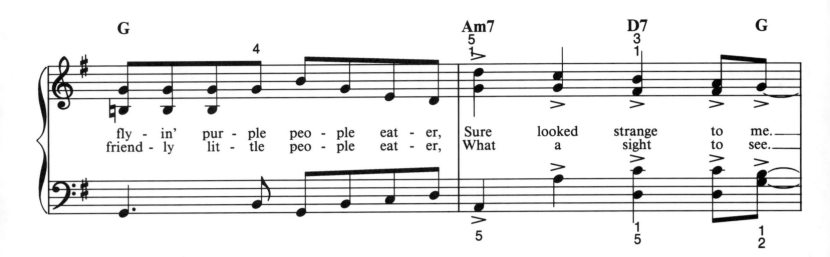

Additional Lyrics

3. I said, "Mister purple people eater, what's your line?"
   He said, "Eatin' purple people, and it sure is fine,
   But that's not the reason that I came to land,
   I wanna get a job in a rock and roll band."
   Chorus

4. And then he swung from the tree and he lit on the ground,
   And he started to rock, a-really rockin' around.
   It was a crazy ditty with a swingin' tune,
   Singa bop bapa loop a lap a loom bam boom.
   Chorus

5. Well he went on his way and then what-a you know,
   I saw him last night on a T.V. show.
   He was blowin' it out, really knockin' 'em dead.
   Playin' rock 'n roll music thru the horn of his head.
   Chorus

ROCKY & BULLWINKLE
from the Cartoon Television Series

By FRANK COMSTOCK

Rather bright

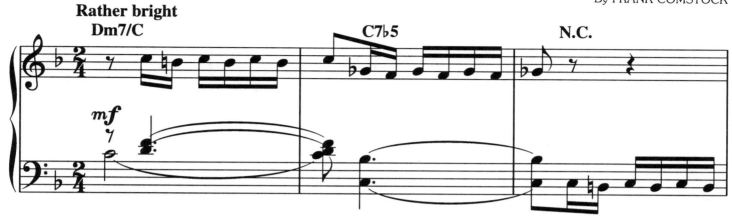

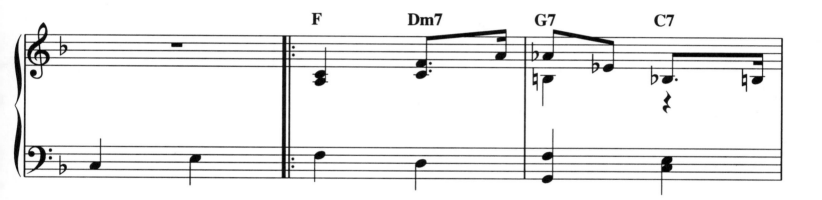

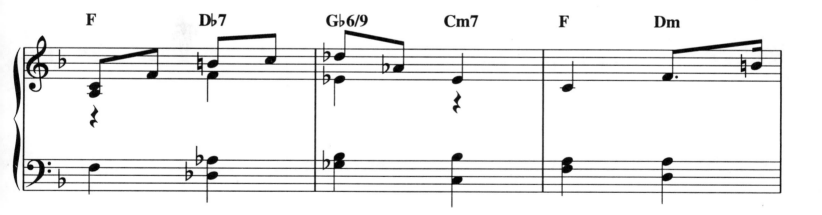

186

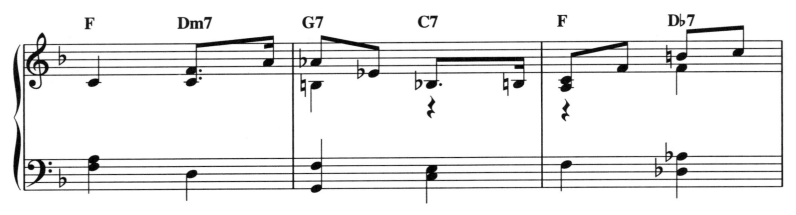

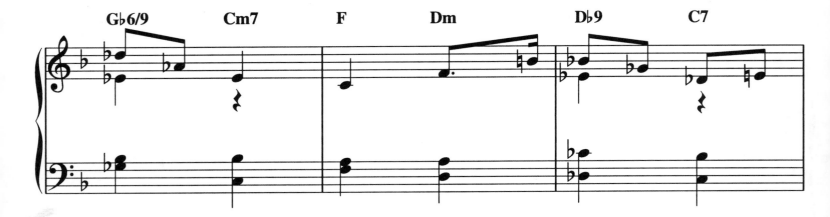

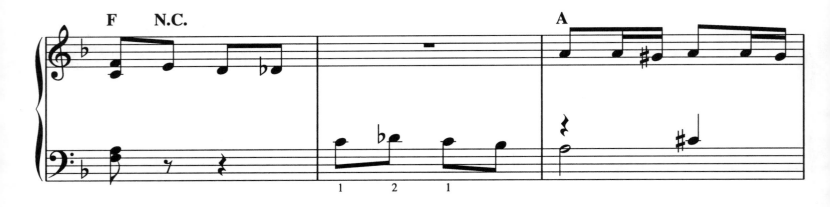

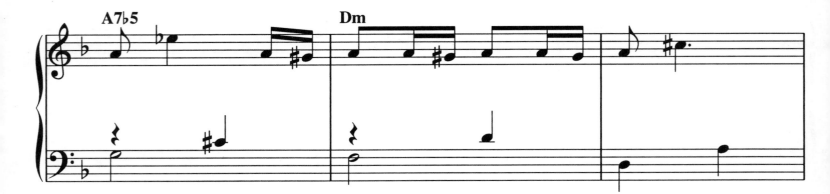

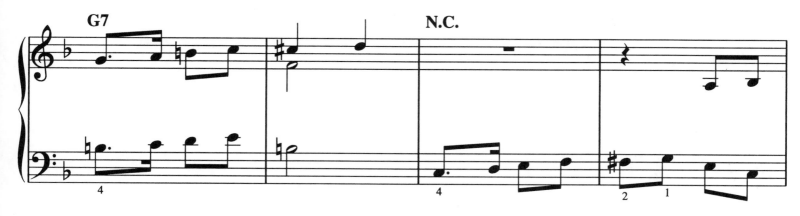

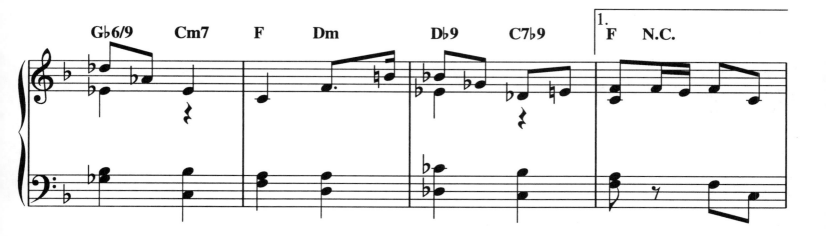

RUMBLY IN MY TUMBLY
from Walt Disney's THE MANY ADVENTURES OF WINNIE THE POOH

Words and Music by RICHARD M. SHERMAN
and ROBERT B. SHERMAN

Hum - dum dee dum
I don't need a

hum - dee dum dum.
pot of hon - ey.
I'm so rum - bly
I'd be grate - ful
in my tum - bly.
for a plate - full.

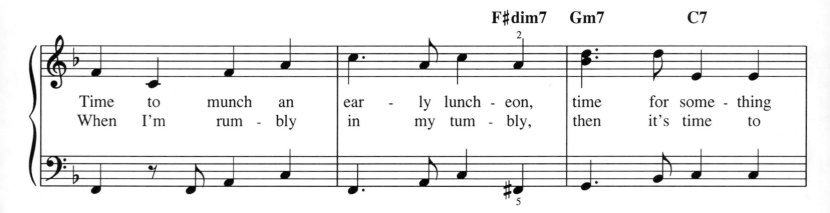

Time to munch an
When I'm rum - bly
ear - ly lunch - eon,
in my tum - bly,
time for some - thing
then it's time to

sweet!   Oh, I   would - n't   climb   this
eat!   It's the   taste - ful   thing   to

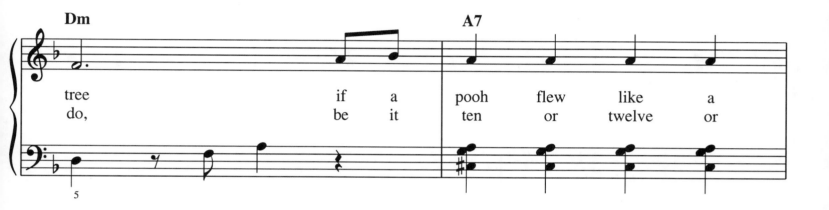

tree   if a   pooh   flew   like   a
do,   be it   ten   or   twelve   or

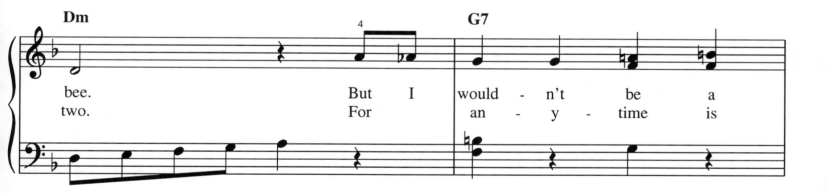

bee.   But I   would - n't   be   a
two.   For   an - y - time   is

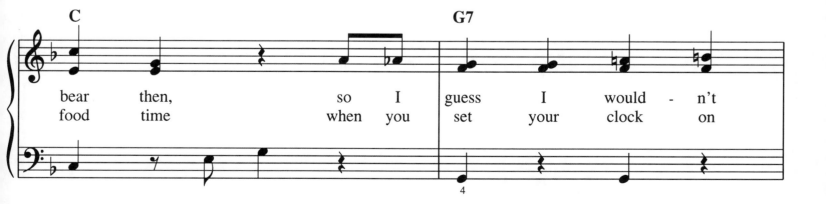

bear then,   so I   guess I   would - n't
food time   when you   set   your   clock   on

190

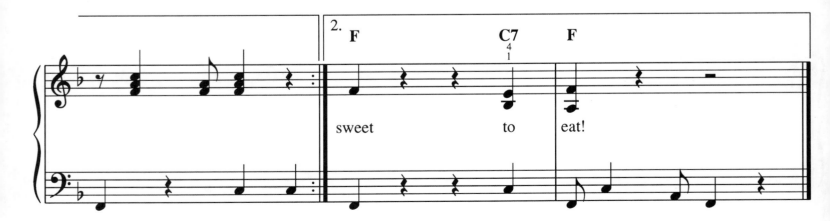

SO LONG, FAREWELL
from THE SOUND OF MUSIC

Lyrics by OSCAR HAMMERSTEIN II
Music by RICHARD RODGERS

Moderately

CHILDREN:

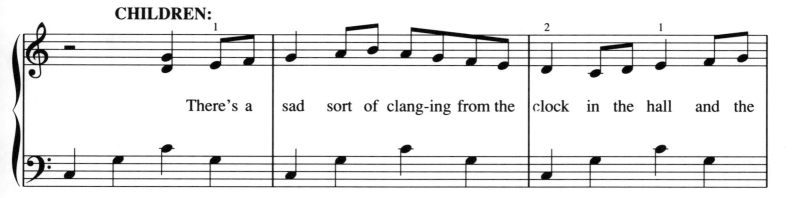

There's a sad sort of clang-ing from the clock in the hall and the

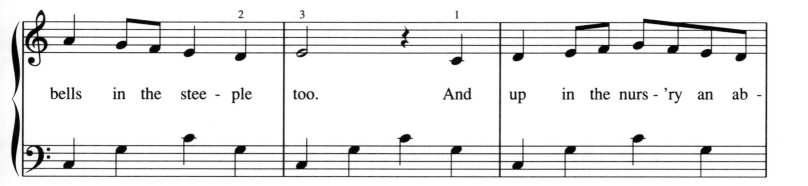

bells in the stee-ple too. And up in the nurs-'ry an ab-

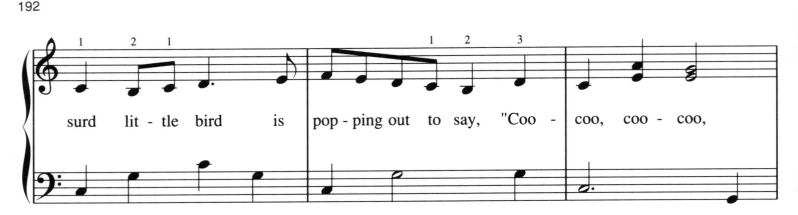

surd lit - tle bird   is   pop - ping out to say, "Coo - coo,   coo - coo,

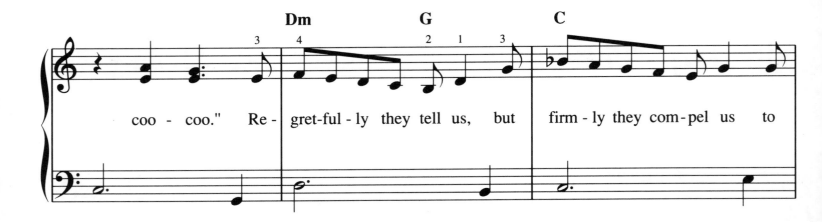

coo - coo."   Re - gret-ful - ly they tell us,   but   firm - ly they com-pel us   to

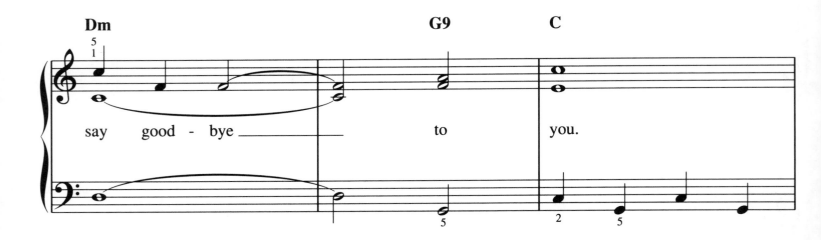

say   good - bye _____   to   you.

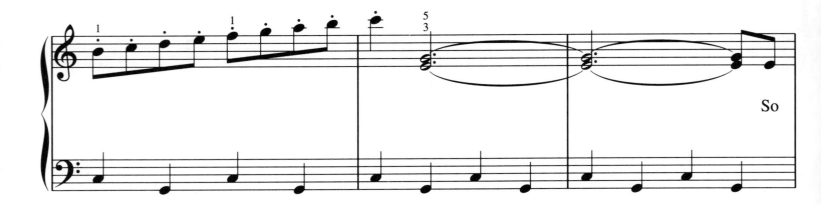

So

MARTA:

long, fare - well, Auf wie-der-sehn, good-night.＿ I hate to go and

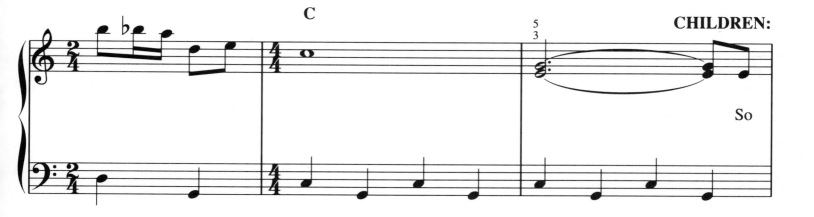

G

leave this pret - ty sight.＿

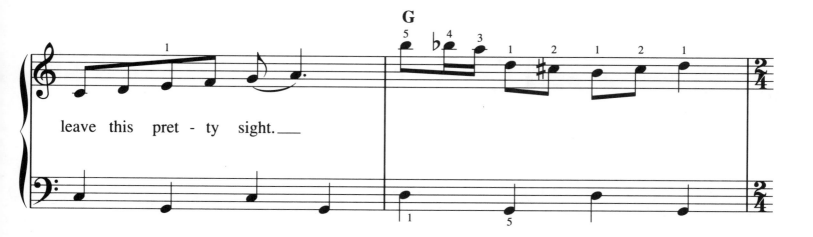

C

CHILDREN:

So

KURT:

long, fare - well, auf wie-der-sehn, a - dieu.＿ A - dieu, a - dieu, to

194

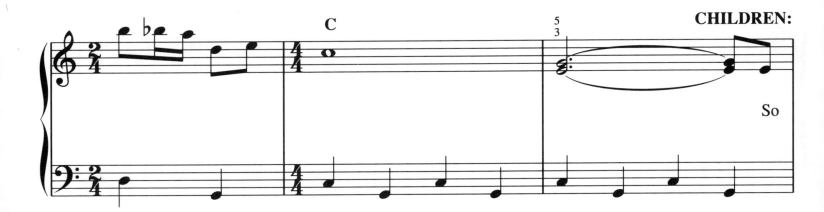

CHILDREN:

So

FRIEDERICH:

long, fare-well, auf wie-der-sehn, good-bye.__ I leave and leave a

sigh and say good-bye, __ Good-bye.

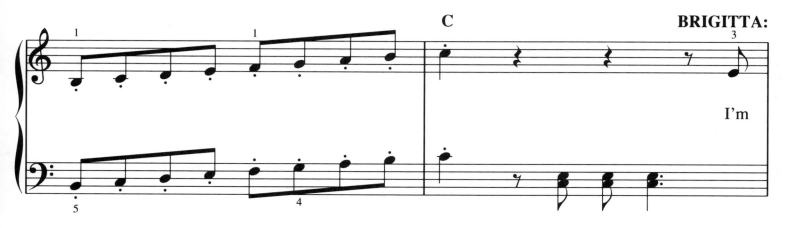

BRIGITTA:

I'm

glad to go, I can-not tell a lie.____ I flit, I float, I

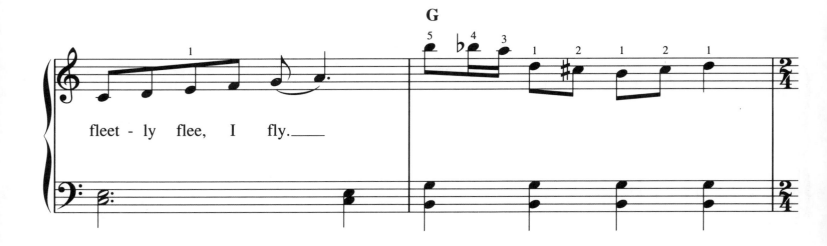

fleet - ly flee, I fly.____

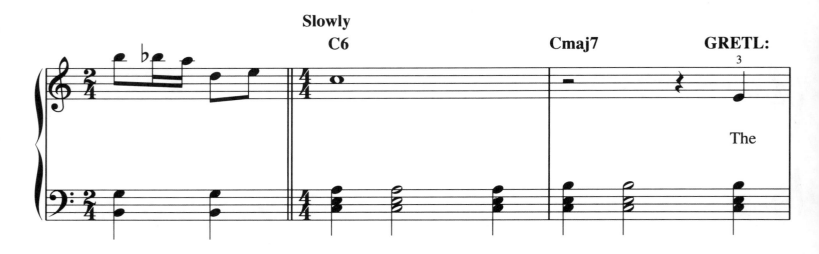

Slowly

GRETL:

The

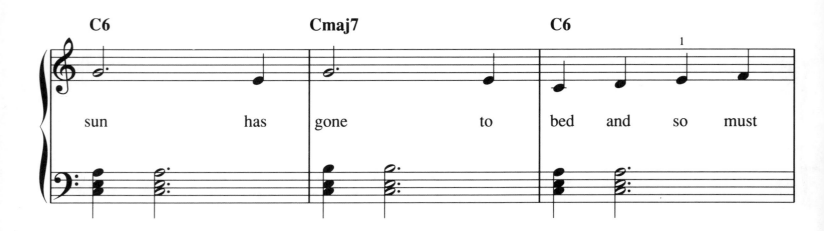

sun has gone to bed and so must

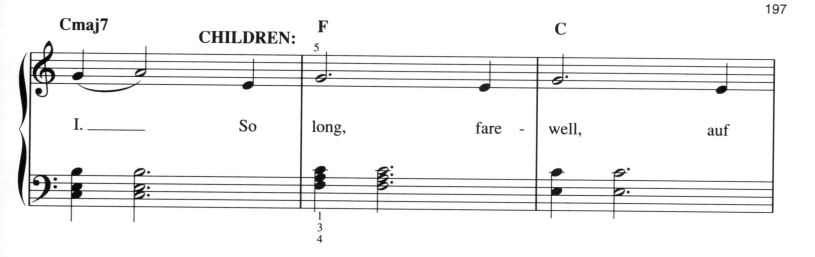

I. _____ So long, fare - well, auf

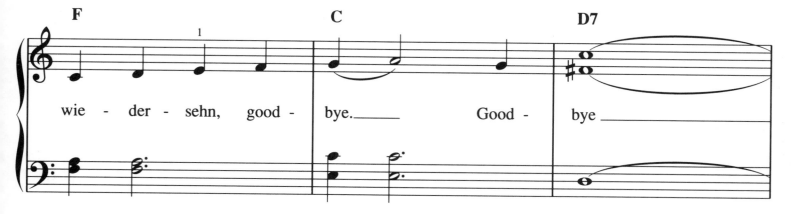

wie - der - sehn, good - bye. _____ Good - bye _____

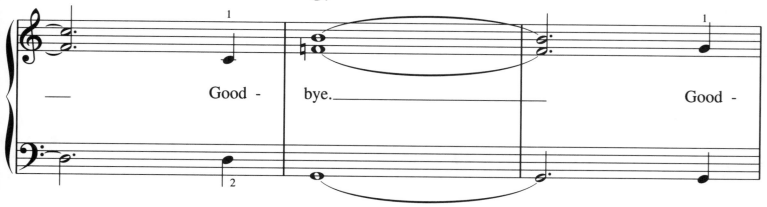

_____ Good - bye. _____ Good -

bye. _____ Good - bye.

SESAME STREET THEME

Words by BRUCE HART,
JON STONE and JOE RAPOSO
Music by JOE RAPOSO

Steady Rock beat

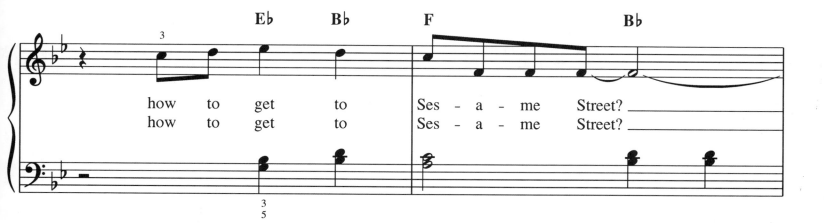

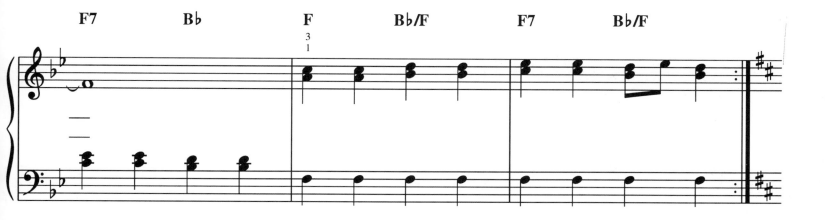

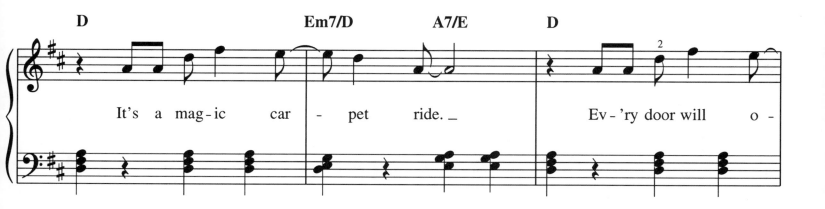

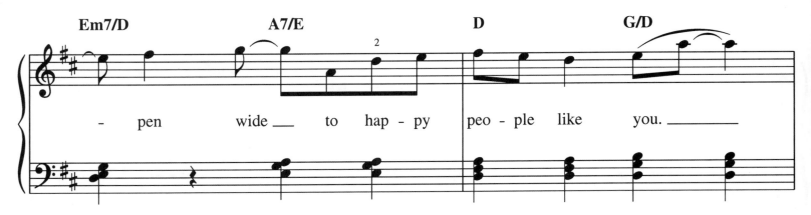

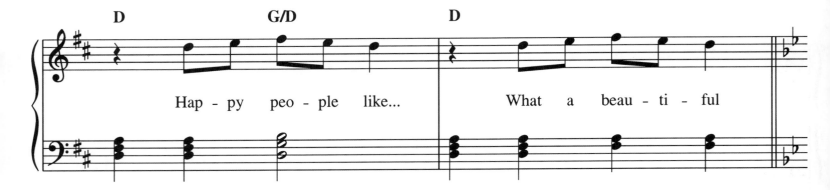

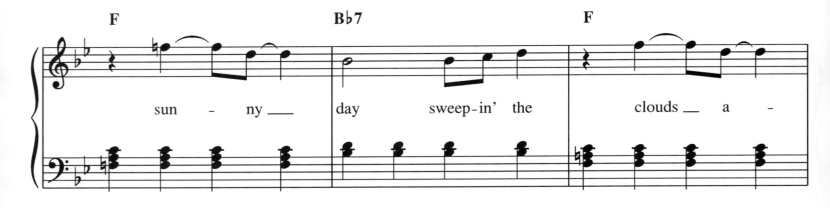

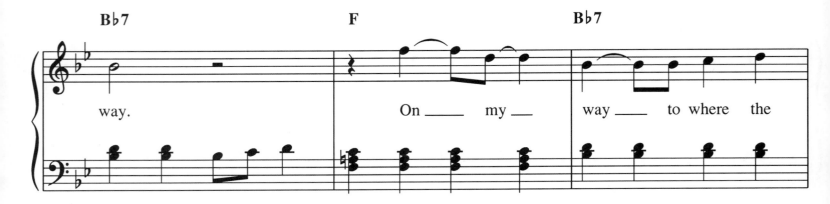

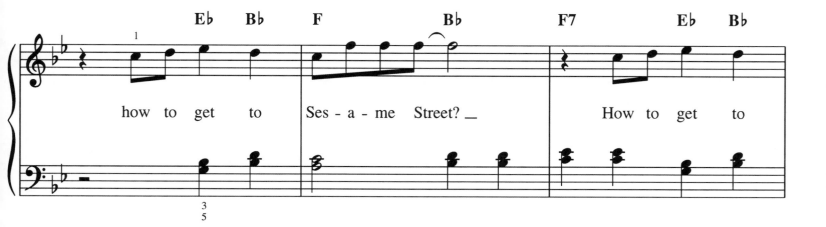

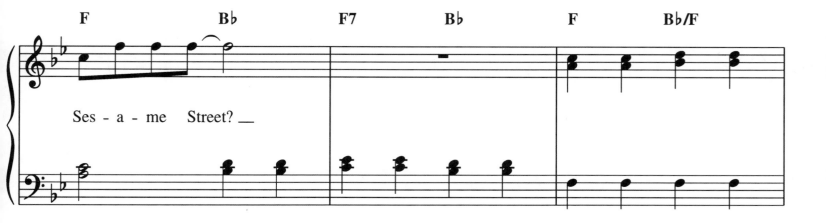

THE SIAMESE CAT SONG

from Walt Disney's LADY AND THE TRAMP

Words and Music by PEGGY LEE
and SONNY BURKE

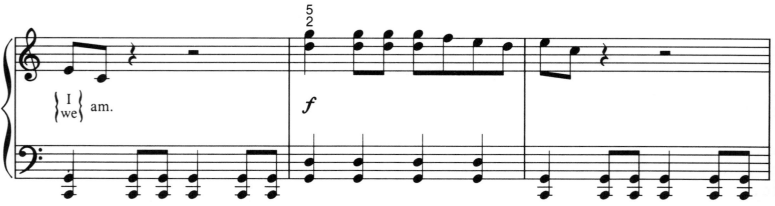

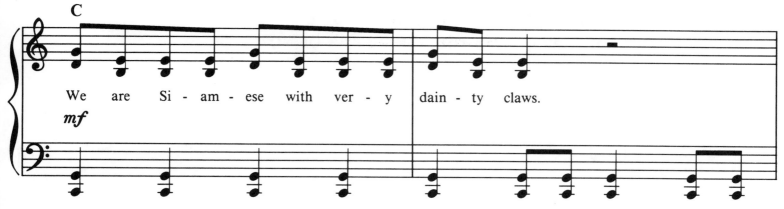

C

We are Si - am - ese with ver - y dain - ty claws.

mf

G7

Please ob - serv - ing paws con - tain - ing dain - ty claws.

Now we look - in' o - ver our new dom - i - cile.

If we like we stay for may - be

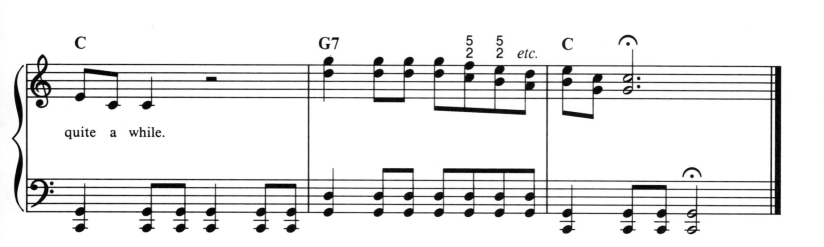

C   **G7**   **C**

quite a while.

SOMEDAY
from Walt Disney's THE HUNCHBACK OF NOTRE DAME

Music by ALAN MENKEN
Lyrics by STEPHEN SCHWARTZ

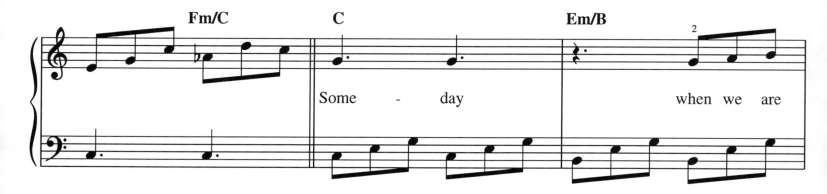

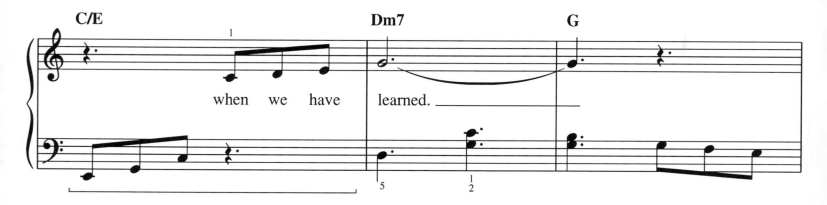

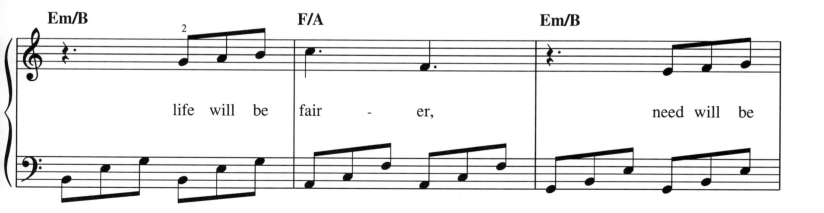

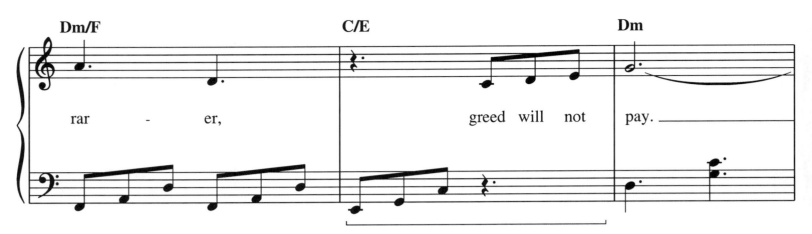

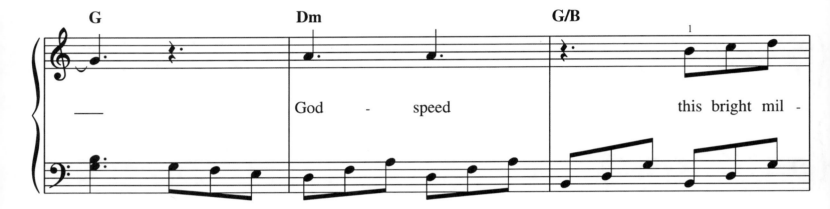

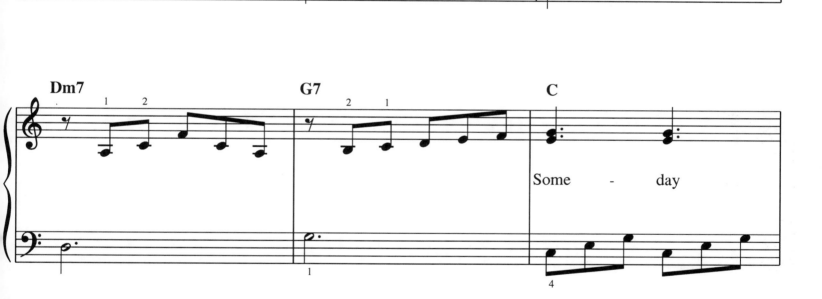

Some - day

our fight will be won then, we'll stand in the

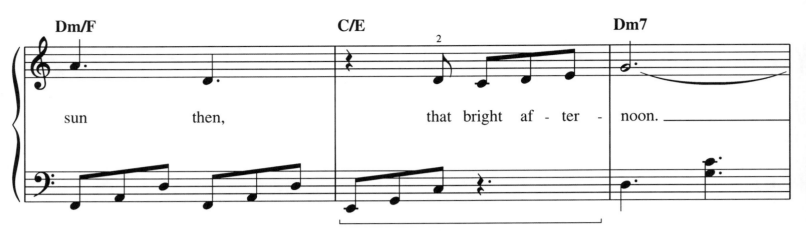

sun   then,   that bright af - ter - noon. _____

_____   Till   then,   on days when the

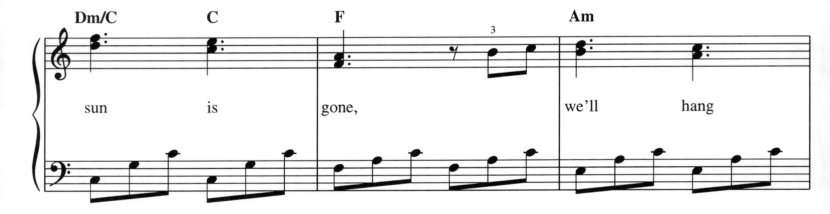

sun   is   gone,   we'll   hang

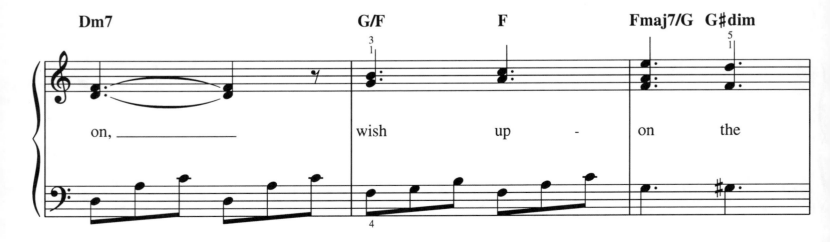

on, _____   wish   up - on   the

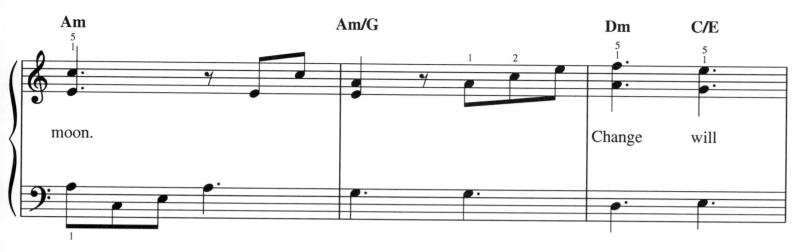

moon.

Change will

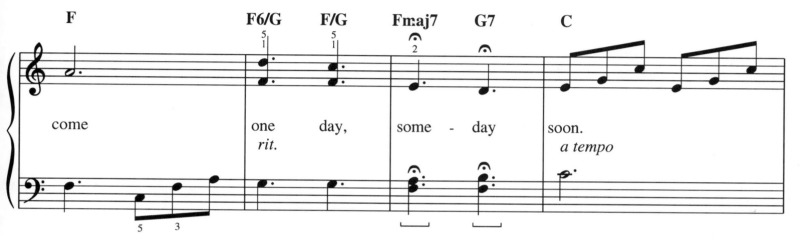

come

one day,

some - day

soon.

rit.

a tempo

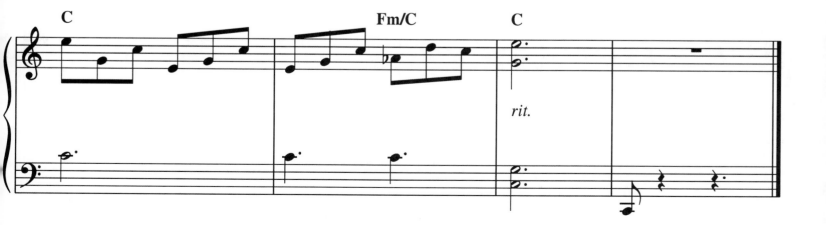

rit.

THE SOUND OF MUSIC

from THE SOUND OF MUSIC

Lyrics by OSCAR HAMMERSTEIN II
Music by RICHARD RODGERS

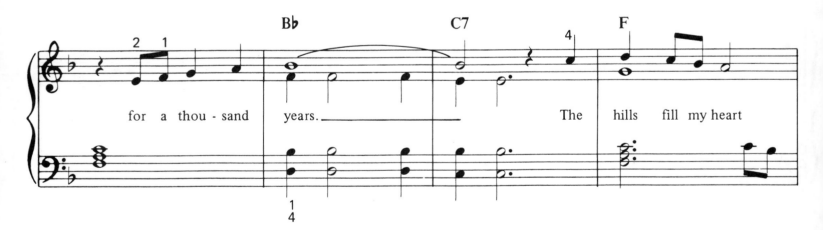

song it hears._____ My heart wants to beat like the wings of the

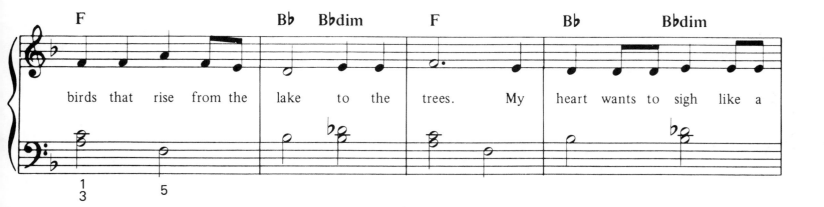

birds that rise from the lake to the trees. My heart wants to sigh like a

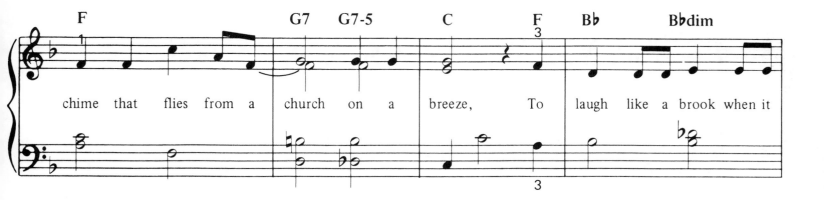

chime that flies from a church on a breeze, To laugh like a brook when it

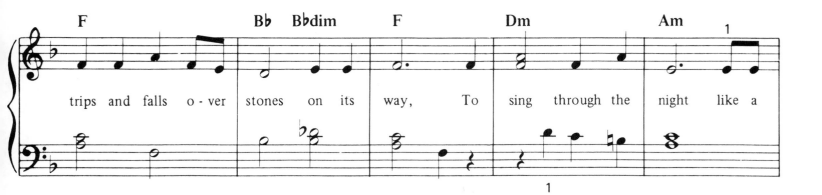

trips and falls o-ver stones on its way, To sing through the night like a

lark who is learn-ing to pray. I go to the hills when my heart is

lone - ly, _____ I know I will hear what I've heard be -

fore. _____ My heart will be blessed with the sound of mu - sic, _

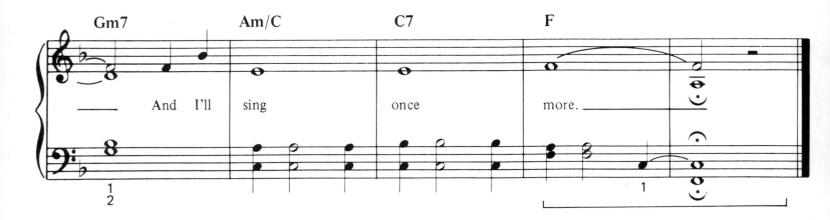

___ And I'll sing once more. _____

THREE LITTLE FISHIES
(Itty Bitty Poo)

Words and Music by
SAXIE DOWELL

Moderately bright

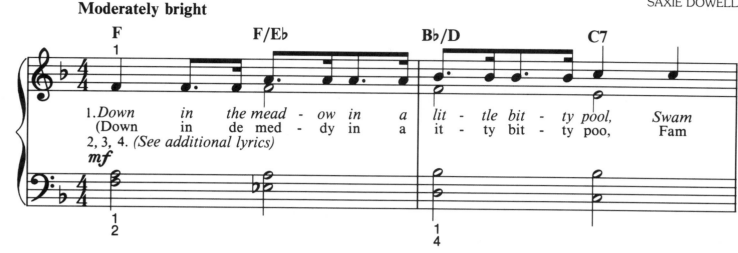

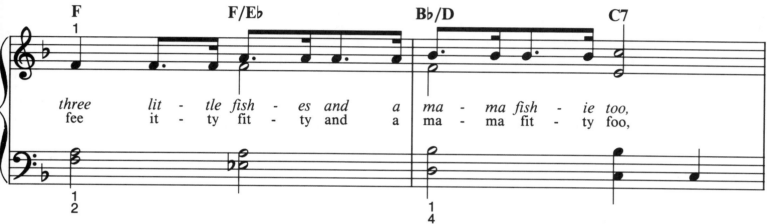

214

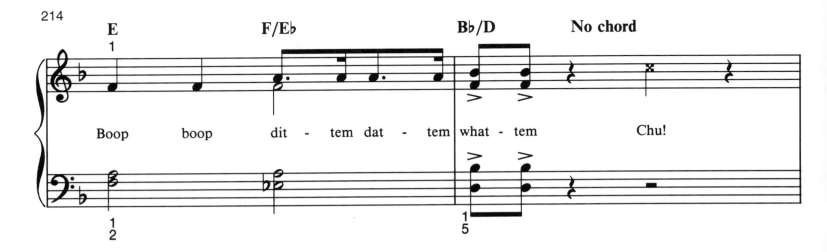

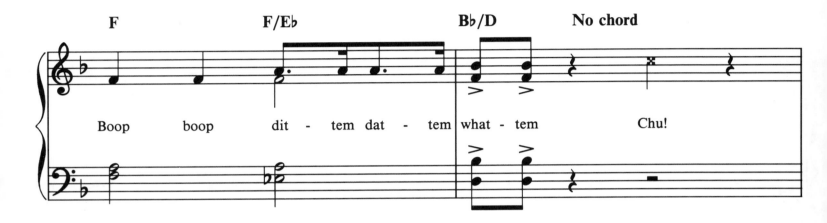

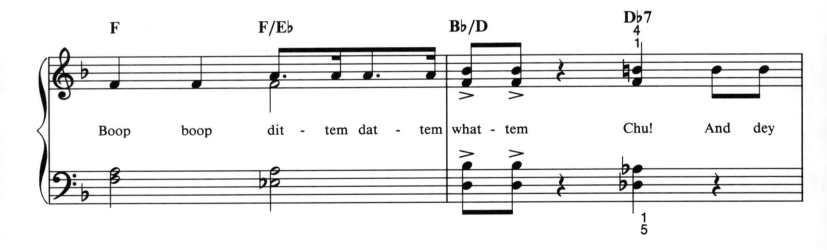

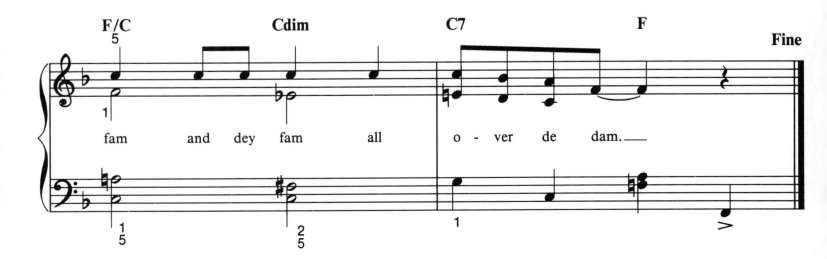

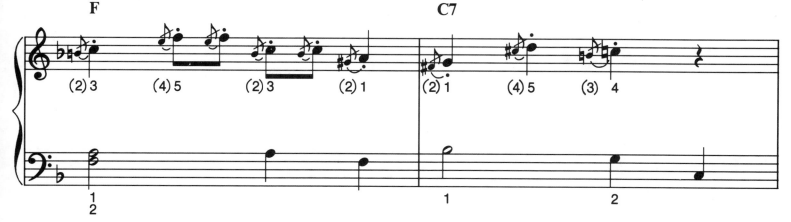

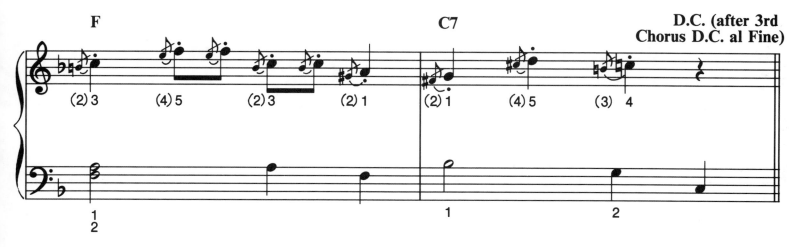

Additional Lyrics

2. "Stop" said the mama fishie "Or you will get lost,"
The three little fishies didn't wanna be bossed.
The three little fishies went off on a spree,
And they swam and they swam right out to the sea.

("Top!" ted de mama fitty "or oo ill det ost,"
De fee itty fitty dinna anna be bossed.
De fee itty fitty ent off on a spwee,
And dey fam and dey fam ight out to de fee.)

Boop boop dit-tem dat-tem what-tem Chu!
" " " " " " " " "
" " " " " " " " "
And dey fam and dey fam ite out to de fee.

3. "Whee!" yelled the little fishies, "Here's a lot of fun,
We'll swim in the sea till the day is done."
They swam and they swam and it was a lark,
Till all of a sudden they met a SHARK!

("Whee!" 'elled de itty fitties "Ears a wot of fun,
Ee'll fim in de fee ill de day is un."
Dey fam and dey fam and it was a wark,
Till aw of a tudden dey taw a TARK!)

Boop boop dit-tem dat-tem what-tem Chu!
" " " " " " " " "
" " " " " " " " "
Till aw of a tudden dey taw a TARK!

4. "Help!" cried the little fishies, "Gee! look at all the whales!"
And quick as they could they turned on their tails.
And back to the pool in the meadow they swam,
And they swam and they swam back over the dam.

("He'p!" tied de itty fitties, "Dee! ook at all de fales!"
And twit as dey tood dey turned on deir tails!
And bat to de poo in de meddy dey fam,
And dey fam and dey fam bat over de dam.)

Boop boop dit-tem dat-tem what-tem Chu!
" " " " " " " " "
" " " " " " " " "
And dey fam and dey fam bat over de dam.

THE THING

Words and Music by
CHARLES R. GREAN

Moderately bright

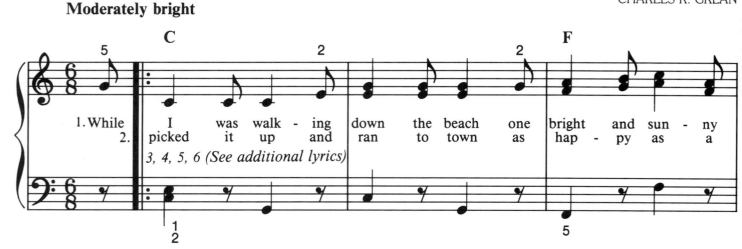

1. While I was walk-ing down the beach one bright and sun-ny
2. picked it up and ran to town as hap-py as a

3, 4, 5, 6 (See additional lyrics)

day.___ I saw a great big wood-en box a-float-in' in the
king.___ I took it to a guy I know who'd buy most an-y-

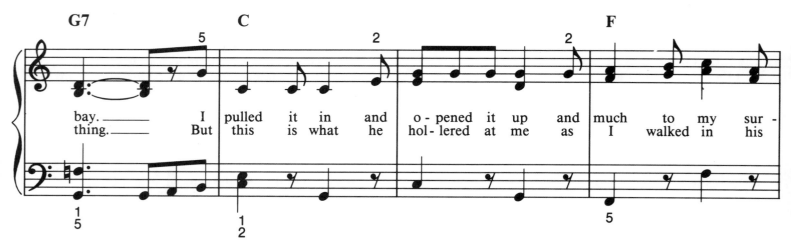

bay.___ I pulled it in and o-pened it up and much to my sur-
thing.___ But this is what he hol-lered at me as I walked in his

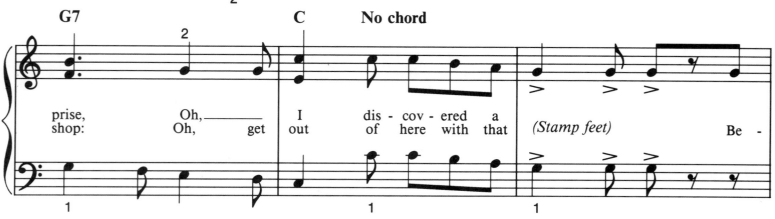

prise, Oh,___ I dis-cov-ered a
shop: Oh, get out of here with that *(Stamp feet)* Be -

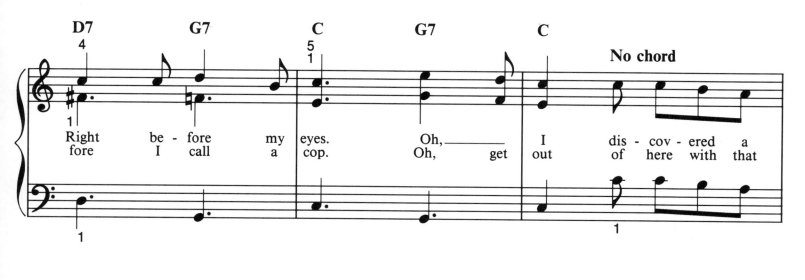

Additional Lyrics

3. I turned around and got right out a-runnin' for my life,
And then I took it home with me to give it to my wife.
But this is what she hollered at me as I walked in the door:
Oh, get out of here with that xxx and don't come back no more.
Oh, get out of here with that xxx and don't come back no more.

4. I wandered all around the town until I chanced to meet
A hobo who was looking for a handout on the street.
He said he'd take most any old thing, he was a desperate man,
But when I showed him the xxx, he turned around and ran.
Oh, when I showed him the xxx, he turned around and ran.

5. I wandered on for many years, a victim of my fate,
Until one day I came upon Saint Peter at the gate.
And when I tried to take it inside he told me where to go:
Get out of here with that xxx and take it down below.
Oh, get out of here with that xxx and take it down below.

6. The moral of the story is if you're out on the beach
And you should see a great big box and it's within your reach,
Don't ever stop and open it up, that's my advice to you,
'Cause you'll never get rid of the xxx, no matter what you do.
Oh, you'll never get rid of the xxx, no matter what you do.

TIE ME KANGAROO DOWN SPORT

Words and Music by
ROLF HARRIS

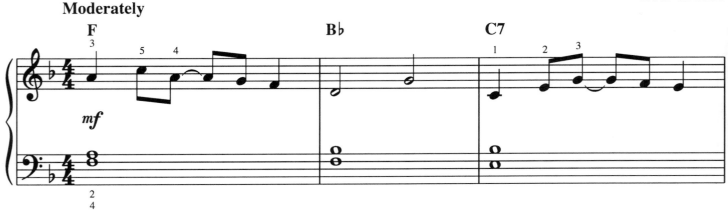

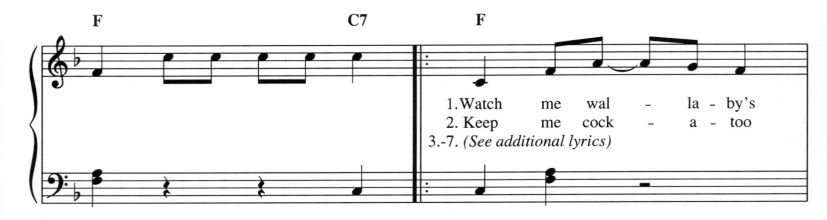

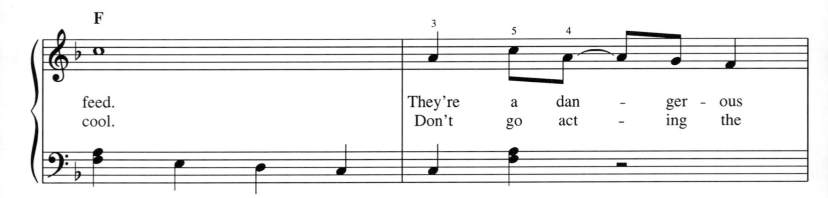

219

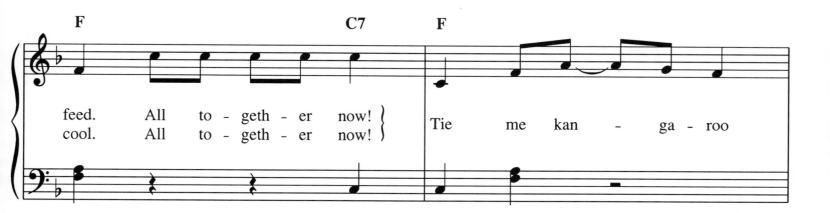

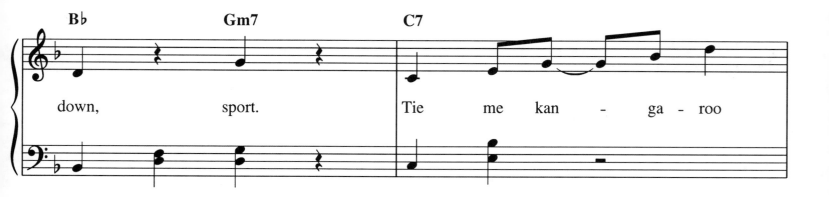

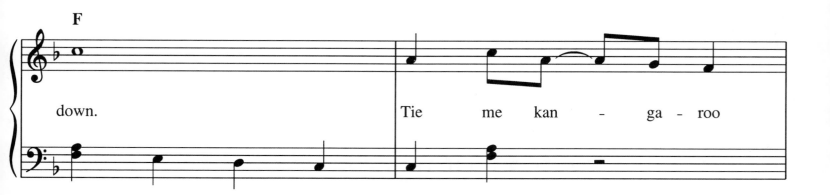

220

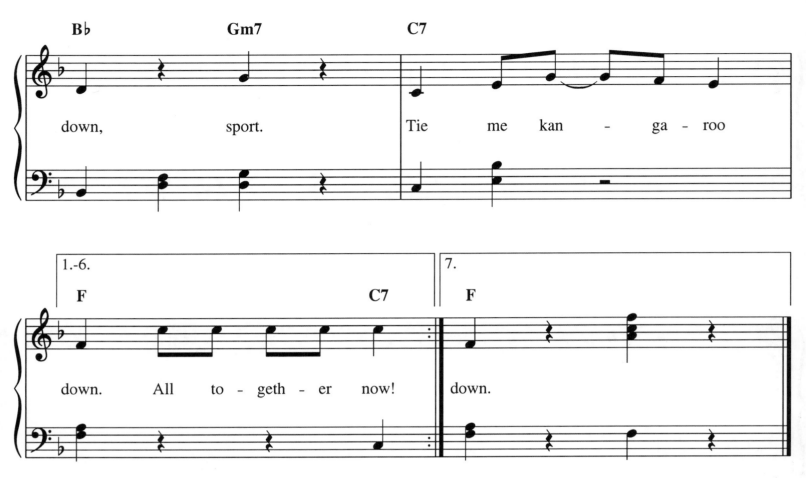

Additional Lyrics

3. Take me koala back, Jack.
Take me koala back.
He lives somewhere out on the track, Mac,
So take me koala back.
All together now!

4. Let me abos go loose, Lew.
Let me abos go loose.
They're of no further use, Lew,
So let me abos go loose.
All together now!

5. Mind me platypus duck, Bill.
Mind me platypus duck.
Don't let him go running amok, Bill.
Mind me platypus duck.
All together now!

6. Play your didgeridoo, Blue.
Play your didgeridoo.
Keep playing till I shoot through, Blue.
Play your didgeridoo.
All together now!

7. Tan me hide when I'm dead, Fred.
Tan me hide when I'm dead.
So we tanned his hide when he died, Clyde,
(Spoken:) And that's it hanging on the shed.
(Sung:) All together now!

TOMORROW
from the Musical Production ANNIE

Lyric by MARTIN CHARNIN
Music by CHARLES STROUSE

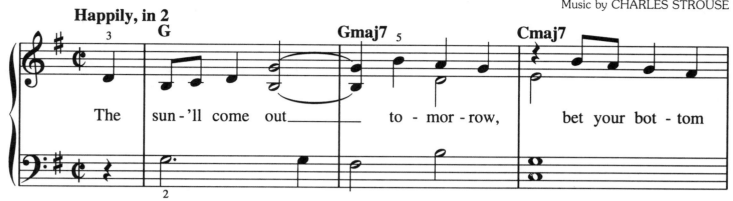

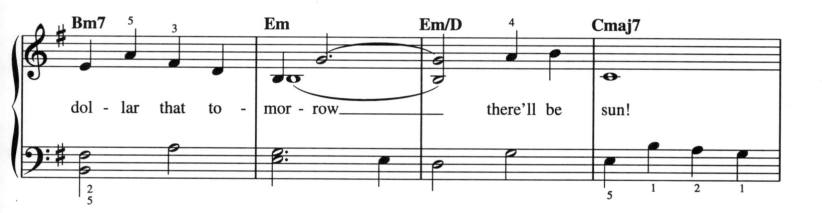

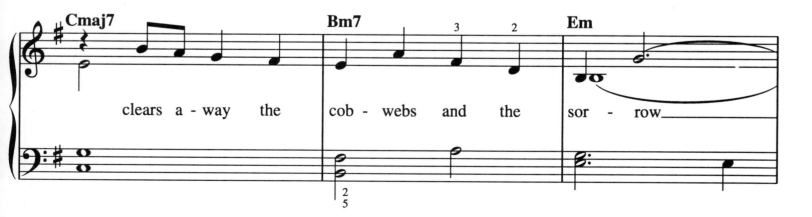

till there's none.
When I'm stuck with a

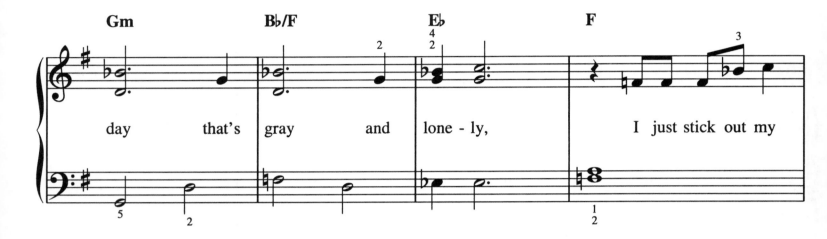

day that's gray and lone - ly,
I just stick out my

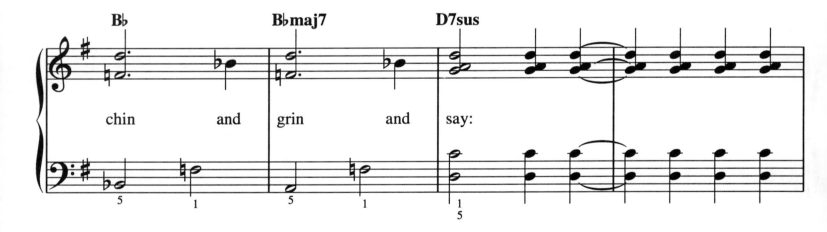

chin and grin and say:

Oh! The sun -'ll come out _____ to - mor - row,

223

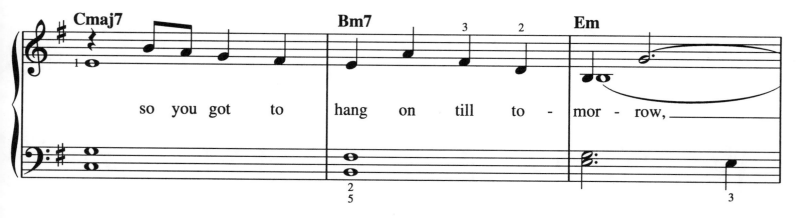

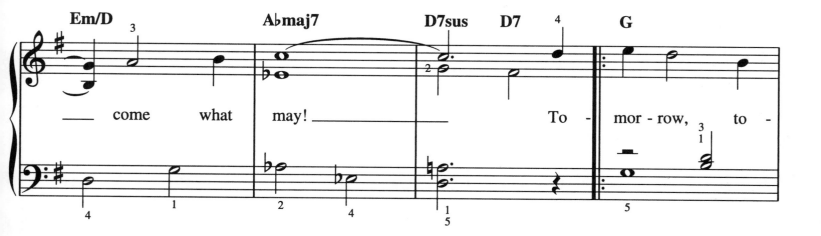

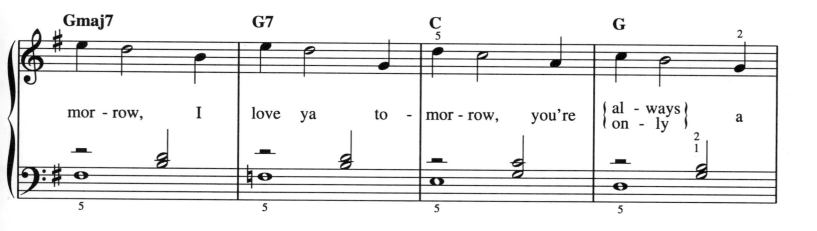

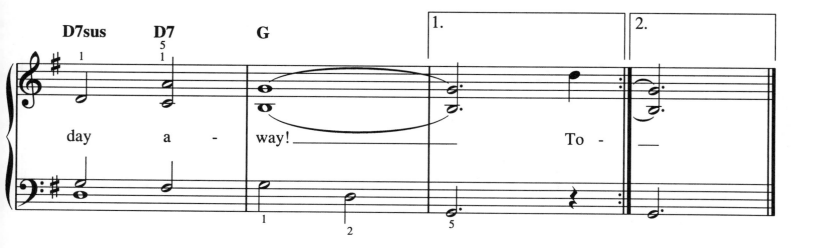

A WHALE OF A TALE
from Walt Disney's 20,000 LEAGUES UNDER THE SEA

Words and Music by NORMAN GIMBEL
and AL HOFFMAN

With a bounce

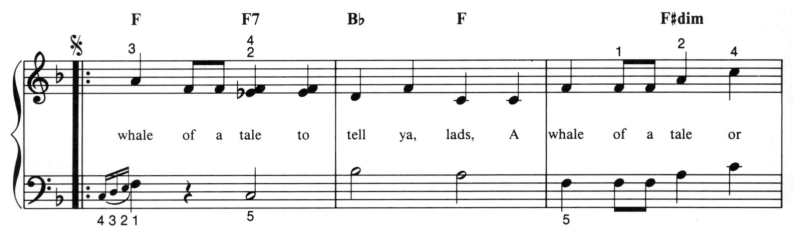

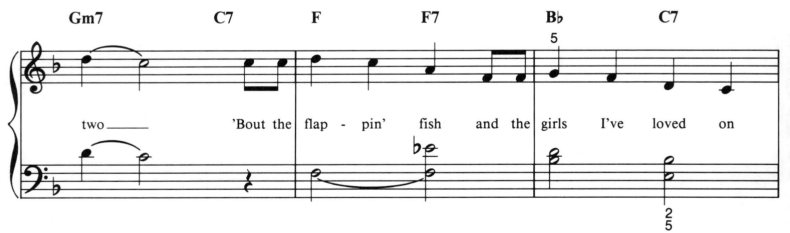

It's all true, I swear — by my tat - too.
{ There was
{ There was

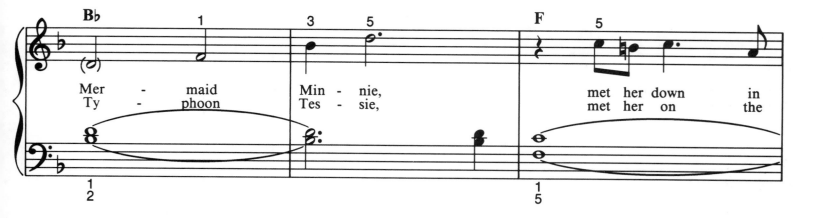

Mer - maid Min - nie, met her down in
Ty - phoon Tes - sie, met her on the

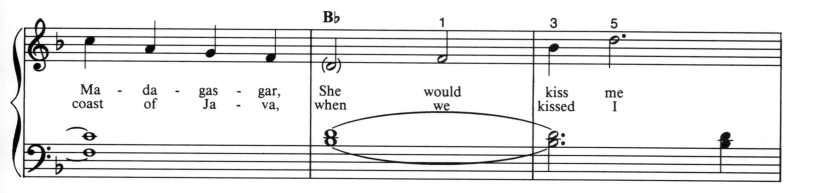

Ma - da - gas - gar, She would kiss me
coast of Ja - va, when we kissed I

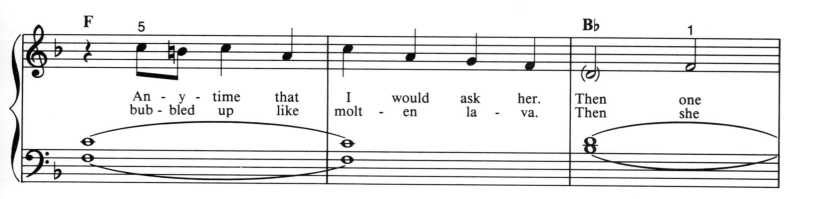

An - y - time that I would ask her. Then one
bub - bled up like molt - en la - va. Then she

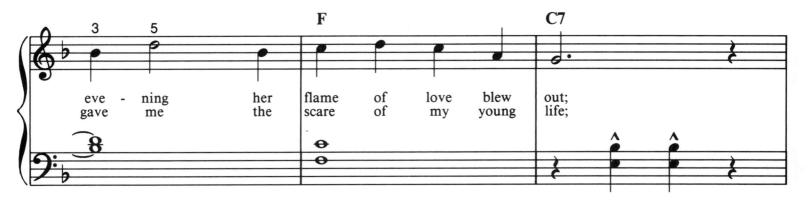

eve - ning her flame of love blew out;
gave me the scare of my young life;

Blow me down and pick me up! She swapped me for a
Blow me down and pick me up! She was the cap - tain's

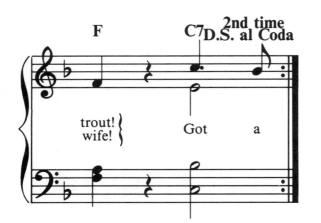

trout!
wife! } Got a

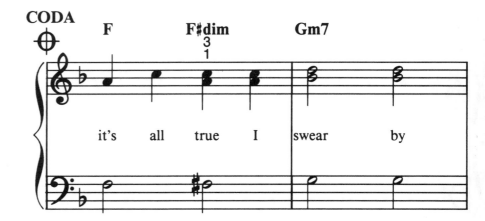

it's all true I swear by

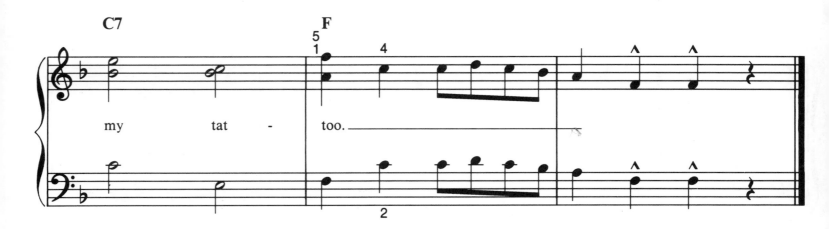

my tat - too.

WHERE IS LOVE?

from the Columbia Pictures - Romulus Film OLIVER!

Words and Music by
LIONEL BART

Slowly

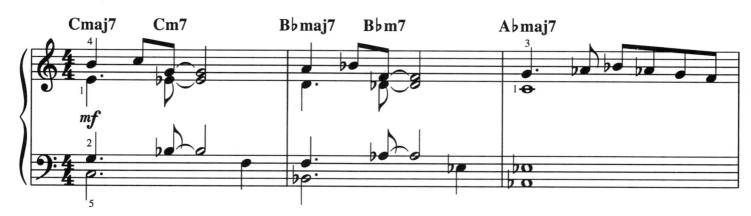

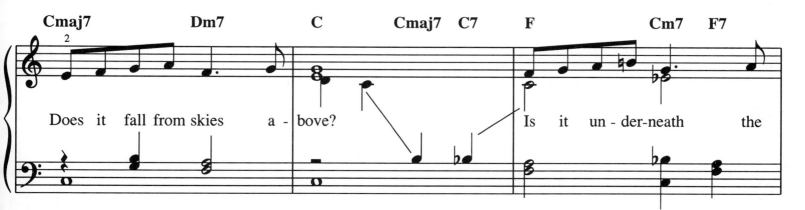

Where _____ is love?

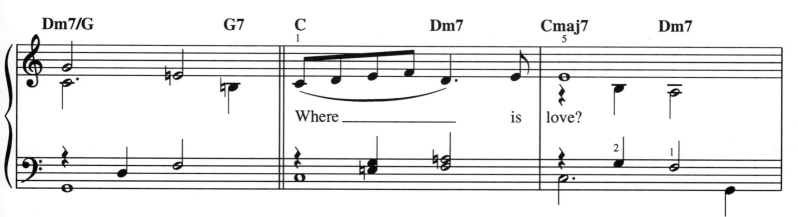

Does it fall from skies a - bove? Is it un - der - neath the

wil - low tree ___ that I've been dream - ing of?

228

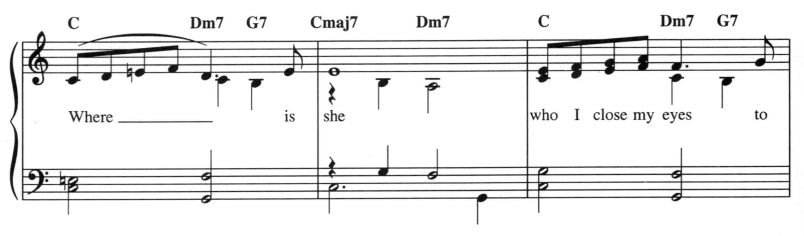

Where _____ is she who I close my eyes to

see? Will I ev-er know the sweet hel-lo _____ that's

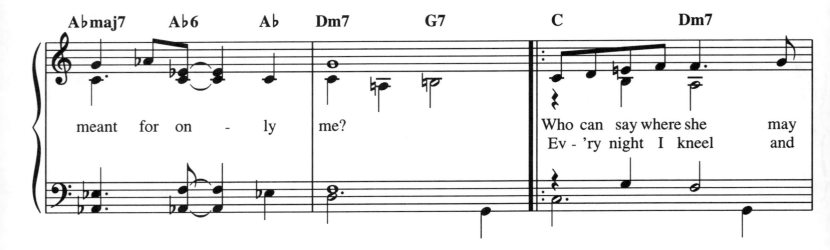

meant for on - ly me? Who can say where she may
Ev - 'ry night I kneel and

hide?
pray, Must I trav-el far and wide
let to-mor-row be the day

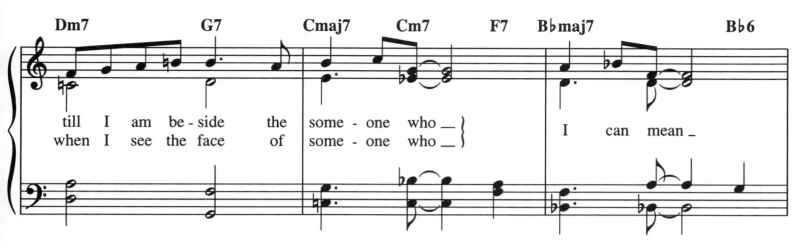

till I am be-side the some-one who —
when I see the face of some-one who — I can mean —

some-thing to? — Where, _____ Where _____ is

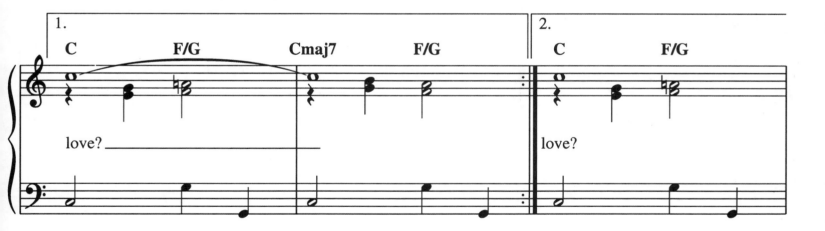

1.
love? _____
2.
love?

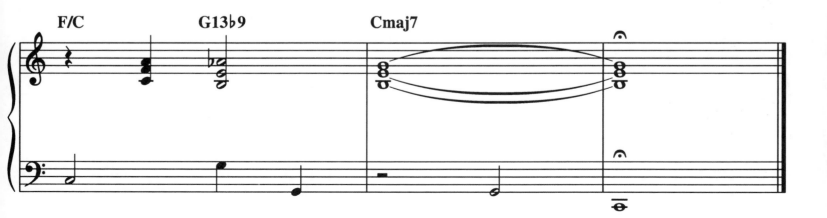

WHEN I'M SIXTY-FOUR

from YELLOW SUBMARINE

Words and Music by JOHN LENNON
and PAUL McCARTNEY

Moderately, with a lilt

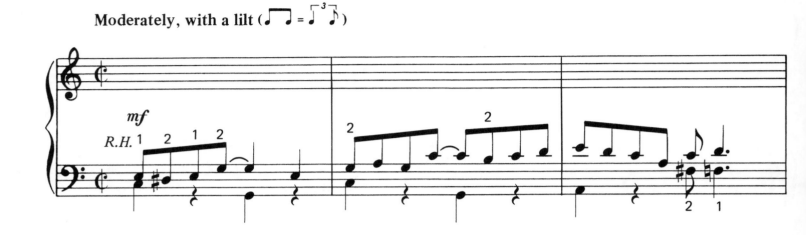

Lyrics:
When I get old-er, los-ing my hair,
I could be hand-y, mend-ing a fuse
Send me a post-card, drop me a line,

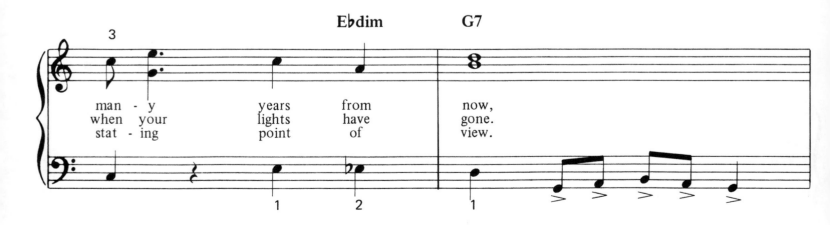

Lyrics:
man-y years from now,
when your lights have gone.
stat-ing point of view.

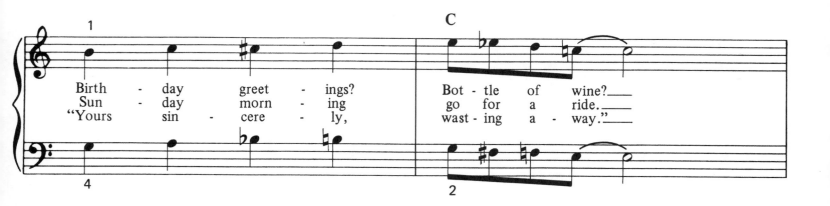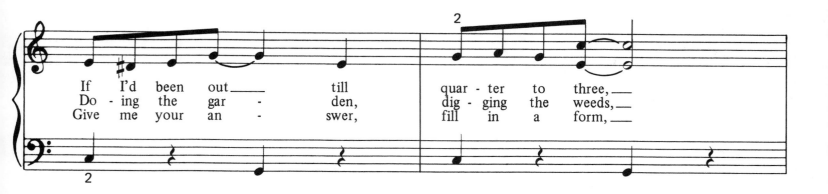

will you still feed___ me When I'm six - ty four?
will you still feed___ me When I'm six - ty four?
will you still feed___ me When I'm six - ty *(to Coda)*

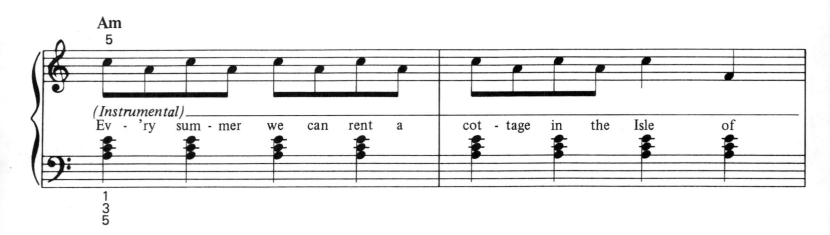

*(Instrumental)*_____
Ev - 'ry sum - mer we can rent a cot - tage in the Isle of

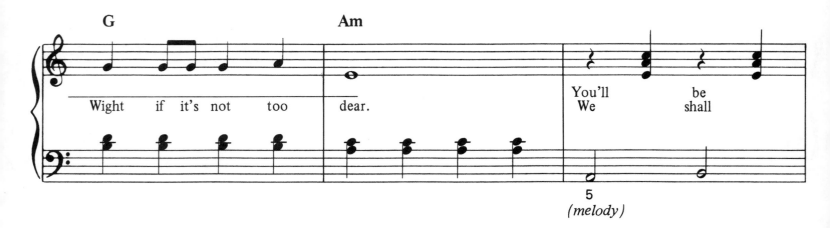

Wight if it's not too dear.
You'll be
We shall
(melody)

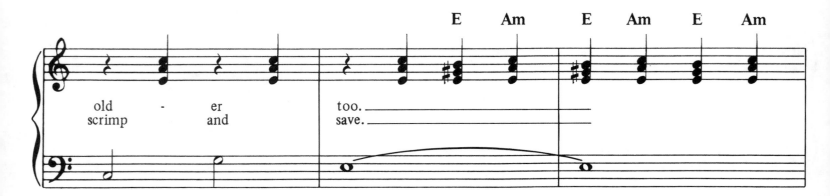

old - er and
scrimp and
too._____
save._____

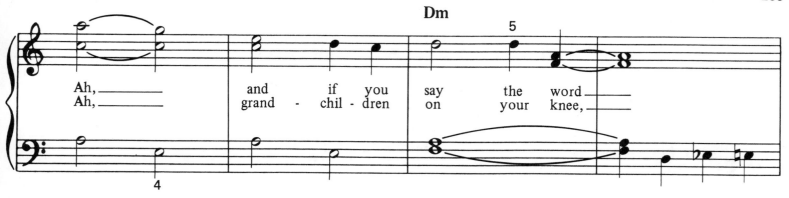

Ah,_____ and if you say the word_____
Ah,_____ grand - chil - dren on your knee,_____

I could stay with you.
Ve - ra, Chuck and Dave.

four?

WON'T YOU BE MY NEIGHBOR?
(It's a Beautiful Day in This Neighborhood)
from MISTER ROGERS' NEIGHBORHOOD

Words and Music by
FRED ROGERS

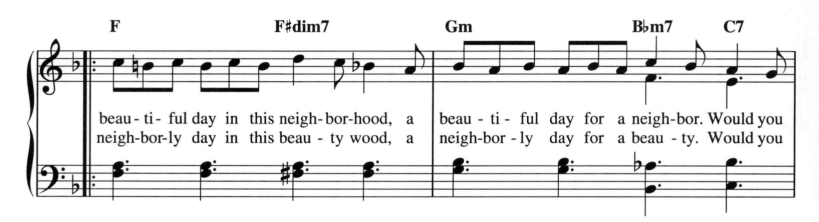

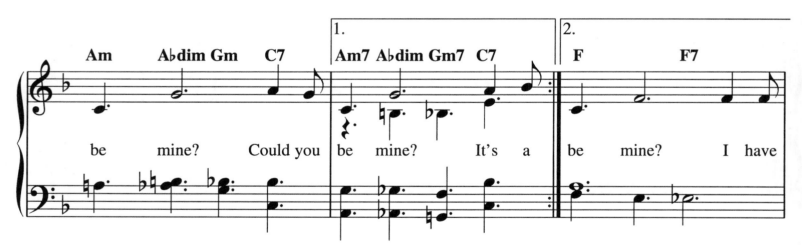

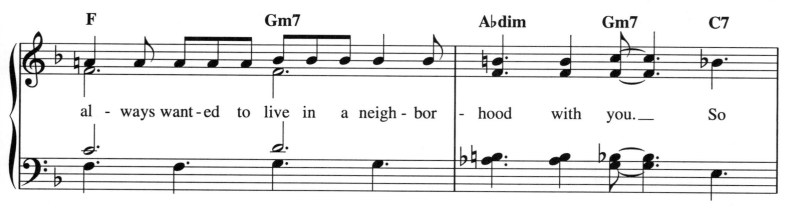

al - ways want-ed to live in a neigh - bor - hood with you.___ So

let's make the most of this beau - ti - ful day, since we're to-geth-er we might as well say;

Would you be mine? Could you be mine? Won't you be my neigh-bor?___

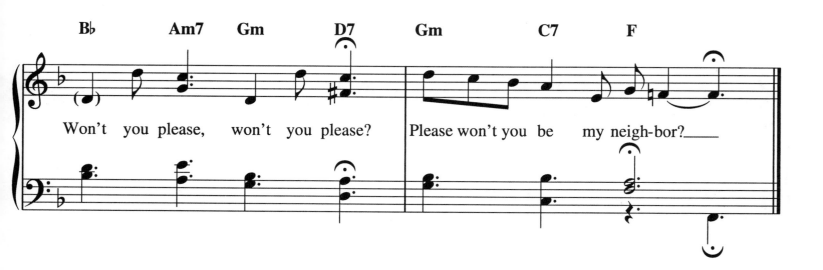

Won't you please, won't you please? Please won't you be my neigh-bor?___

YOU'RE A GRAND OLD FLAG

Words and Music by
GEORGE M. COHAN

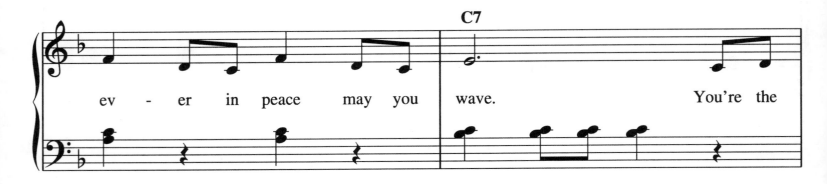

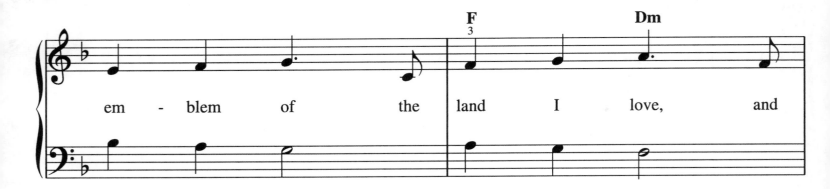

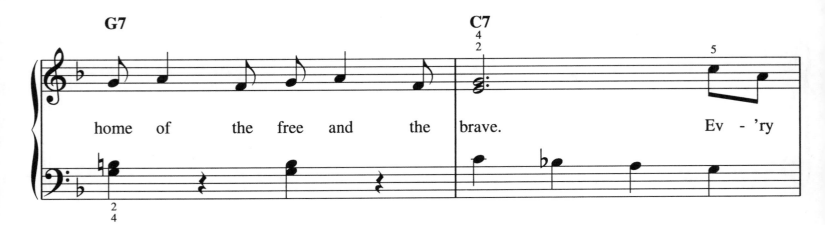

heart   beats   true   un - der   red, white   and   blue,   where there's

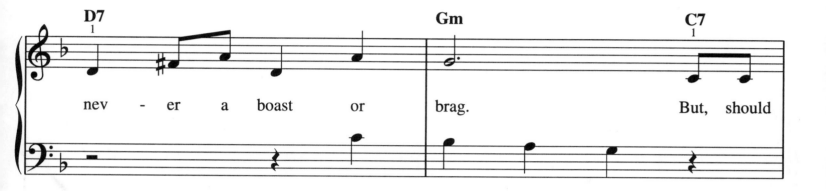

nev - er   a   boast   or   brag.   But,   should

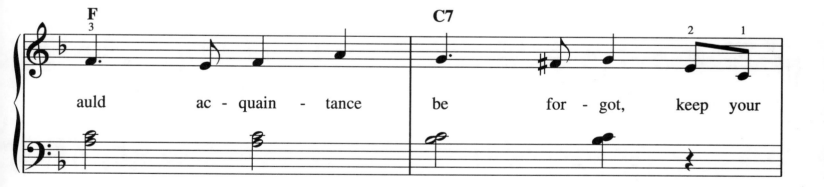

auld   ac - quain - tance   be   for - got,   keep your

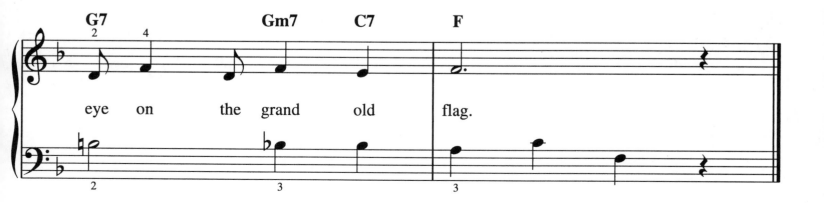

eye   on   the   grand   old   flag.

YOU'VE GOT A FRIEND IN ME

from Walt Disney's TOY STORY

Music and Lyrics by
RANDY NEWMAN

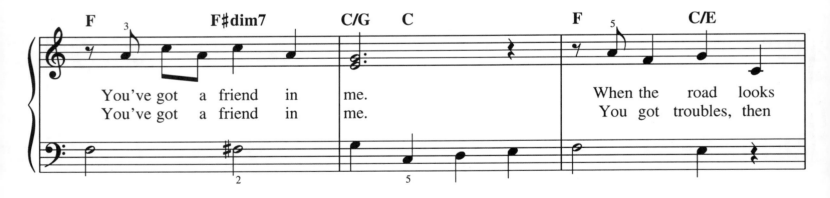

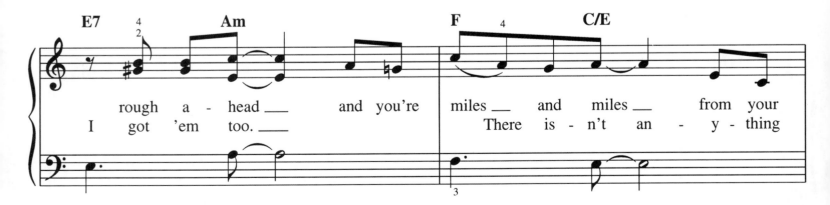

nice warm bed,
I wouldn't do for you.   If we stick to - geth - er we can

old pal   said. Son,   you've got a friend in
see it   through, 'cause   you've got a friend in

me.   Yeah, you've got a friend in me.
me.   Yeah, you've got a friend in

me.

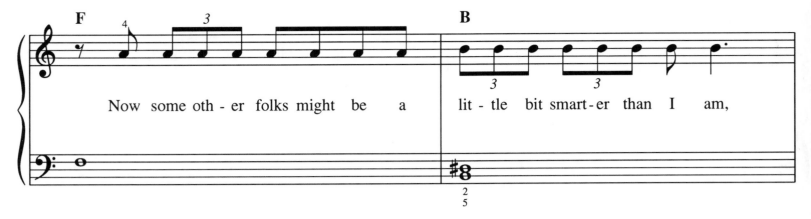

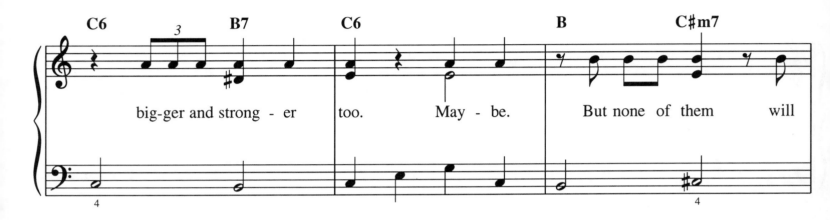

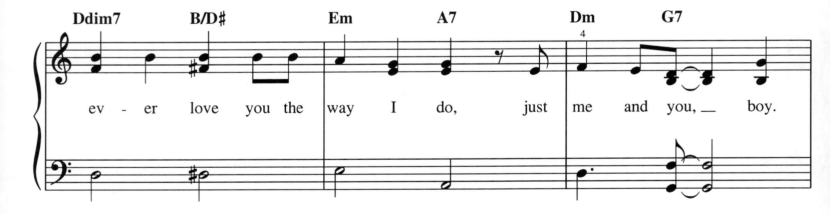

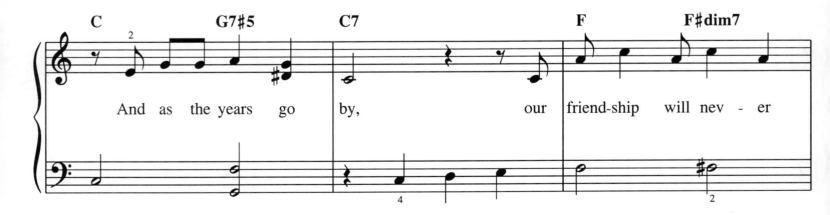

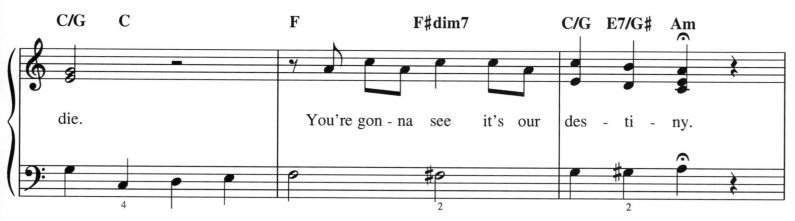

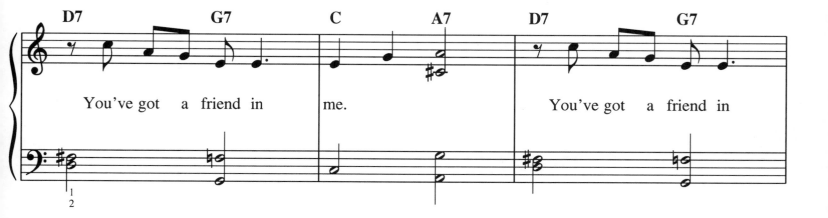

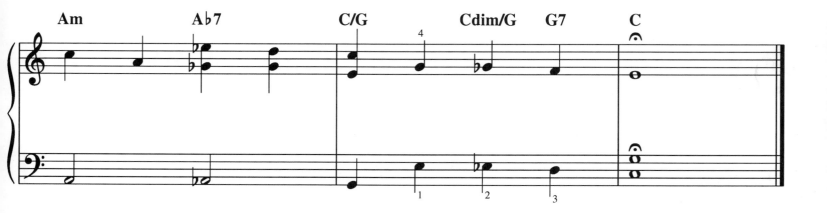

ZERO TO HERO

from Walt Disney Pictures' HERCULES

Music by ALAN MENKEN
Lyrics by DAVID ZIPPEL

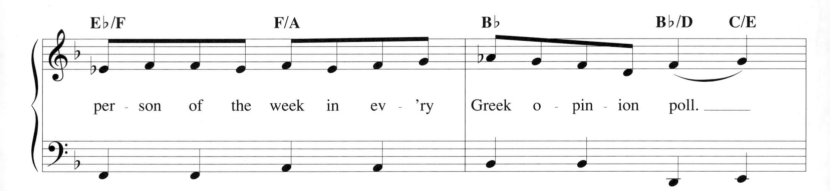

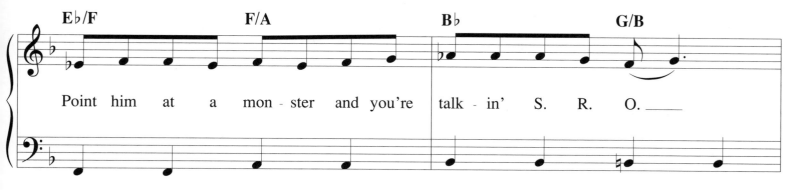

Eb/F **F/A** **Bb** **G/B**

Point him at a mon-ster and you're talk-in' S. R. O. _____

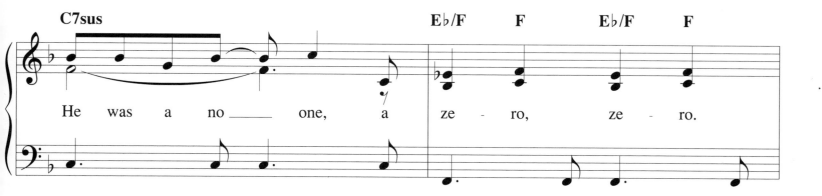

C7sus **Eb/F** **F** **Eb/F** **F**

He was a no _____ one, a ze - ro, ze - ro.

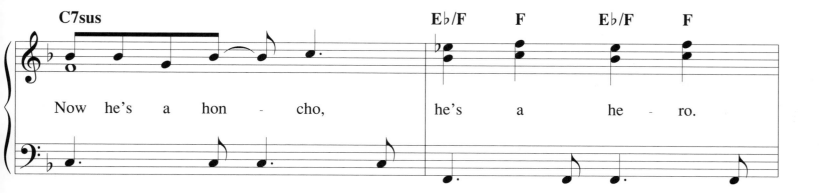

C7sus **Eb/F** **F** **Eb/F** **F**

Now he's a hon - cho, he's a he - ro.

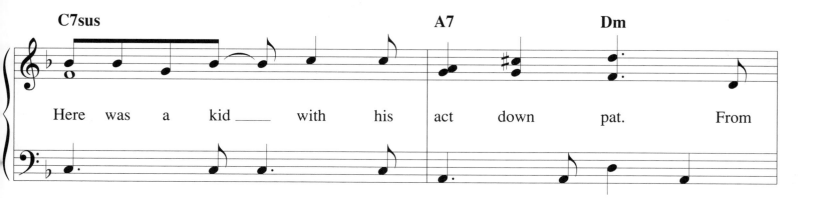

C7sus **A7** **Dm**

Here was a kid _____ with his act down pat. From

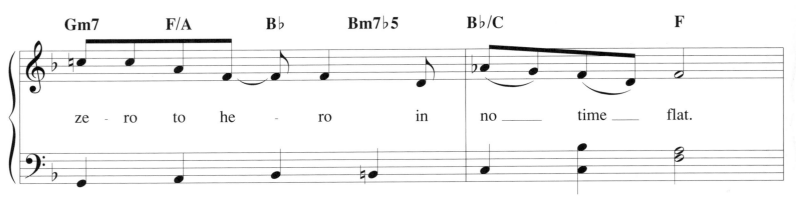

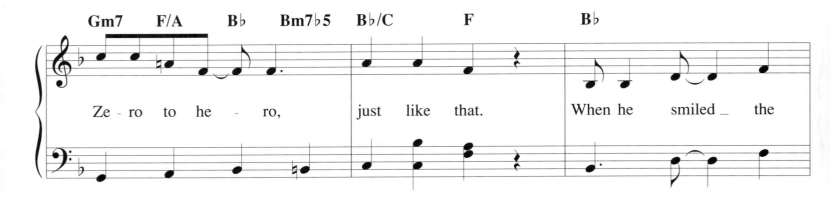

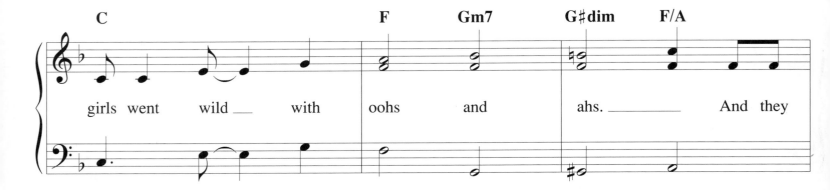

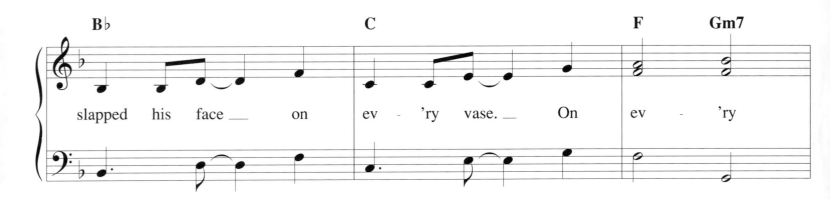

vahse. ____ From ap - pear-ance fees ___ and roy - al - ties ___ our

Herc had cash to burn. ___ Now nou - veau riche and

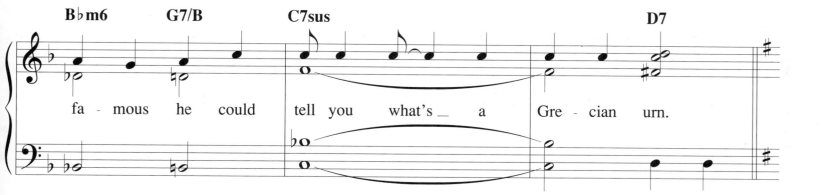

fa - mous he could tell you what's ___ a Gre - cian urn.

Say a - men, there he goes a - gain.

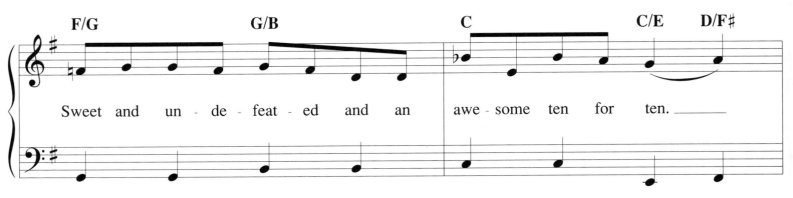

Sweet and un - de - feat - ed and an awe - some ten for ten. _____

Folks lined up just to watch him flex,

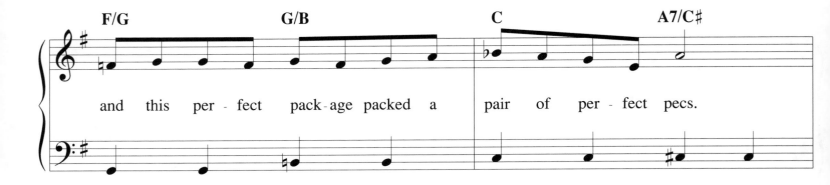

and this per - fect pack - age packed a pair of per - fect pecs.

Herc - ie, he comes, _ he sees, he con - quers.

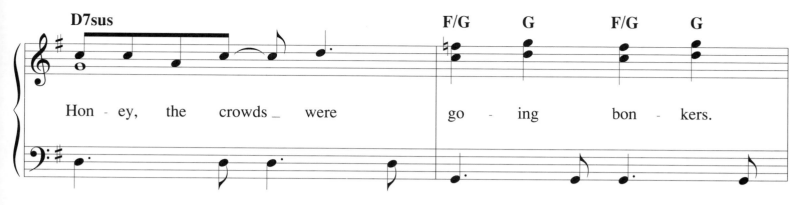

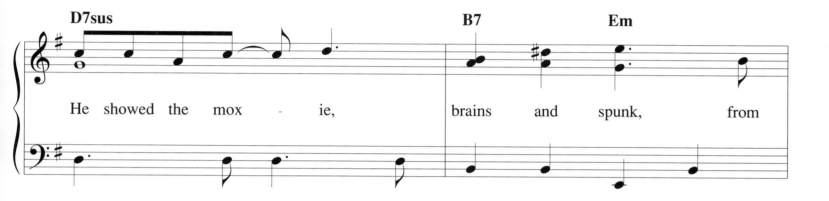

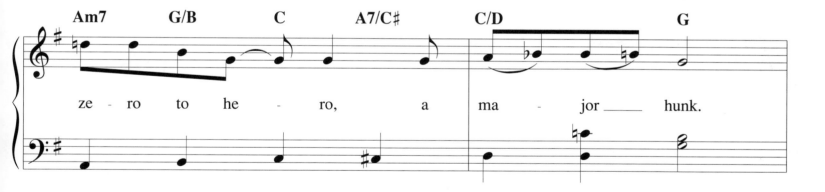

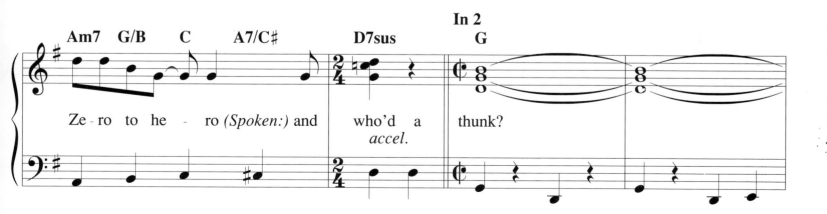

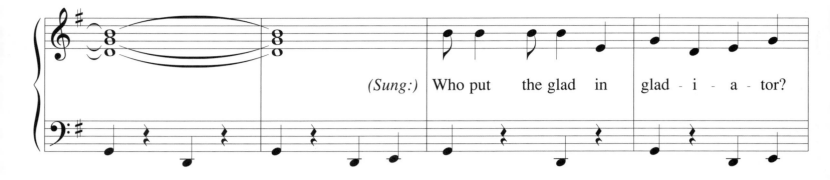

(Sung:) Who put the glad in glad - i - a - tor?

Her - cu - les. Whose dar-ing deeds _ are great the - a - ter?

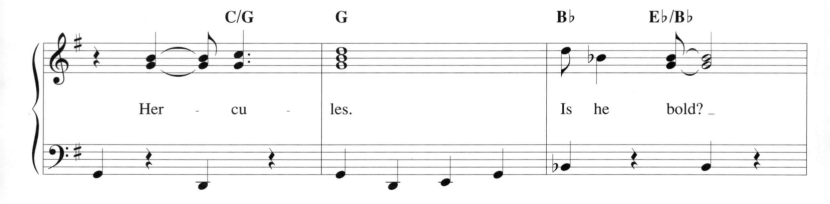

Her - cu - les. Is he bold? _

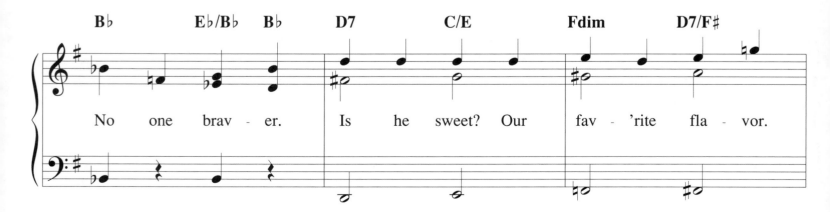

No one brav - er. Is he sweet? Our fav - 'rite fla - vor.

Her - cu - les.   Her - cu - les.

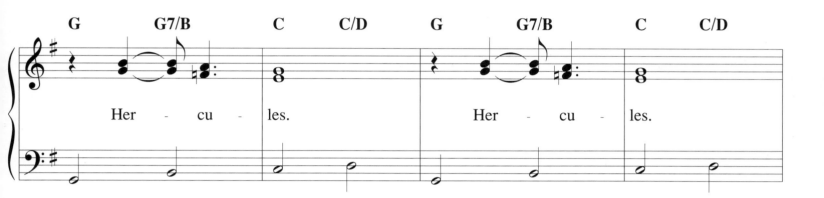

Her - cu - les.   Her - cu - les.

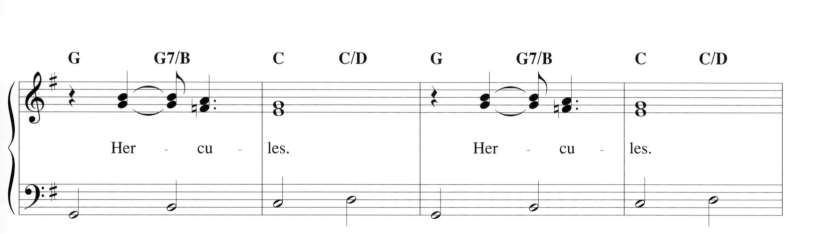

Her - cu - les.   Her - cu - les.

Bless my soul,   Herc was on a roll,   un - de -

250

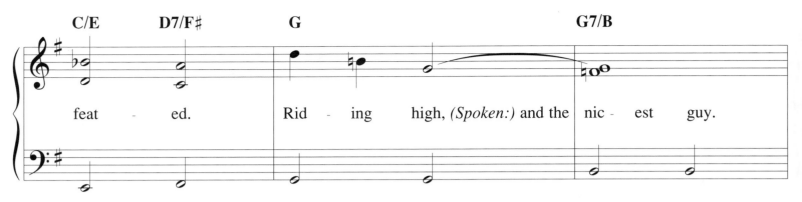

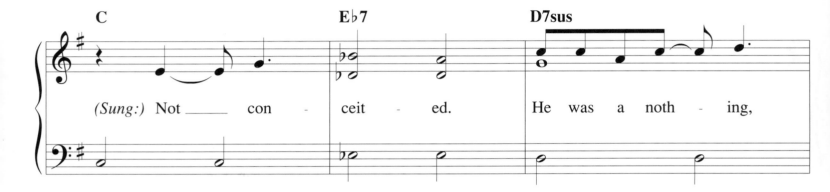

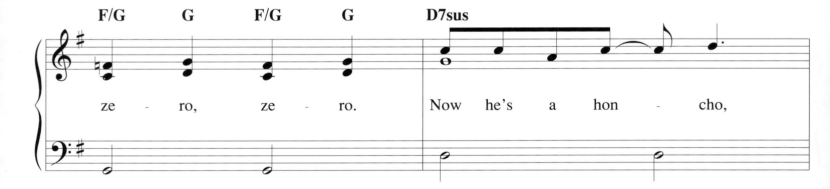

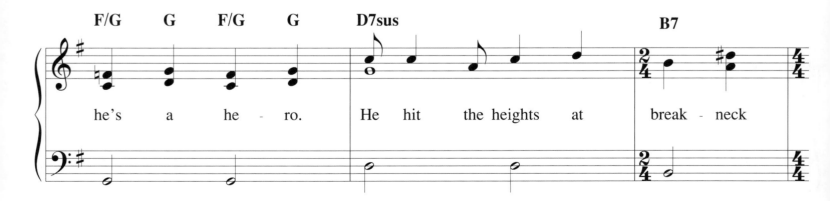

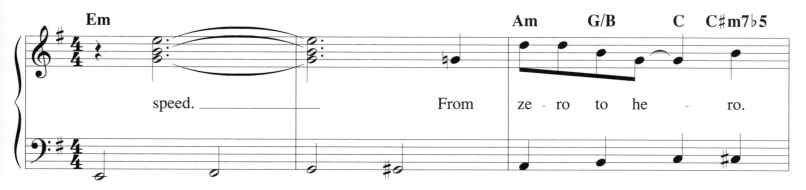

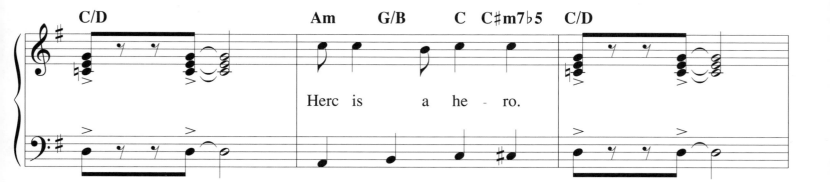

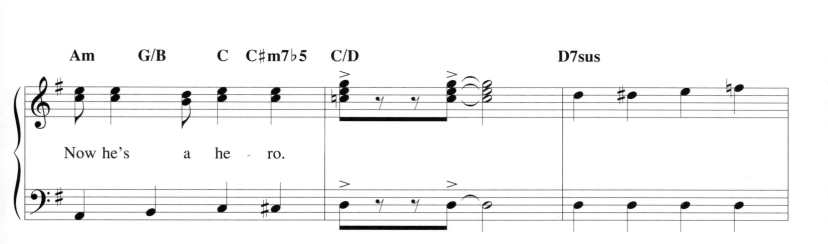

WINNIE THE POOH
from Walt Disney's THE MANY ADVENTURES OF WINNIE THE POOH

Words and Music by RICHARD M. SHERMAN
and ROBERT B. SHERMAN

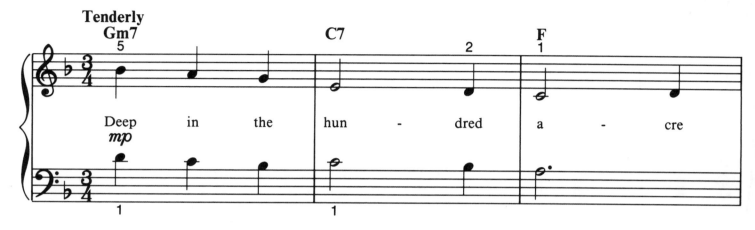

Deep in the hun - dred a - cre

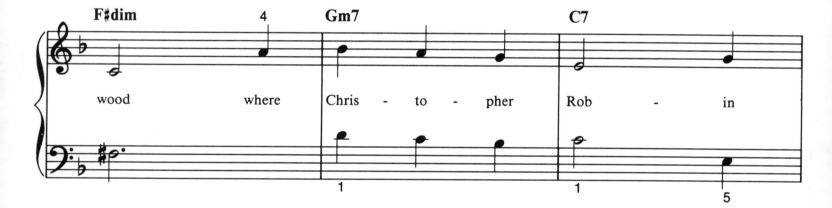

wood where Chris - to - pher Rob - in

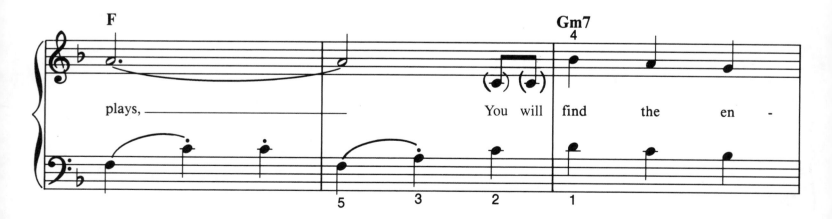

plays, _____ You will find the en -

253

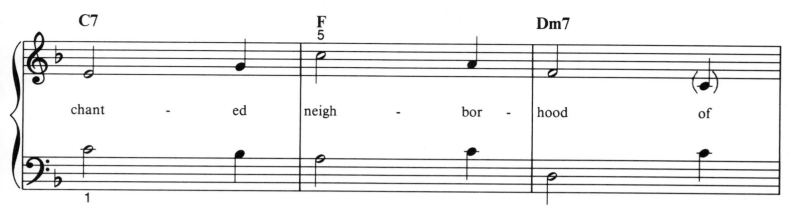

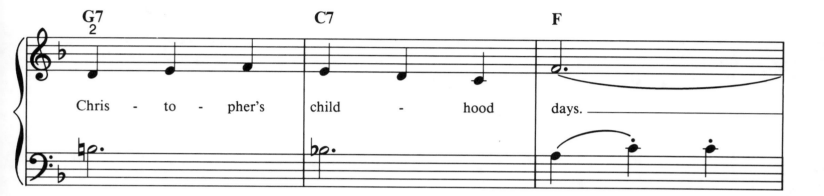

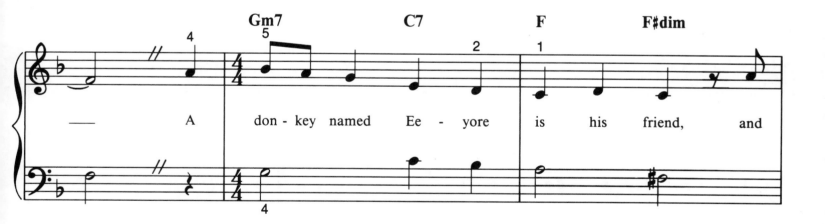

PIANO PLAYING THAT'S FUN & EASY

EASY PIANO BOOKS FROM HAL LEONARD

Irving Berlin's Children's Songbook
13 of his classics, including: Alexander's Ragtime Band • Count Your Blessings Instead of Sheep • Easter Parade • God Bless America • Happy Holiday • White Christmas • and more.
00306047 Easy Piano $7.95

Cartoon Tunes
15 favorite songs from Saturday mornings, including: I'm Popeye the Sailor Man • Jetsons Main Theme • (Meet) The Flintstones • Rocky & Bullwinkle • This Is It • and more.
00222570 Easy Piano $9.95

Children's Favorites For Easy Piano
49 songs children love to play and sing, including: AB-C-DEF-GHI • Bein' Green • C Is for Cookie • Do-Re-Mi • My Favorite Things • Rainbow Connection • Rubber Duckie • Sing • Somebody Come and Play • Won't You Be My Neighbor • and more!
00110014 Easy Piano $10.95

Disney's Silly Songs
Matching easy piano songbook to the album of the same name. 20 humorous songs, including: Baby Bumblebee • Little Bunny Foo Foo • I'm My Own Grandpaw • Three Little Fishies • When I See an Elephant Fly.
00290187 Easy Piano $9.95

Favorite Songs From Jim Henson's Muppets
15 favorite tunes including: Mah-Na-Mah-Na • The Muppet Show Theme • The Rainbow Connection • Rubber Duckie.
00356867 Easy Piano $10.95

The Disney Collection
Over 50 Disney delights, including: The Ballad of Davy Crockett • The Bare Necessities • Bibbidi-Bobbidi-Boo • Candle on the Water • Chim Chim Cher-ee • A Dream Is a Wish Your Heart Makes • Heigh Ho (The Dwarfs' Marching Song) • It's a Small World • Kiss the Girl • The Siamese Cat Song • Someday My Prince Will Come • Supercalifragilisticexpialidocious • Under the Sea • When You Wish upon a Star • Winnie the Pooh • Zip-A-Dee-Doo-Dah • and more.
00222535 Easy Piano $17.95

Disney's Hercules
9 vocal selections, including: The Gospel Truth I, II and III • Go the Distance • Zero to Hero • and more. Includes beautiful full-color art from the movie.
00316020 Easy Piano $14.95

Disney's The Lion King
8 selections, including: Be Prepared • Can You Feel the Love Tonight • Circle of Life • Hakuna Matata • I Just Can't Wait to Be King. Includes both film versions and Elton John solo versions of the songs. Filled with beautiful full-color scenes from the film.
00110029 Easy Piano $14.95

An Illustrated Treasury Of Songs For Children
56 traditional American songs, ballads, folk songs, and nursery rhymes for easy piano. Each song is beautifully complemented with full-color reproductions of famous artworks from the National Gallery of Art, Washington. Songs include: America, The Beautiful • Clementine • The Farmer in the Dell • Hush, Little Baby • I've Been Working on the Railroad • Jingle Bells • Oh, Susanna • On Top of Old Smokey • and more. A wonderful gift idea for a parent or beginning piano student.
00490439 Easy Piano $14.95

Willy Wonka & The Chocolate Factory
What child can resist this sweet collection of 6 songs from their favorite movie, including The Candy Man • Pure Imagination • Oompa Loompa Doompadee-Doo • and more.
00222530 Easy Piano $6.95

FOR MORE INFORMATION, SEE YOUR LOCAL MUSIC DEALER, OR WRITE TO:

HAL•LEONARD® CORPORATION
7777 W. BLUEMOUND RD. P.O. BOX 13819 MILWAUKEE, WI 53213

Prices, contents, & availability subject to change without notice. Some products may not be available outside the U.S.A.

0298

The Greatest Songs Ever Written

The Best Ever Collection
Arranged for Easy Piano with Lyrics.

The Best Broadway Songs Ever

Over 65 songs in all! Highlights include: All I Ask of You • All the Things You Are • As Long as He Needs Me • Bess, You Is My Woman • Bewitched • Cabaret • Camelot • Climb Ev'ry Mountain • Comedy Tonight • Don't Cry for Me Argentina • Everything's Coming Up Roses • Getting to Know You • I Could Have Danced All Night • I Dreamed a Dream • If I Were a Rich Man • It Might as Well Be Spring • The Last Night of the World • Love Changes Everything • Memory • My Funny Valentine • Oklahoma! • Ol' Man River • People • Send in the Clowns • Seventy-Six Trombones • Try to Remember • Younger Than Springtime • and many more!

00300178 ....$18.95

The Best Children's Songs Ever

A great collection of 97 songs, including: Alouette • Alphabet Song • The Ballad of Davy Crockett • The Bare Necessities • Be Kind to Your Parents • Beauty and the Beast • Bingo • The Brady Bunch • The Candy Man • A Dream Is a Wish Your Heart Makes • Eensy Weensy Spider • The Farmer in the Dell • Frere Jacques • Friend Like Me • Hakuna Matata • Hello Mudduh, Hello Fadduh! • I Whistle a Happy Tune • I'm Popeye the Sailor Man • Jesus Loves Me • The Muffin Man • My Favorite Things • On Top of Spaghetti • Puff the Magic Dragon • The Rainbow Connection • A Spoonful of Sugar • Take Me Out to the Ball Game • Twinkle, Twinkle Little Star • Winnie the Pooh • and more.

00310360 ....$19.95

The Best Christmas Songs Ever

A collection of 72 of the most-loved songs of the season, including: Auld Lang Syne • Blue Christmas • The Chipmunk Song • The Christmas Song (Chestnuts Roasting on an Open Fire) • Feliz Navidad • Frosty the Snow Man • Grandma Got Run Over by a Reindeer • Happy Holiday • Happy Xmas (War Is Over) • A Holly Jolly Christmas • Home for the Holidays • I Heard the Bells on Christmas Day • I'll Be Home for Christmas • Jingle-Bell Rock • Let It Snow ! Let It Snow ! Let It Snow! • My Favorite Things • Old Toy Trains • Parade of the Wooden Soldiers • Rudolph, The Red-Nosed Reindeer • Santa, Bring Back My Baby (To Me) • Silver Bells • Suzy Snowflake • Toyland • You're All I Want for Christmas • and more.

00364130 ....$18.95

The Best Country Songs Ever

Over 65 songs, featuring: Always on My Mind • Behind Closed Doors • Could I Have This Dance • Crazy • Daddy Sang Bass • Daddy's Hands • Forever and Ever, Amen • Friends in Low Places • God Bless the U.S.A. • Help Me Make It Through the Night • I Fall to Pieces • I Was Country When Country Wasn't Cool • Islands in the Stream • Jambalaya • King of the Road • Love Without End, Amen • Mammas, Don't Let Your Babies Grow Up to Be Cowboys • Paper Roses • Rocky Top • She Thinks I Still Care • Sixteen Tons • Stand by Your Man • Through the Years • To All the Girls I've Loved Before • You Decorated My Life • Your Cheatin' Heart • and more.

00311540 ....$16.95

The Best Love Songs Ever

A collection of 66 favorite love songs, including: Always • And I Love Her • The Anniversary Song • Beautiful in My Eyes • Can You Feel the Love Tonight • Can't Help Falling in Love • (They Long to Be) Close to You • Endless Love • Feelings • Have I Told You Lately • Isn't It Romantic? • Just the Way You Are • Longer • Love Takes Time • Misty • My Funny Valentine • Saving All My Love for You • So in Love • Vision of Love • When I Fall in Love • You Needed Me • Your Song • and more.

00310128 ....$17.95

The Best Movie Songs Ever

Over 70 songs, including: Alfie • Almost Paradise • Beauty and the Beast • Born Free • Circle of Life • Endless Love • Funny Girl • Isn't It Romantic? • It Might As Well Be Spring • Theme from "Jaws" • Theme from "Jurassic Park" • Moon River • Pennies from Heaven • Puttin' on the Ritz • River • Somewhere Out There • Sooner or Later (I Always Get My Man) • Speak Softly, Love • Star Trek® – The Motion Picture • Take My Breath Away • Tears in Heaven • Theme from "Terms of Endearment" • Thanks for the Memory • Unchained Melody • Up Where We Belong • The Way We Were • A Whole New World • and more.

00310141..$19.95

The Best Songs Ever

Over 70 must-own classics, including: All I Ask of You • All the Things You Are • Blue Skies • Body and Soul • Candle in the Wind • Crazy • Edelweiss • Endless Love • The Girl from Ipanema • Have I Told You Lately • Imagine • In the Mood • Isn't It Romantic? • Longer • Love Me Tender • Memory • Moonlight in Vermont • My Favorite Things • My Funny Valentine • People • Piano Man • Satin Doll • Save the Best for Last • Send in the Clowns • Somewhere Out There • Strangers in the Night • Tears in Heaven • Unforgettable • The Way We Were • When I Fall in Love • You Needed Me • and more.

00359223 ....$19.95

Prices, contents and availability subject to change without notice. Not all products available outside the U.S.A.

0298